6485644

S0-BTD-810

WITHDRAWN

TALLULAH BANKHEAD

As Sadie Thompson in the 1935 American revival of *Rain*. Courtesy of the Hampden-Booth Theatre Library at the Players, New York City.

TALLULAH BANKHEAD

A Bio-Bibliography

Jeffrey L. Carrier

Bio-Bibliographies in the Performing Arts,
Number 21

GREENWOOD PRESS
New York • Westport, Connecticut • London

Library of Congress Cataloging-in-Publication Data

Carrier, Jeffrey L.
    Tallulah Bankhead : a bio-bibliography / Jeffrey L. Carrier.
      p. cm. — (Bio-bibliographies in the performing arts, ISSN
0892-5550 ; no. 21)
    Includes bibliographical references and index.
    ISBN 0-313-27452-5 (alk. paper)
    1. Bankhead, Tallulah, 1902-1968. 2. Bankhead, Tallulah,
1902-1968—Bibliography. 3. Actors—United States—Biography.
I. Title. II. Series.
PN2287.B17C37   1991
792'.028'092—dc20   91-24008
  [B]

British Library Cataloguing in Publication Data is available.

Copyright © 1991 by Jeffrey L. Carrier

All rights reserved. No portion of this book may be
reproduced, by any process or technique, without the
express written consent of the publisher.

Library of Congress Catalog Card Number: 91-24008
ISBN: 0-313-27452-5
ISSN: 0892-5550

First published in 1991

Greenwood Press, 88 Post Road West, Westport, CT 06881
An imprint of Greenwood Publishing Group, Inc.

Printed in the United States of America

The paper used in this book complies with the
Permanent Paper Standard issued by the National
Information Standards Organization (Z39.48-1984).

10 9 8 7 6 5 4 3 2 1

Every reasonable effort has been made to trace the owners of copyright
materials in this book, but in some instances this has proven impossible.
The author and publisher will be glad to receive information leading to
more complete acknowledgements in subsequent printings of the book
and in the meantime extend their apologies for any omissions.

For my father

Contents

Illustrations   ix

Acknowledgments   xi

Alphabetical Listing of Films and Plays   xiii

Preface   xv

1. Biography: Looking at Tallulah   1

2. Chronology   47

3. Stage Work   57

4. Film Work   117

5. Radio   153

6. Television   169

7. Discography   175

8. Awards, Honors, Tributes   177

9. Bibliography   183

Appendix A: Film Roles Considered and Film Tests   249

Appendix B: The Use of Her Name in Books and Films   251

Index   255

Illustrations

As Sadie Thompson in *Rain* (1935)   *frontispiece*

As Miss Flood in *Reflected Glory* (1936)   xx

With Tom Moore in *Thirty A Week* (1918)   5

As the dancer, Maxine, in *The Dancers* (1923)   10

As Carlotta in *My Sin* (1931)   17

With Robert Montgomery and Maurice Murphy in *Faithless* (1932)   18

Mr. and Mrs. John Emery (1937)   23

With Charles Dingle in *The Little Foxes* (1939)   24

With William Eythe in *A Royal Scandal* (1945)   31

With Henry Hull in *Foolish Notion* (1945)   32

With President and Mrs. Harry Truman (1948)   34

Attending a New York Giants game (circa 1950)   37

With Joan Blondell and Estelle Winwood in *Crazy October* (1958)   41

As Mrs. Trefoile in *Die! Die! My Darling!* (1965)   43

As Elsa Carlyle in *The Cheat* (1931)   45

As the Queen in *The Eagle Has Two Heads* (1947)   56

As Constance Porter in *Lifeboat* (1944)   116

With Jeff Chandler in the radio dramatization of *Lifeboat* (1950)   152

With Adam West and Burt Ward in an episode of *Batman* (1967)   168

A glamour portrait from the early 1930s   181

Acknowledgments

No human being can possibly research the life and career of Tallulah Bankhead without help, and I have had a great deal of support from day one, especially from William K. Everson and his wife, Karen Latham Everson, whose proofreading and fact-checking skills are unequaled. James Robert Parish also rates high in the same areas. Aiding me in my photo research were Reg Shrader, of the Wisconsin Center for Film and Theatre Research, Mary Corliss and Terri Geeskin at the Museum of Modern Art, the staff of the New York Public Library at Lincoln Center, Movie Star News, Jerry Vermilye (who also made his collection of Bankhead clippings available to me), and Ray Wemmlinger of the Hampden-Booth Theatre Library at the Players. Maryann Chach, of the Shubert Archive, opened up their Bankhead files for me, and Dawn Dickerson (Belk Library, Boone, North Carolina), Donald Hardy (Library of Congress), Ken Richards, Brooks McNamara (New York University), Joe Savage, Richard Bojarski, Richard Stoddard, Wynn Mathias (Library of Congress, Recorded Sound Division), Radio Yesteryear, Pat Wilks Battle (New York Post), Aggie Carroll, and the Boston Public Library were all helpful in my search for articles as well as for radio and television information. Geraldine Duclow, of the Free Library of Philadelphia's Theatre Collection, deserves a special thank you for her efficiency and cheerfulness in responding to my monthly requests for obscure information, and researching Miss Bankhead's career in England would not have been possible without assistance from The Mander-Mitchenson Theatre Collection, the British Newspaper Library and Mr. Stephen Bourne of the British Film Institute. And I am eternally grateful to Paul and Judy Caputo, for so many things. And to those who graciously responded to my queries – Mr. Vincent Price, Miss Stefanie Powers, Mr. Dick Van Patten, Miss Katharine Hepburn, Mr. Joseph Campanella, Mr. George Abbott, Miss Pia Zadora, Mr. Adam West, Mr. Charles Bennett and Mr. Hume Cronyn – my sincere appreciation. Finally, I must thank Marilyn Brownstein, my editor, for giving me the opportunity to research the exciting career and fascinating life of Tallulah Bankhead.

Alphabetical Listing of Films and Plays

Films

Boy Who Owned a Melephant, The, 146
Cheat, The, 128-129
Daydreamer, The, 149-151
Devil and the Deep, The, 132-134
Die! Die! My Darling!, 146-149
Faithless, 134-136
His House in Order, 122-124
Lifeboat, 139-141
Main Street to Broadway, 143-146
Make Me a Star, 131-132
My Sin, 126-128
Royal Scandal, A, 141-143
Stage Door Canteen, 136-139
Tarnished Lady, 124-126
Thirty a Week, 120-121
Thunder Below, 129-131
Trap, The, 121-122
When Men Betray, 119-120
Who Loved Him Best?, 117-119

Plays

Antony and Cleopatra, 84-85
Blackmail, 74-75
Circle, The, 86-87
Clash By Night, 90-91
Conchita, 65-66
Craig's Wife, 112-113
Crazy October, 102-103
Creaking Chair, The, 67-68
Dancers, The, 64-65

Danger, 62
Dark Victory, 80-81
Dear Charles, 97-98, 110
Eagle Has Two Heads, The, 94
Eugenia, 101-102
Everyday, 61
Exciters, The, 63-64
Fallen Angels, 68
Foolish Notion, 93-94
Foot-Loose, 59-60
Forsaking All Others, 79-80
Garden of Eden, The, 72-74
Glad Tidings, 113-114
Gold Diggers, The, 72
Good Gracious, Annabelle, 107
Green Hat, The, 68-69
Her Cardboard Lover, 75-76, 108-109
Her Temporary Husband 62-63
Here Today, 113
He's Mine, 76-77
House on the Rocks, 111-112
I am Different, 87-88
Lady of the Camellias, The, 77-78
Let Us Be Gay, 78-79
Little Foxes, The, 88-90
Midgie Purvis, 103-105
Milk Train Doesn't Stop Here Anymore, The, 105-106
Mud and Treacle, 75

Nice People, 60-61
Private Lives, 96-97, 109-110
Rain, 81-82
Reflected Glory, 83-84
Scotch Mist, The, 69-70
Second Mrs. Tanqueray, The,
        107-108
Skin of our Teeth, The, 91-93
Sleeping Partners, 107
Something Gay, 83
Squab Farm, The, 57-58
Streetcar Named Desire, A,
        98-100
*They Knew What They
        Wanted,* 70-72
39 East, 58-59
This Marriage, 66-67
Welcome, Darlings, 110-111
Ziegfeld Follies, 100-101

Preface

I've been a film buff since the age of ten, and I hold responsible an elderly widow who lived next door. Mrs. Harry Goodman must have been at least 80, with a memory that stretched back to the nickelodeon. She still thought Pearl White was the greatest star of them all, and I used to sit crosslegged at her feet, spellbound, as she would describe, in great detail, *The Perils of Pauline*.

To Mrs. Goodman, the motion picture was the greatest form of entertainment. Make no mistake about that! She had no patience for live theatre, although she had seen one professional play. *One!* I asked her once why she hadn't seen others. Her reply was quick and to the point: "If you've seen the best, why see another?"

She had been to New York City only once, to visit the 1939 World's Fair, and her traveling companion had dragged her into the National Theatre to see Lillian Hellman's *The Little Foxes*. Three hours and four curtain calls later, she had to be dragged out.

"I thought if I stayed, they might do it again," she laughed. "I had seen Tallulah Bankhead in several movies, and hadn't particularly liked her, but her performance on that stage is almost as vivid as if I had seen it last week. There have been few truly memorable experiences in my life, but that was definitely one of them."

When the 1941 film version made it to our small-town theatre, Mrs. Goodman was the first in line. "But I was disappointed," she said. "Compared to Bankhead, Bette Davis was like the understudy."

*****

It had to have taken a formidable actress to melt Mrs. Goodman's icy disdain for the theatre, and from all accounts, Tallulah Bankhead fit the bill, both as actress and as woman. No one who met her was ever quite able to forget her. As Nathaniel Benchley once remarked, "she makes her presence felt with something of the force of a hailstorm."

She conquered practically every medium of entertainment -- stage, screen, radio, television -- yet she was bettered in every one of them. As an actress her talent was undeniable (although largely unappreciated), but her greatest achievement had nothing to do with talent. It was sheer force of personality that made Tallulah Bankhead a legend. And her legend as an unconventional, uninhibited, free-spirited woman continues to thrive, nearly a quarter century after her death. She was also known as a shrewd business woman (she was her own agent and her stage contracts always stipulated that she receive 15% of the weekly gross profits and 25% of the producer's share of all subsidiary profits from motion picture rights, radio rights and amateur performances), but she had a human side as well: the side that kneeled before a gold-framed photograph of her parents prior to every performance, crossed her heart and prayed silently, "Dear God, don't let me make a fool of myself tonight."

Born into a famous political family in Alabama and given to tantrums as a child, she found acting to be the only logical outlet for her boundless energy. At the age of 15, her schooling was abandoned and Tallulah Bankhead was set loose upon the world. From then on, until her death in 1968, at age 66, she lived to the fullest, making headlines almost daily, scaling the heights (and depths) of her profession, flaunting conventions, puzzling physicians with a series of strange ailments, stripping at parties, making many friends (and just as many enemies) and generally having one helluva time.

She arrived in New York in 1917, took up residence at the fashionable Algonquin Hotel, sat herself down at its famous Roundtable and proceeded to charm and amuse the literati of the day. By 1923 she had made her mark both socially and dramatically with four films and nine plays to her credit; but success wasn't coming quickly enough to suit her. A fortune teller told her that fame lay "across the water," so she accepted an offer to appear in a London play, and off she sailed to England with never a backward glance.

She caused a sensation in her first scene, doing a spirited Indian dance (the play was appropriately titled *The Dancers*), and suddenly she was the talk of the town. She remained in London for the rest of that "roaring" decade, becoming the *outre* darling of madcap Mayfair and one of the brightest lights on the West End. Word of her popularity in England spread quickly, fueled by the mania she caused among that country's population of shopgirls. They copied her speech, her hairstyle, and chanted "Tallulah! Tallulah!" before her every performance. In 1931, Paramount attempted to cash in on her fame by luring her back to American shores with a lucrative film contract. Plagued by a fear of poverty, she accepted, leaving England a little less merry.

She starred in six films over the next two years, but none was especially successful. It was not so much a case of Tallulah failing Hollywood as Hollywood failing her. Paramount touted her as a second Marlene Dietrich and cast her in roles in which she was more sinned against than sinful. Her fiery personality was smothered in such films as *Tarnished Lady*, *The Cheat* and *Thunder Below*, and the public quickly lost interest. She turned her back on Hollywood and returned to the footlights of Broadway, opening on March 1, 1933, in *Forsaking All Others*. It failed, as did her next several plays.

It was not until 1939 and *The Little Foxes* that she found the right vehicle and scored a success. The play lasted 408 performances at the National Theatre before Tallulah took it on the road for another year, never missing a performance. It was unquestionably the highest point of her career, and although she did have other successes, she would never be at the top again. She did make an impression on radio, however, hostessing *The Big Show* for NBC in the early 50s (being named 1951's most popular woman in that medium), but the last two decades of her life were marked mostly by summer stock engagements, Broadway failures and guest appearances on radio and television, where her ribald wit was always appreciated.

That she was never universally recognized as a major talent is probably her own fault. As many critics have noted, the potential for greatness was there, but, regretfully, the discipline wasn't. By living exactly as she wanted – with reckless abandon – she allowed her antics to upstage her art. A lack of good judgment also held her back. Many of the roles she chose were hardly suited to her talents, but as she admitted many the time and oft, a fear of landing in the poorhouse forced her to accept whatever came along. (Ironically, at her death she left an estate valued at more than one million dollars.)

Even if she didn't have the world's admiration as an actress, she certainly had its interest as an unconventional woman. Her basso voice, likened by comedian Fred Allen to the sound of a man pulling his foot out of a pail of yogurt, her questionable sexual behavior ("My family warned me about men, but they never mentioned women!"), her fondness for profanity and unwavering devotion to the New York Giants and the Democratic Party were known the world over. And the throaty "dahling" with which she greeted both friends and strangers, passed into the language and has been copied by many, especially Zsa Zsa Gabor.

Aiding and abetting her exploits was her press agent, Richard Maney, who saw to it that her name was in print as often as possible. He even ghostwrote her autobiography, *Tallulah*, which became a 1952 best-seller and confirmed most of the legends. By the time of its appearance she was already considered high camp. Wherever she appeared, an audience always gathered, but people came not to see a great actress, but to watch an outrageous performance. Tallulah knew what her fans wanted, and they were seldom disappointed. When she tried to break free of the campy stereotype (*A Streetcar Named Desire*, 1956), it was too late. The audience wouldn't let her; they laughed at every line that seemed a reflection of Bankhead's own life and though she tried valiantly to control her mannerisms, she was ultimately unsuccessful. She didn't try again to stretch her acting muscles.

She became a parody of herself, and the caricature that she presented on radio and television was a tragic distortion of a rare and original talent, a talent that fell victim to the whims and caprices of the formidable Tallulah Bankhead.

*****

Tallulah Bankhead's greatest portrayal was Tallulah Bankhead, but her qualifications as a serious actress should not be minimized. The body of work she produced in her fifty years as a professional is astounding, but her accomplishments are too rarely noted. Although she has been the subject of four biographies, all of them tend to dwell on the seamier side of her life. Granted her life *was* seamier than most, hedonism being an important part of her personality, and although no book about the actress would be complete or accurate without giving *some* attention to her frenzied search for pleasure, it is Tallulah Bankhead, the actress, whom this book honors.

The book is divided into 10 major sections:

1.   A short biography.

2.   A chronology noting the highlights of her life.

3.   A complete listing of her appearances on stage, the medium in which she achieved her greatest success and for which she is best known. The plays have been subdivided according to the period of her career into which they fall: *Broadway Beginnings* (1918-1922), *London Acclaim* (1923-1930), *Broadway Stardom* (1933-1964), and *Summer Stock*. A complete listing of cast and credits, review summary and commentary has been included for each play. A listing of additional professional appearances, including the lecture circuit, nightclubs and fund raising events, follows.

4.   An examination of her work in film, including synopsis, complete cast and credits, a review summary, sources for study and commentary for each motion picture.

5.   Appearances on national radio, including her series and guest appearances.

6.   Appearances on television, including her brief series and guest appearances on other programs.

7.   A discography of song and dramatic recordings.

8.   A listing of awards, honors and tributes to her memory, talent and achievements.

9.   An annotated bibliography of books and magazine articles about her or referring to her.

10.   A complete index of names and titles.

There are also two appendixes: (1) film roles considered and film tests and, (2) the use of her name in books and films.

As Miss Flood in *Reflected Glory* (1936). Courtesy of the Billy Rose Theatre Collection, New York Public Library at Lincoln Center, Astor, Lenox and Tilden Foundations.

1

Biography: Looking at Tallulah

It came as no surprise to the Bankheads of Alabama when Tallulah became an actress. As she herself later admitted, she wasn't fit for anything else, acting being the only logical outlet for her unbridled energy. Considered the greatest natural talent of her time by the equally great Lynn Fontanne, she was already starring on Broadway at the age of 19 in a play written expressly for her, and her death forty-seven years later rated the front page of the *New York Times*.

During those forty-seven years, Tallulah Bankhead became a legend, making her mark in theatre, film radio and television. She conquered the stages of two continents and tried to conquer Hollywood as well. But as a movie star, she never really clicked, and it was in the theatre that she honed her talent and perfected her unusual style, a combination of verve, acerbic wit and a deep voice that, as one critic said, "caressed the ears like the tones of a violincello." Maurice Zolotow called her the most flamboyant stage personality of her time, but there are other adjectives just as well suited. Compared to her peers – sedate Helen Hayes, sober Katharine Cornell, quietly sophisticated Gertrude Lawrence and safely married Lynn Fontanne – Tallulah was dangerous, daring, dynamic, whimsical, unconventional and utterly unpredictable. When put to the test, Tallulah's talents were as great as anyone's, but she relished being Tallulah Bankhead and her greatest performance was playing herself. And for 66 years she had her audience's undivided attention.

Tallulah was known primarily for promiscuity, a passion for foul language and unprecedented outspokenness, but a little known – and highly admirable – part of her life was her involvement with the Foster Parents Plan. She rarely discussed it, probably because it didn't fit in with her image. Never a natural mother, she was a foster parent to several orphaned children, including twin Spanish boys, a Maltese boy whom she adopted in 1944, several Chinese youngsters and a badly injured girl from Greece, the only one of her foster children whom she actually met. (See B156.) Tallulah would contribute $180 a month toward the upkeep of her "children" and was highly interested in their lives. She wrote them letters, cherished their answers and expressed genuine sorrow when they reached the age of seventeen and were taken out of the program.

Tallulah Brockman Bankhead was born on January 31, 1902, in the little North Alabama town of Huntsville. She was named for her paternal grandmother, who had been named for Georgia's Tallulah Falls. Who the falls were named for is anybody's guess, but legend has it that "tallulah" is an Indian word meaning "terrible."

The Bankheads were well known in Alabama. Tallulah's grandfather, John Hollis Bankhead, was a United States senator, as was his son, John Hollis Bankhead, Jr., and his son-in-law, Dr. Thomas Owen, was head of the rather pretentious-sounding Department of Archives and History of the State of Alabama, a position his wife, Marie Bankhead Owen, later inherited. Tallulah was the daughter of another son, William, whose political position was not as exalted, but who was doing nicely as Huntsville's city attorney. William (called Will by friends and family) had married Adelaide Eugenia Sledge, a celebrated beauty from Virginia, in 1900, and their first child, Eugenia, was born the following year. Tallulah was their second child and, as it turned out, their last. At the age of 22, Ada died, three weeks after the baby was born.

Deeply saddened by his wife's premature death, Will sent his two daughters to his parents' home in Jasper, just north of Birmingham, while he remained in Huntsville tending to morning hangovers and afternoon politics. Three years later, his broken heart apparently mended, he rejoined his family in Jasper. He eventually remarried, but not until 1916.

Under the large roof of her grandparents' home, Tallulah grew to be a difficult child, frequently flying into screaming rages that usually ended with her grandmother sloshing a pail of cold water over her head. Her willful spirit was probably born of a desire to wrestle attention from her sister. Tallulah was a chubby child, and not especially pretty, whereas Eugenia was slim and cute and was obviously her father's favorite. To be noticed, young Tallulah resorted to histrionics. It worked, but the family wasn't particularly amused by her crying, screaming and sudden aerobic displays, although a string of cartwheels did impress the state's governor who was visiting one afternoon.

Until she was ten, Tallulah attended school in Jasper, where, as schoolmate Zora Ellis recalled in a 1990 telephone interview, she was a show-off.

"Sometimes we would walk home together after school," said Miss Ellis, 90, now of Talledega, Alabama, "and if something tickled her, she would get down and roll on the sidewalk, laughing as hard as she could. She was a real show-off."

Zora and Tallulah went through four years of school together, but Tallulah did not linger in Jasper for a fifth. In the autumn of 1912, Will sent his two daughters to New York City where they were enrolled at the Academy of the Sacred Heart. They remained there for two terms, and for the next three years were shuffled from school to school, making their last academic stand at Washington's Fairmont Seminary in 1916, the same year Will was elected to the House of Representatives from Alabama's tenth district.

With Tallulah's formal education ended, her family was left to speculate on the direction the 14-year-old's life would take. A difficult task. She didn't seem to fit into Washington's congressional society, with its dull dinner parties and formal cotillions. She was too restless, too free-spirited. Tallulah had some ideas of her own, and one of them was a life on the stage; the problem was how to get to New York. It wasn't a problem for long. Her eye was caught by the June 1917 issue of *Picture Play* Magazine which encouraged would-be actresses to enter a screen opportunity contest. According to the advertisement, twelve winners would be chosen, and each was guaranteed "a real part, not that of an extra" in a film which would be shot in New York City. The winners would have their traveling expenses to New York paid, and would receive an additional $25 a week for as long as the film was in production. She saw her chance and responded. At 15, Tallulah was growing out of her chubby, unattractive stage, and the photo she had taken for the contest showed a lovely, sophisticated-looking girl wearing a fur and a wide-brimmed hat.

The September issue contained the winning photographs, and Tallulah's picture was one of the twelve chosen. She had won the contest! The family, led by her stern grandmother, strongly objected toTallulah's going to New York, but the girl's excitement and enthusiasm finally won out, and she was soon on her way, with a promise from her grandfather to underwrite her stay (paying her fifty dollars a week) and a doting aunt along to chaperone.

They arrived in late 1917, and the now trim, fair-haired, pseudo-sophisticated 15-year-old Tallulah went to work as a film actress. The promised film role was not a plum part, however; her few scenes took less than three weeks to shoot, and when the film, titled *Who Loved Him Best?*, was released in January 1918, her name was at the bottom of the cast list. Dell Henderson (a Griffith protegée) was credited with direction, and Sol Polito, who would later become one of Hollywood's most respected cinematographers, chalked up one of his first credits as cameraman. Tallulah apparently forgot about the film because she never referred to it, and although records prove that she appeared in four films before 1920, she later acknowledged only two.

By the time of the film's release, Tallulah and her aunt had moved into the elegant Algonquin Hotel at 59 West 44th Street, the gathering place of the city's most glamorous theatre and literary personalities. It was the home of the famous "round table" where the likes of Dorothy Parker, Alexander Woollcott, Herbert Ross, Charles MacArthur and Robert Benchley sat and exchanged quotable bon mots and epigrams. Anita Loos was a fringe member of this illustrious group and years later, in an article published after Tallulah's death, Miss Loos remembered the young actress's first day at the Algonquin: "Her first move was to take up a post in the hotel lobby where she could sit and gaze at the show folk. But her roseleaf beauty was so dazzling that in no time at all the show folk were gazing back" (see B237).

With her quick wit, deep blue eyes and mane of blonde hair, Tallulah quickly became a favorite at the hotel. Besides Anita Loos, she formed close and lasting friendships with Ethel Barrymore and Estelle Winwood and even charmed Frank Crowninshield, the world-renowned editor of *Vanity Fair*, who saw to it that she was invited to the lavish parties of Condé Nast, the publisher of *Vanity Fair* and *Vogue*.

By the spring of 1918, Tallulah Bankhead was a name becoming more and more familiar in New York's social and theatre circles; it was easy for her to amuse party guests (her imitations of famous stars were the hit of many an evening), but finding work in the theatre wasn't as easy. She did manage to land a part in *The Squab Farm*, a Broadway production that opened on March 13, 1918, but the part was a mute walk-on and the play closed after 45 performances. It wasn't a debut to be especially proud of, and her search for another theatre job ended in disappointment. But through some friends at the Algonquin (and partly due to her grandfather's influence), the Graphic Film Corporation offered her a supporting role in *When Men Betray*, a six-reeler with a complicated plot involving marriage infidelity. Robert Elliott starred, and Tallulah played his younger sister. She had only one scene to really get her teeth into – a discreet, but effective rape scene and her performance warranted a favorable mention in the June 8th edition of *Exhibitors Trade Review*, her first critical notice (see F2).

The next film offer came from Samuel Goldwyn, who, in the summer of 1918, was still using his real name, Goldfish, and whose base of operation was still in New York. He was also still trying to cast his soon-to-be-produced film *Thirty a Week*. Tom Moore, a popular leading man of the day, was already set to star, and Tallulah was persuaded to sign as his leading lady. She and Moore made a handsome team (as a young married couple battling professional setbacks and a villainous father-in-law) and under Harry Beaumont's able direction, performed well enough to please the critics. Said *Variety*, "Tallulah Bankhead makes a sweet little ingenue as the young wife."

With three films now to her credit, Tallulah seemed to be building a sturdy foundation for a movie career, but her heart was not in it; she preferred the stage and concentrated even harder on finding a job in the theatre. While spending a few weeks in Washington that autumn, she wrote to her grandfather's friend Joseph L. Rhinock, a former congressman from Kentucky then acting as a financial backer for the Shubert brothers in New York. "I am writing you a little note to remind you that I am still very anxious to go on the stage in preference to pictures," the sixteen-year-old Tallulah wrote. "I would be so very grateful to you if you would get me a good part in a dramatic show." Rhinock's answer (dated November 12, 1918) encouraged the young stage-struck girl to keep in touch with the Shubert's secretary.

Having a contact in the Shubert's front office did not help Tallulah to find additional stage roles, but in the spring of 1919, when stage and screen star Constance Binney announced she would be leaving the cast of *39 East* for weekend vacations and would be replaced, Tallulah rushed to the theatre to read for the part. The play had a special significance for her; she had seen it in Washington in 1916 and was certain that she could play

With Tom Moore in *Thirty A Week* (1918). Courtesy of the Wisconsin Center for Film and Theatre Research.

the part of the young actress as well as Miss Binney. None of her enthusiasm for the role had diminished and when her turn came to read, the seventeen-year-old's performance won her the part and made a lasting impression on the playwright, Rachel Crothers, who would later pen several plays with Tallulah in mind (see B003).

Henry Hull, who was Miss Binney's leading man, also decided to leave the play on weekends, and his replacement, Sidney Blackmer, began rehearsing with Tallulah early in the summer. Their first weekend to star in *39 East* was July 25th and 26th. ("Tallulah Bankhead gave to her performance of Penelope Penn the idyllic beauty which it demands," said one New York critic.) Tallulah was finally on Broadway in a speaking part, and the lead at that! She was also causing something of a sensation by refusing to wear stockings on stage and lacquering her one-inch fingernails a Chinese red. She was often glimpsed riding through Central Park in a hansom cab, a young man at her side and a sprig of purple lilacs in her lap.

Her exhilaration was short-lived, however; she and Blackmer (who were also set to head the Chicago company in the fall) had only appeared in *39 East* six times (on two weekends), when Broadway was shaken by the Actors Equity Strike of 1919. It eventually marked the first substantial victory of actors over the hitherto all-powerful theatre owners and managers, but it also closed the show and cut off Tallulah's income. The doting aunt had long since succumbed to her niece's tantrums and fled back to Alabama, and although Tallulah was still getting fifty dollars a week from her grandfather, her suite at the Algonquin went for twenty-one, and never one to live on a budget, she had also hired a French maid for twenty-five dollars a week. The remaining four dollars a week just wasn't enough for the extravagant Tallulah Bankhead to live on, and to eat, she resorted to scrounging food from the Algonquin's dining room at meal times. But Tallulah suffered very little, if any; she had many friends, and she was as popular as ever at those lavish Park Avenue parties.

According to some Bankhead biographers, she spent at least four weeks during the late summer of 1919 making her debut in summer stock as an apprentice in Somerville, Massachusettes, and Baltimore, Maryland. There is apparently no official record as to what the plays were, but official records *do* exist to prove that sometime during that summer, she found time to enact the second feminine lead in *The Trap*, a Universal film starring Olive Tell. (Olive's sister, Alma Tell, had been the star of *The Squab Farm*.)

As 1919 became 1920, and Tallulah turned 18, she began to feel discouraged. She had been in New York two years and fame was still eluding her. Feigning ill health she was let out of her *39 East* touring contract because she thought her chances for stardom were better in New York than on the road. But those chances seemed very slim.

Sam Harris, the Broadway producer, came to her rescue in February, by offering her the lead in *The Hottentot*, a horse-racing comedy by Victor Maples. She was to earn $200 a week, a goodly sum for an untested Broadway talent. The ecstatic young actress began rehearsing with co-stars William Collier and Donald Meek, but on the second day of rehearsals, Harris dismissed her and hired Ann Andrews for the part. He didn't think her voice was strong enough. (For an actress later known as the "Alabama Foghorn," this seems an unlikely excuse.) Next in line to offer her a professional engagement was John Barrymore, who wanted her to play the fiancée in *Dr. Jekyll and Mr, Hyde*, a film he was scheduled to make for Paramount. In her 1952 autobiography, Tallulah writes that when she met with Barrymore to discuss the part, talking wasn't what he had in mind: "He started to make little animal noises... rose and took my hands in his and started to lead me to a convenient couch" (see B001). According to Tallulah, she resisted his advances and lost the part to Martha Mansfield. Her account of Barrymore's unsuccessful attempt at seduction went unchallenged for decades, but Douglas Fairbanks, Jr., in his 1987 autobiography, *The Salad Days*, gives a different version: "She told her friends that she had pleaded with him to seduce *her*," writes Fairbanks, "but he was so afraid of her youth and the trouble such an act might bring in its wake that he brusquely refused" (see B054). Fairbanks, who was a mere lad of twelve at the time, doesn't reveal the source of his information.

Tallulah was once more out of work, but not for long. The playwright Zoë Akins, who had seen and admired her impersonations at parties, offered her a supporting role in *Foot-Loose*. Miss Akins had revamped Merivale and Grove's play *Forget-Me-Not*, and with the competent George Tyler as producer and director, the show opened on May 10 at the Greenwich Village Theatre. As the young widow in a cast headed by Emily Stevens, O.P. Heggie and Elisabeth Risdon, Tallulah got fine notices. The play did not, closing after 32 performances, but Tallulah maintained fond memories of the experience and once said that observing Emily Stevens's performance and off-stage conduct "was an education beyond that I could have gained in a drama school" (see B001). Miss Stevens (1883-1928), a blonde, aristocratic-looking actress, had a distinguished stage career, beginning about 1900 in plays starring her legendary aunt, Mrs. Fiske, and continuing until her death.

Tallulah left New York after her final performance in *Foot-Loose* and spent the summer and following winter with her family in Washington. But the New York theatre circles had a hard time forgetting Tallulah Bankhead, and when *Nice People*, went into rehearsals in February 1921, the playwright, Rachel Crothers, summoned her to the city to take on one of the roles. As the title suggests, *Nice People* was an innocuous little play, a diverting comedy that caused no great stir when it opened on March 4, yet found its audience and enjoyed a decent run. Tallulah had a supporting role (as did Katharine Cornell, another relative newcomer), yet it gave her good notices ("There should be a special word of appreciation for the comely and competent Tallulah Bankhead who luxuriates in a feline role," wrote Alexander Woollcott of the *New York Times*) and, more important, steady employment. *Nice People* lasted 20 weeks at the Klaw Theatre, but Tallulah left before it closed to take on the lead in *Everyday*, a play Rachel Crothers wrote expressly for her.

It was well-received in Atlantic City, where it opened on October 27. The critic for the *Gazette* thought it was the "finest play that has been offered from the even-tempered pen of Rachel Crothers." Of Tallulah, he wrote that she was little known to the local stage, but he had enjoyed her performance. "She carried the art of expression without over-emphasis, to a most satisfying degree." After additional performances in Baltimore and Washington, *Everyday* opened on November 16, 1921 at New York's Bijou Theatre.

In her first starring role, Tallulah played Phyllis Nolan, an American girl who returns to her small town after five years of eye-opening education abroad to find herself at odds with the folks at home. She causes a tempest, naturally, but things settle down nicely and everyone learns a lesson in time for the final curtain. Frank Sheridan and Minnie Dupree were the perplexed parents of Tallulah's character, and other roles went to Lucile Watson, Don Burroughs and Henry Hull. Everyone had high expectations for the play, but critics dismissed it and it closed after 30 performances. Alexander Woollcott's review, published in the *New York Times*, was one of the more favorable. He thought the play was "good enough to recommend genially for general consumption and not good enough to get excited about." He did not seriously discuss the play's star, but did say the "beauteous Tallulah Bankhead quite justifies the choice of her for the central role." Other critics agreed.

Tallulah was inactive professionally during the winter of 1921/22 (except for a brief stint as Kathlene McDonnell's replacement in *Danger* at the 39th Street Theatre), but socially she was more active than ever. She was introduced to cocaine, which came in little packages the size of tea bags that sold for $50 each, probably engaged in a few lesbian affairs (Estelle Winwood is rumored to have been her first lover) and began running around with a young English crowd, including Noël Coward, Jeffrey John Archer Amherst, the fifth Earl of Amherst, and Napier Alington, the third Alington baron, with whom she fell in love. They had an on-again, off-again affair for several months until he returned to England the following spring. Tallulah said years later that he was the only man she had ever loved (see B006).

In April 1922, it was announced that Tallulah would star in H.H. Frazee's production of *Her Temporary Husband*. The play was set to open at the Frazee Theatre on May 22, and the pre-Broadway tour commenced in Stamford, Connecticut, where it opened on May 9, with Robert Elliott starring opposite Tallulah. In its review, The *New York Times* said the play had several problems, especially a cast that seemed nervous and unfamiliar with its lines, but the reviewer waxed enthusiastic about Tallulah, particularly complimenting her "poise, good voice and exceedingly good looks" (see S7). *Her Temporary Husband* went on to play New Haven, Waterbury and Hartford, but didn't open in New York on May 22; it opened on August 31 and without Tallulah. Ann Andrews had replaced her. No one apparently knows what went wrong. Tallulah doesn't mention the play in her memoirs, nor is it mentioned in the Bankhead biographies.

Although her plans for a Broadway play that summer fell through, she was back on stage that fall, opening on September 22 in a comedy by

Martin Brown, but *The Exciters* belied its title and was considered artificial and unexciting. It succumbed to popular disapproval after 43 performances. As Rufus Rand, a carefree heiress who gets involved with a bogus burglar, Tallulah received excellent notices ("She does well with the role of the heroine," declared the *New York World*), but her vitality was unable to overcome poor material. When the play closed, Tallulah paid fifty dollars to Evangeline Adams, the leading psychic of the day, for an astrology reading. She had only one question: when will I achieve fame? "Your future lies across the water," was the seer's advice. "Go if you have to swim."

Tallulah didn't know it but the machinery to make Miss Adams's prediction come true was already being put into place. Charles B. Cochran, the famous London impresario, had seen Tallulah in *The Exciters*, and was certain that she would be a hit in London. As Tallulah was having her cards read, Cochran was in London trying to interest Sir Gerald Du Maurier, the playwright and actor, in hiring the girl for *The Dancers*, a play Du Maurier had written with Viola Tree. One of the female roles was that of a high-spirited American, and Cochran thought Tallulah was perfectly suited for it. Du Maurier agreed to meet the actress and consider her, and the elated Cochran immediately cabled Tallulah with the news. A few days later she was aboard the Majestic, sailing across the Atlantic, with a letter of credit for $1,000, a letter of introduction to Basil Dean, the noted theatre producer and director, and a great deal of enthusiasm.

A day or so before she sailed, however, Du Maurier had decided against the unknown American actress and had hired another girl for the part. Cochran sent an urgent cable advising Tallulah not to come, but she ignored it and sailed on. "What seemed the most foolhardy venture of the century – born of my pride, my inability to face up to defeat," Tallulah writes in her autobiography, "flowered into rapturous success. It touched off eight triumphant years in London" (see B001).

Upon her arrival, Tallulah was introduced to Du Maurier who, after seeing the lovely determined girl with the dark blue eyes and beautiful blonde hair, changed his mind and gave her back the part. She never had to use the letter to Basil Dean, but she certainly took advantage of her letter of credit.

The Dancers opened on February 15, 1923, at Wyndham's Theatre, and although it was, by her own admission, a second-rate melodrama, it was performed 344 times and made Tallulah Bankhead a star. The October 10 edition of *The Tatler*, an English magazine, called Bankhead "one of the most brillant actresses of the present day." In her first scene, wearing a buckskin dress with a headdress of long white feathers, she performed an Indian dance that was more likely a cross between the Charleston and a Harlem nightclub number. As Brendan Gill wrote in his biography of the actress, "nothing as young and wild and beautiful had been seen in London and she became literally the talk of the town" (see B003).

For the next eight years she was something of a West End cult, her fans often lining up 24 hours outside the theatre before an opening. Her

As Maxine in *The Dancers* (1923). Courtesy of the Hampden-Booth Theatre Library at the Players, New York City.

following consisted almost entirely of young women, an oddity which the press of the day was at a loss to explain (and which over the years has fueled rumors of her bisexuality). According to Gill, to these young women she represented flaming youth, "the newfound, postwar freedom to do and say and become whatever one pleased" (see B003). Tallulah herself was unable to explain the frenzy she caused, but made a feeble attempt in her autobiography: "My hoarse laugh, my American accent, the defiant tosses of my mane, the oddity of my given name, all these may have contributed to my worship" (see B001).

Before long all of England was abuzz with news of Tallulah. Her name was in every gossip column and was soon as common a household term as God Save The King! She lived a wild and unrestrained life, made enemies to be sure, but also made many friends, among them T.E. Shaw (better known as Lawrence of Arabia), Lord Beaverbrook and Winston Churchill. And she had lovers aplenty, including old flame Napier Alington. Although Tallulah would later achieve greater *critical* acclaim, she would never again be the center of such worshipful attention.

As a young actress, she lacked discipline, relying on personality rather than skill to get through a performance, and she had already formed the life-long habit of not preparing for a role, but simply walking on stage and *doing* it. Her antics consistently received more press coverage than her performances, but from 1923 to late 1930, seldom a season passed without the opening of a new Tallulah Bankhead play.

The Dancers took up most of 1923, but 1924 saw her in *Conchita*, an outright failure which lasted only 37 performances at the Queen's Theatre, *This Marriage*, which fared only slightly better, and *The Creaking Chair*, a spooky melodrama that was played for laughs. It didn't excite the critics, but the the public loved it and kept it going for 30 weeks. According to its star, that was more than it deserved (see B001).

Tallulah's popularity continued to soar, and the next year – 1925 – could have been one of the happiest of Tallulah's life. Instead it contained one of her bleakest hours. Before *The Creaking Chair* closed in February, Tallulah was approached by Basil Dean. He was set to direct the London stage adaptation of Somerset Maugham's *Rain*, then playing to raves in New York, and he wanted Tallulah for the lead! "I felt my hour had struck," Tallulah said in her memoirs. "At last I could get my teeth into a role that had guts and swagger and shock" (see B001). Indeed, the role of South Seas' prostitute Sadie Thompson seemed perfectly suited for Tallulah's talents.

She signed a contract with Dean to open in *Rain* on June 30, at a weekly salary of forty pounds, and to get a better feel for the role, even went to New York to catch Jeanne Eagels's performance, an expensive journey that took several days. She learned the part quickly and was pleased with her reading on the first day of rehearsals. But Maugham was not pleased and fired her. He did not tell her himself, however; he let her read in the paper three days later that Olga Lindo was taking over the role. "I wanted to drain the hemlock cup," Tallulah later wrote, and that is precisely what she tried to do (though probably not seriously).

Late that night, in her flat on Farm Street, Tallulah put on Sadie's Pago-Pago costume, turned on Sadie's jazz record, swallowed twenty aspirin tablets, and lay down to die... but not before scribbling on a piece of paper, the words, "It ain't goin' to rain no moh" (see B001).

She awakened the next morning feeling fine, and a phone call from Noël Coward made her feel even better. Margaret Bannerman, one of the leads in his latest play, *Fallen Angels*, had withdrawn from the production due to nervous exhaustion. It was scheduled to open in four days. Could she learn the part?

Could she, indeed. The play opened as planned and Tallulah was a resounding success, although her vehicle was labeled obscene by critics and shameful by conservative theatergoers. Nevertheless, it ran for nearly twenty weeks and helped ease Tallulah's sorrow over losing out on Sadie. But she never got over it entirely, and in her autobiography (published 27 years later) wrote that when Olga Lindo opened in *Rain*, "It was an immediate failure" (see B001). It was not an immediate failure, and Miss Lindo sued the publishers for libel. She won, and those five words were ordered stricken from all subsequent editions.

After *Fallen Angels*, Tallulah starred in an adaptation of Michael Arlen's novel *The Green Hat*. Katharine Cornell was having a huge success with it on Broadway at the same time, but Tallulah's version was not as fortunate. The critics were complimentary of Tallulah's performance ("Miss Tallulah Bankhead may not have that combination of dignity with passionate abandon with which great actresses have shown, but she has tears in a voice often husky with the monotony of anguish and a lightning-like quickness of emotional response," wrote the observant critic of *Punch*), but theatergoers were not as impressed and the play closed before the year was spent. Another play was always waiting for Tallulah, and in January 1926, she was back in the theatre as the promiscuous wife of a British Cabinet minister in *The Scotch Mist*. The critics despised it, as did the Bishop of London who denounced it from his pulpit, but it was the type of role Tallulah's fans had come to love and they made the play a commercial success.

In early 1926 Tallulah was riding the crest of her popularity. It was said that she and Steve Donohue, the English jockey, were the only two people in the British empire who were instantly known by their first name alone. (An exaggeration. There were others, notably Gracie Fields.) Despite her stardom, critics complained that she had not yet had a play worthy of her talents, that she had wasted her gifts by playing prostitutes, Jezebels and unfaithful wives. Tallulah agreed with their verdict and admitted in an interview, "You don't for a minute think I enjoy doing sex plays. But when you're climbing, you've got to take what the Gods offer" (see B004).

The Gods soon offered something different, and when Tallulah opened in *They Knew What They Wanted* on May 18, 1926, the critics shouted huzzahs. "Miss Bankhead, tested at last for restraint and some subtlety, passes the test with honour," announced the *London Times*. In Sidney Howard's Pulitzer prize-winning play, Tallulah had no gorgeous costumes to wear, no glamorous sets to slink around in and was not pursued by handsome young men; she was an ex-waitress from a cheap spaghetti joint in San Francisco, and the love interest was supplied by an aging illiterate Italian immigrant and a drifter named Joe (magnificently played by American actor Glenn Anders). Tallulah was delighted with her critical success and the prestige the play brought her, but concerned that her legion of gallery fans weren't as excited as usual. Bankhead biographer Lee Israel says most of Tallulah's followers were unsophisticated as well as uneducated, and in *They Knew What They Wanted*, their idol was "as poor as they were poor, as ignorant as they were ignorant. They preferred her in the gaudy appurtenances of exhibition rather than in the austere garb of her art. They wanted escape, not catharsis" (see B004). The play closed after 14 weeks.

She was back on familiar ground with her next play, *The Gold Diggers* (which opened on December 14, at the Lyric Theatre), a bawdy comedy about showgirls and their efforts to land rich sugar daddies. As "Jerry Lamar" (a character first impersonated by Ina Claire in New York), Tallulah titillated her fans by wearing gold pajamas and doing a wild dance number. *The Gold Diggers* was performed 180 times and her next play was even more popular. *The Garden of Eden* was part comedy and part melodrama and found little favor with critics, but the gallery girls loved it. In one scene Tallulah scorned the advances of a lecher and stripped down to her underwear in another. It was an easy role for her to enact, which critics were quick to make note of. "She is not asked to impersonate a human being," wrote the critic for the *London Times*. "She is asked to display charm... and this she does almost with more competence than the dramatist allows her." And the *Sunday Times* said that since her role did not require serious acting, Tallulah "substituted her own personality and charm, so that this piece might with justice be described as 'A Cadenza in the Key of Tallulah'" (see S18). *The Garden of Eden* kept Tallulah busy for most of 1927, earning her £500 a week. Later in the year she added another £500 to her weekly salary by starring in *His House in Order*, a silent British film based on the Pinero stage success. The London papers said her salary for making the film was the highest ever paid a film star in the British Isles. "An exaggeration," Tallulah later admitted (see B001).

She crowded three plays into 1928: *Blackmail* (which Hitchcock made into a film the following year), *Mud and Treacle*, and *Her Cardboard Lover*. None of them was particularly successful, but Tallulah's popularity continued to soar. On the opening night of *Her Cardboard Lover* (which was the most successful of the three), thousands of fans, mostly female, mobbed the theatre, stopped traffic, and rushed Tallulah's creme-colored Bentley, almost overturning it. She was a little shaken, but unhurt, and the only comment she made to the press about the increasing rowdiness of her fans was, "I cannot pretend not to enjoy it. That would be hypocritical. I feel greatly complimented by these demonstrations" (see B004).

On the social front, Tallulah was making headway with a handsome Englishman named Tony Wilson, but she lost him to her sister, Eugenia, who had also come to England to play. (Eugenia never did much in her life but play. She traveled extensively and before her death in 1979, had been married seven times, three times to the same man.) Tallulah's beau-less period was brief; she was soon involved with Count Anthony de Bosdari, a cousin to the King of Italy. When he moved into her flat in the fall of 1928, the stuffy press demanded an explanation. They got it. Tallulah announced her engagement to the count, and in a letter to her father she said the ceremony would be performed on December 22 (see B003). It wasn't, and in April 1929, the papers announced that the relationship was kaput. Tallulah didn't have much time to herself that year to reflect on the shattered engagement; she took *Her Cardboard Lover* on a tour of Scotland and the provinces (opening in Glasgow on April 15), followed by a long holiday in the south of France. She also took time out to make a short film in Berlin – the telephone scene from *Her Cardboard Lover*. It ran five minutes and was directed by Clayton Hutton. (It is unclear why this film was made, as it was unusual for an English-speaking short to be made in Berlin at the time, and the outlet for such a film would have been limited. Possibly it was intended as publicity for the play.) She was back on stage in late October in a comedy titled *He's Mine*. Her reviews were excellent, but the play closed after a few weeks.

1930.   The United States had slipped into a depression, but in London, Tallulah was in high spirits. She followed Bernhardt and Duse by opening on March 5 as *The Lady of the Camellias*. Alexandre Dumas's play had been a resounding success earlier in the century for the two legendary actresses, but critics didn't care much for Tallulah's rendition. "Miss Bankhead's monotony of delivery (which in contemporary plays is part of her appeal) and a certain pervasive modernity of manner and style tell against her," said one critic, who added hastily, "But make no mistake about it, she is worth seeing" (see S23). Her loyal fans certainly thought she was worth seeing and kept the play going for seventeen weeks, weeping openly during the death scene. A month after the play closed she was back on stage again in *Let Us Be Gay*, a light comedy by Rachel Crothers. It opened at the Lyric Theatre on August 18, and at the same time, a few blocks away, the MGM film version of the play was showing at the Empire. Norma Shearer had the leading role, and several reviews compared the two performances. Tallulah won, and the play was also preferred to the film.

Let Us Be Gay lasted four months, and when Tallulah Bankhead took her final bow in mid-December, it was the last time she would ever appear on the stages of London's West End. Troubled by a dwindling bank account and charges by the British government that she owed thousands of pounds in back taxes, she signed a contract with Paramount for five pictures and $5,000 a week (or roughly $50,000 per film). In January 1931, she boarded the Aquitania and set sail for New York, determined to be just as smashing a success in her homeland as she had been abroad.

In her autobiography, Tallulah wrote of her time spent in London: "I had advanced from comparative obscurity to international recognition. I had feasted on fame, rejoiced in stardom, reveled in page one note. My eight years in London were the happiest and most exciting in my life" (see

B001).

Tallulah's most prized possession dated from the London period. Probably the only time in her life when she was still was in early 1930 when she posed for a portrait done in oils by famed artist Augustus John. She made John promise that once the painting was exhibited, he would sell it to her for one thousand pounds. He kept his promise, and she kept the portrait near her the rest of her life. She treasured it above all other possessions, and wherever she lived, it always hung across from her bed. After her death, it was auctioned off at the Parke-Bernet Gallery in New York where John Hay Whitney successfully bid $19,000 for it. It now hangs in the National Portrait Gallery in Washington, D.C.

When the boat docked in New York and Tallulah stepped off, ready to begin her new adventure as a movie star, scores of reporters and photographers were there to greet her. "I've heard a great deal about you," said Walter Winchell, the news columnist and radio commentator. "It's all true," was her quick retort. She took a large suite at the Elysee Hotel and reported to Paramount's East Coast studio at Astoria for her first film assignment – *Tarnished Lady*.

Donald Ogden Stewart wrote the screenplay and George Cukor was hired to direct his first feature film, having previously co-directed three films. Paramount flooded the theatres with advance publicity touting Tallulah as a second Marlene Dietrich, an exotic creature who drives men mad, but Tallulah Bankhead was too original, too unique to be a second anybody. In *Tarnished Lady* she portrayed Nancy Courtney, an impoverished Long Island lass who marries wealthy Clive Brook to keep her society-minded mother out of the poor house. She sacrifices her own happiness by marrying a man she does not love, but when she finally finds the courage to leave him, decides that she loved him after all.

It is surprising that Paramount would choose this particular film to launch their new star for it is difficult to imagine a character more contradictory to Paramount's Bankhead publicity than Nancy Courtney. One could hardly describe her as a creature who drove men mad! *Tarnished Lady* smothered Bankhead's flamboyant personality and caused audiences to wonder what the fuss over her was all about.

Bankhead later admitted the story was wrong for her, but said at the time she didn't know how to judge film stories. "I, who could appreciate a play at first reading, could not fathom the possibilities of a complicated scenario after hours of study. *Tarnished Lady* sounded like a good story. They told me it was a good story. Why should I have doubted them? Perhaps it was a good story, just wrong for me" (see B285).

Her next two films, also made at the Astoria studios, fared no better. *My Sin* paired her with Fredric March and *The Cheat* with Irving Pichel. Both were directed by George Abbott. In 1990, at 102, Abbott still remembered Tallulah vividly. "She was a lot of fun," he said in a telephone interview from his home in Florida. "She used to sit on my lap between scenes. I told her people would think we were lovers, and she said, 'I hope they do!'" Abbott said he didn't get to know Tallulah very well off the set, "but we did go out once, with several other people. It was pretty late when we got back to Tallulah's suite at the Elysee. There were several men there, and I remember her saying, 'which one of you is going to help me take my bath?' I'm sure someone took her up on the offer, but I don't know who," Abbott laughed. "I didn't stay long enough to find out!"

In late 1931, Paramount shipped her off to Hollywood to make three more movies. The studio bosses told her she would get better scripts and a fatter paycheck – a thousand dollars fatter! They still had confidence in her, and so did she, but her first "Hollywood" film did little to justify that confidence. *Thunder Below*, with its Equatorial setting, had its share of steam (her body and soul were fiercely struggled over by Charles Bickford and Paul Lukas, eventually leading to her suicide) but little fire. *The Devil and the Deep* followed, and although Tallulah (and the critics of the day) dismissed it as being second-rate, it holds up fairly well. For one thing it has a marvelous cast – Charles Laughton (having a great time in his first American film), Gary Cooper, Cary Grant – but it also has some clever dialogue, good photography and a central character a little closer to the type of role that had made her so famous in England: a promiscuous wife of an insane submarine commander.

The set of *The Devil and the Deep* was not a happy one. Tallulah loathed Charles Laughton (she once ridiculed him at a party, pointing at him, laughing and calling him ugly) and Cary Grant strongly disapproved of *her*. She was also unhappy because Paramount had cut her salary (but only slightly) due to financial woes, and the United States government had sent her a $15,000 bill for unpaid taxes (see B004).

By mid 1932, she had made five films for Paramount (plus a cameo as herself in *Make Me a Star*), but all of them had failed to establish her at the box office. The studio was paying her a great deal of money, but her films were barely making back their negative cost. Her contract was up on November 7, 1932, and since she had one film remaining on her contract, Paramount loaned her to MGM where she was paired with Robert Montgomery in *Faithless*. Harry Beaumont, with whom Tallulah had worked in 1918, directed, and although film critic Richard Watts, Jr. called the film "the worst of her dramas," this seems an unfair criticism. It's a Depression story of young newlyweds trying to overcome impossible odds to make a go of marriage. Tallulah's character even resorts to prostitution at one point to pay for her husband's medical bills. The film admirably captured the sobering mood of the period, but Tallulah's personality was again at odds with the material. Although she did get to utter some comical lines in the opening scene, she spent the remainder of the film suffering.

Despite her movie failures, and despite her promiscuous off-screen behavior (which she discussed with such frankness in an interview for *Motion Picture* Magazine [see B215], studio heads ruled that a publicity representative must be present at all interviews from then on), both MGM and Paramount expressed an interest in keeping her on. Louis B. Mayer wanted to put her in *Red Dust* as a replacement for Jean Harlow, whose husband had killed himself, but Tallulah expressed no interest and in December 1932, she jumped aboard a train headed back to New York and the stage. "I wanted a rest," she said in a 1933 interview. "I wanted to get

As Carlotta in *My Sin* (1931). Courtesy of Jerry Vermilye.

With Robert Montgomery and Maurice Murphy in *Faithless* (1932). Courtesy of the Museum of Modern Art/Film Stills Archive.

away from Hollywood and think things over. I had no grudge against the movies. I simply felt that, through nobody's fault in particular, I had been the victim of the weakest stories that any star of my standing has ever had. But I didn't know, myself, what roles would best fit me on the screen. I knew nothing about films. I knew nothing of lights and angles and retakes" (see B285).

In her autobiography (see B001), Tallulah blamed her failure in Hollywood on the disorganization of the movie studios. "Too many people were involved," she wrote. "No one had the authority to fuse conflicting elements. Cameraman, star, director and writer worked at cross purposes. They reminded me of humorist Stephen Leacock's knight who jumped on his horse and rode off in all directions." But she was also willing to take some of the blame herself. In a 1964 interview with John Kobal (see B083), she said her fame in the theatre was based on a vitality "which, if I showed in pictures, made me look as though I had St. Vitis dance. In calming myself down, I lost a certain naturalness, part of my own personality." Other explanations have been offered – George Cukor said it was because she didn't photograph well (see B087) – but Paramount appears to have been the real culprit by consistently casting her as a victim buffeted by fate. A personality as dynamic as Tallulah Bankhead obviously – like Garbo – should be the catalyst who affects the lives and destinies of others.

For her return to Broadway, she searched for a play that would re-establish her professionally and lessen the embarrassment and humiliation at having failed as a film star. She finally selected *Forsaking All Others*, a frothy comedy in the Philip Barry style, and decided to produce it herself. After a stormy pre-Broadway tour during which three directors were hired and then fired (Thomas Mitchell, a few years before becoming a favorite character actor in Hollywood, was the final director tested and approved), it finally opened on March 1, 1933, the same day President Roosevelt declared a bank holiday. The term has a festive ring to it, but it meant that all the banks were closed and no one could get any money out of them. Theatre attendance was naturally affected and audiences probably weren't in the mood to laugh. The undaunted Tallulah tried her best and got good notices for her performance, but few saw it. She kept the doors open as long as she could, but finally closed the play after fourteen weeks, taking a $40,000 loss.

She decided to find another vehicle as soon as possible, and a month later signed to star as the spoiled Julie in *Jezebel*. The play was scheduled to open at the Martin Beck Theatre on September 25, 1933, but in mid-August, Tallulah became ill and was hospitalized with a mysterious abdominal ailment. Guthrie McClintic, the play's director (and the husband of Katharine Cornell), suspended rehearsals for a time, but as Tallulah's condition worsened, he replaced her with Miriam Hopkins, another actress from the South. The show finally opened on December 19, only to close 30 days later. Warner Bros. filmed the story in 1938, and Bette Davis won her her second Oscar for her performance as Julie.

As weeks passed and Tallulah did not improve, doctors decided to perform exploratory surgery. "What they found in my abdominal cavities and adjacent areas was hair-raising," Tallulah said in her memoirs. "My trunk lines were matted, meshed and fouled up" (see B001). According to biographer Lee Israel, what they found was an advanced case of gonorrhea, death-threatening even, and only by removing all of her reproductive organs (a five-hour operation), were the doctors able to save her life (see B004). The illness kept her in the hospital for fifteen weeks and set her back another $40,000.

Six failed films, a flop play and a near-fatal illness were a little much for the usually spunky actress. She was sure that only in England would she be successful, so after spending the winter in Alabama, she sailed for her beloved London in early May 1934. She was interested in staging *Serena Blandish* as a showcase for herself and Constance Collier, but was unable to find an agreeable producer.

Tallulah had been in England barely a month when she received an urgent message from New York. Jock Whitney was putting up the money for a production of *Dark Victory*, and he wanted Tallulah to be the star. She was reluctant, he was insistent, and on November 9, 1934, she opened in *Dark Victory* at the Plymouth Theatre. Tallulah played Judith Traherne, a young Long Island socialite who learns that she's dying of a brain tumor. Bette Davis later had a hit with it as a movie, but on Broadway, business was bad, and when Tallulah was ironically stricken with a rare head infection (fortunately *not* a fatal brain tumor), the play closed after 51 performances.

The failure didn't send her scurrying back to England. Instead, she stayed on in New York, and six weeks later, in February 1935, she finally got to lock horns with Sadie Thompson. The revival of *Rain* was expected to be Tallulah's big American success and her chance to avenge herself on Maugham. It wasn't. Although most critics were impressed by her interpretation of Maugham's salty heroine, and at least one (writing for the *New York American*) thought her performance *better* than the late Jeanne Eagels's, audiences were disappointed, and the play closed after a few weeks. She then unwisely agreed to star in *Something Gay*, opposite Walter Pidgeon. It opened on April 29 and closed soon after. "The adventurous Miss Bankhead is adrift again in an untrustworthy drama," said one critic, "and the usual condolences are in order" (see S28).

She was inactive for nearly a year, but the following spring (1936) she took on the lead in George Kelly's *Reflected Glory*, a comedy about an actress who must choose between a career and marriage. *Gone with the Wind* hit the bookstores at the same time. David O. Selznick bought the screenrights for a record $50,000, and began a nation-wide search for a suitable Scarlett. In mid-summer, *Reflected Glory* was in Los Angeles on its pre-Broadway tour and Selznick happened to see it, liked Bankhead, and thought she would be ideal as Margaret Mitchell's Southern vixen. Tallulah had read the book and couldn't have agreed more. As she admitted in her autobiography, "I was inflamed with the desire to play Scarlett. I had the looks, the Southern background and breeding, the proper accent" (see B001). With Selznick on her side, she thought it was a sure thing.

   Reflected Glory opened on Broadway in September, and a month later, Tallulah was summoned to the coast for a screen test (photographic only). It was December before she could fly out – and then for only a weekend – but she went eagerly and made three tests, one in color (see R159). She was the first actress tested, and for a few months afterward was the leading contender, but her name began to slip lower and lower on the list, before disappearing altogether. At 35, she was considered too old to portray the Scarlett who appears at the beginning of the film, the Scarlett who is not yet twenty years old. Twenty-five-year-old Vivien Leigh played Scarlett instead.

   "I'll go to my grave convinced that I could have drawn the cheers of Longstreet and Beauregard and Robert E. Lee had I been permitted to wrestle with Rhett Butler," Tallulah later wrote (see B001). Perhaps, but it's hard to imagine a better Scarlett O'Hara than Vivien Leigh.

   Reflected Glory held its own on Broadway for sixteen weeks, then Tallulah toured with it across the country until the following June. By that time *Gone With the Wind* was no longer an obsession, an actor named John Emery was.

   She had met the tall, distinguished-looking actor during her *Reflected Glory* try-out, when he was touring in *Saint Joan* with Katharine Cornell. She saw him again a few months later while he was appearing in *Busman's Holiday* at the Country Playhouse in Westport, Connecticut. Tallulah happened to catch a performance and cornered him after the show. They spent the night together, and he moved in with her the next day (see B003). A few weeks later, on August 31, 1937, they were pronounced man and wife by a kindly judge in Jasper, Alabama. Will Bankhead (who had been named Speaker of the House the previous year) gave his daughter away.

   Tallulah envisioned the two of them as a distinguished acting team, not unlike the Lunts, and she chose Shakespeare's *Antony and Cleopatra* as a vehicle to launch their joint career. Under the direction of Reginald Bach, with Virgil Thompson supplying the music and Jo Mielziner the lighting, the play opened on November 10, 1937, and closed five performances later. It was an unmitigated disaster.

   According to Brendan Gill, the critics blamed her for the play's failure. Tallulah blamed herself as well, but a closer look at the reviews doesn't justify that opinion. While it is true that her acting *did* come under fire – the reviews were the least complimentary of any she received, excepting *Variety*'s, which called her "glamorous and magnetic" – her leading man, Conway Tearle, took an even harsher beating. But the *real* villain, agreed the critics, was William Strunk, the professor from Cornell who had adapted Shakespeare's tragedy for the stage. The only cast member to escape the fiasco unscathed was John Emery, who enacted the role of Octavius Caesar. He was actually complimented! That must have irked Tallulah, and it couldn't have done their marriage any good. Actually, it's questionable if the marriage was ever "good." Tallulah never claimed to have loved him, and since he bore a striking resemblance to John Barrymore, it's probable that was the basis of her infatuation with him, especially when considering Barrymore's alleged attempt to seduce her in 1918.

The winter of 37/38 was a bleak one for the newlyweds; neither was working and no money was coming in. Tallulah signed a contract with the Shuberts in January to co-star with Clifton Webb in *By Candlelight*, a comedy-with-music adapted by Cole Porter, but her salary demands (10% of the gross weekly box office receipts) were considered too high, so she was replaced by Lupe Velez long before rehearsals began. The title was changed to *You Never Know* when it opened later that year. (It's very odd that Tallulah would be signed to co-star in a *musical*, and perhaps her questionable singing ability had something to do with her contract being dissolved.)

Tallulah's Hollywood savings were depleted and she had pawned as many jewels and furs as she dared, but a revival of *The Circle* brought her back to Broadway in the spring of 1938 and put some cash in her pocket. She was Elizabeth and Grace George was Lady Kitty in Somerset Maugham's brittle comedy which had first appeared on Broadway in 1921 (with Estelle Winwood as Elizabeth), and was most recently revived in 1989 with Rex Harrison, Glynis Johns and Stewart Granger. Tallulah's version was well received and would probably have continued throughout the summer had a heat wave not forced it to close after nine weeks. (Air conditioned theatres were a rarity in those days.)

A few months later the Emerys went on the road with *I am Different*, Lily Hatvany's Hungarian play which Zoë Akins had translated into English. It opened in San Diego that August, but closed in D.C. on Thanksgiving Day. Plans for a Broadway opening were scrapped. It seemed that whatever Tallulah touched, failed: her plays had flopped, her films hadn't made money and even her marriage was deteriorating, but her professional status was about to improve – and fast! (The marriage, however, did not improve, finally ending in divorce on June 13, 1941.)

On February 15, 1939, Tallulah Bankhead finally had her great American success: *The Little Foxes,* Lillian Hellman's play about the predatory Hubbard family of the deep South of a century before, opened at the National Theatre and stayed there a year, playing to capacity crowds night after night. Tallulah never missed a performance, and what's more, she took it on the road for another year. The play won tremendous critical and public acclaim and gave Tallulah the greatest role of her career. "She plays with a superb command of the entire character," raved the *New York Times,* "sparing of the showy side, constantly aware of the poisonous spirit within" (see S33.) It was undoubtedly her finest hour, and she was cited by *Variety* as the Best Actress of the 1938/39 Broadway season.

Tallulah knew that Regina Giddens would not be a sympathetic character. "[She] was a rapicious bitch, cruel and callous," wrote the actress in her autobiography. "She was soulless and sadistic, an unmitigated murderess" (see B001). But she was fascinated by the role, and knew that it would establish her once and for all as an actress of merit and mettle.

Herman Shumlin had the difficult task of directing Tallulah in *Foxes*, and he met the challenge admirably, forcing her to become a *disciplined*

Mr. and Mrs. John Emery (1937). Courtesy of the Hampden-Booth Theatre Library at the Players, New York City.

As Regina Giddens in *The Little Foxes* (1939), with Charles Dingle.

actress for the first time in her professional life. She resented Shumlin's taskmaster-like direction at first, but eventually came to realize that he was right, and in later rehearsals would point to him and announce, "There sits teacher" (see B004). Her respect for Shumlin didn't last long, however; before the play had finished its run, political differences had made them enemies. Tallulah also grew to loathe Miss Hellman (for the same reasons) and the two didn't speak for twenty-five years. Political differences hadn't mattered to Tallulah before, but with a war raging in Europe, 1939 was a serious year politically, and she became intensely interested in the situation. She was first and foremost a Democrat, a fierce anti-Communist, a New Dealer, and she became one of the more active members of the Committee to Defend America by Aiding the Allies. When Hitler invaded Finland, Bankhead wanted the profits from a special performance of *The Little Foxes* to go to a Finnish relief fund. Both Shumlin and Hellman refused, making them, in Bankhead's mind, as evil as Hitler himself. Undeterred, Tallulah became the leading spirit of the Stage and Artists Committee for Finnish Relief and for three months she donated her salary ($1,000 a week) to the fund.

In *The Little Foxes*, Tallulah headed a marvelous cast, including Dan Duryea, Patricia Collinge, Carl Benton Reid and Charles Dingle, and she became particularly fond of Eugenia Rawls, the understudy for the role of Alexandra, Regina's seventeen-year-old daughter. Miss Rawls took over the role when the play went on tour, and she and Tallulah became as close as real-life mother and daughter, a relationship that lasted until Tallulah's death. When Eugenia married Donald Seawell, Tallulah engaged him as her personal lawyer; when their children were born, Tallulah became their godmother; and when Tallulah made out her will, she rewarded them generously.

Several of the original cast members were later transported to Hollywood for the 1941 film version of *The Little Foxes*. Tallulah wasn't one of them; she wasn't considered a box office draw. It's hard to find a written account of Tallulah's reaction to the news (she avoids the issue entirely in her autobiography) but John Emery, still her husband at the time, said she threw bric-a-brac at the walls until her apartment "looked like the London blitz had hit it." (See B118). The role was assigned to Bette Davis, who received an Oscar nomination for her performance.

Besides marking the date of Tallulah's career pinnacle, 1939 was also the year she was introduced to baseball. One night after a performance, she was introduced to outfielder Mel Ott and catcher Harry "the horse" Danning at Billy La Hiff's Tavern. They played for the New York Giants and she became a fanatical rooter for the team, shouting and cheering wildly from the stands. She once said that one of the saddest days in her life was when the Giants moved to San Francisco.

The Little Foxes began its tour in February 1940, in Washington, with Tallulah's proud father in the audience. From there it moved to Philadelphia, Boston, Toronto, Detroit and Chicago before its stars returned to New York in June. Eugenia Rawls kept a daily diary during the tour (and the subsequent national tour that followed) and portions of that diary are reprinted in her book, *Tallulah, a Memory* (see B005), providing an interesting look at the hardships and rewards a touring company experiences.

On July 1, in Maplewood, New Jersey, Tallulah and Eugenia opened in Cheryl Crawford's production of *The Second Mrs. Tanqueray*, which made the summer circuit rounds until the beginning of September. This has often been noted as Tallulah Bankhead's debut in summer theatre, but she had actually been introduced to summer stock several years before, twenty-one to be exact, if the reports of her summer activities of 1919 are accurate. The first *official* record of Tallulah's involvement with summer stock dates from 1922. In June of that year, after leaving the cast of *Her Temporary Husband*, she joined the George Marshall Players for a two-week engagement at Baltimore's New Lyceum Theatre doing *Sleeping Partners* and *Good Gracious, Annabelle*. A young Chester Morris was her leading man. Baltimore was in the clutches of a record-breaking heat wave that month, but the plays were so amusing, said local critics, that no one gave a thought to the heat (except between acts).

After her 1940 foray into summer stock, Tallulah went back on the road as Regina Giddens. The national tour of *The Little Foxes* began in Princeton, New Jersey, on September 14, 1940, and ended in Philadelphia on April 5, 1941. During those seven months, the cast covered some 2,500 miles by train, zigzagging from coast to coast, giving a total of 87 performances. It ended on a happy note, with Eugenia's marriage (Tallulah served as matron of honor), but the opening performance had been marred by sadness. Shortly before curtain time, Tallulah received an urgent message that her father was gravely ill in a Washington hospital. Will Bankhead, at 66, had been in failing health since suffering the first of several heart attacks in 1933. He had been in Maryland the week before to open the Democratic Convention, but had suffered another heart attack minutes before he was to have delivered his speech. He had recovered slightly, enough to be moved to Washington, but had suddenly relapsed. Tallulah decided to go ahead with the play, and catch a train to Washington immediately following. By the time she arrived, he was dead. Tallulah was unable to attend the funeral, but a touching passage from Eugenia's diary describes an early morning a few months later when the cast of *Foxes* was passing through Alabama: "the train pulled into a siding and I wondered why the stop until, looking through the train window, I saw Tallulah, a small and gallant figure... walking down the track to be met and driven to her father's grave" (see B005).

In late 1941, after a summer stock tour of *Her Cardboard Lover* with Fred Keating and Harry Ellerbe, she spent six weeks in Reno getting a divorce from Emery, adopted a lion cub whom she christened Winston Churchill (she had a veritable menagerie of animals including several dogs, cats, a parrot and a monkey) and opened in a new play, *Clash by Night*. In the bleak drama by Clifford Odets, Tallulah was a humdrum Staten Island housewife who clashes with husband Lee J. Cobb and lover Joseph Schildkraut. She also clashed with the producer, Billy Rose, who was fresh from his water circus triumph at the 1939 World's Fair. As a dry land producer he was all wet, however, and the production was beset with flaring tempers and wounded egos. The off-stage tension naturally affected the on-stage performances, and although Tallulah received generally good notices, the play did not and closed early in 1942 after 49 performances. It was rewritten slightly in 1952 and gave Barbara Stanwyck one of her meatier film roles.

With *Clash by Night*, Tallulah lost some of the ground she had gained in *Foxes*, but she was back in top form as the star of *The Skin of Our Teeth,* which opened on November 18, 1942. It was an allegorical play by Thornton Wilder, in which the Antrobus family of Excelsior, New Jersey (Fredric March, Florence Eldridge, their maid, Tallulah, and two children) survive the ice age, the great flood and a great war, but only by the skin of their teeth. As Sabina, the flippant maid, Tallulah had a field day. She was the play's backbone, and gave it its humor, especially in scenes where she would suddenly step out of character and address the audience with such ad-libbed lines as "I don't understand a word of this play, not a word," and "I didn't want to be in this silly play, but I needed the work." Reviewers loved her, and thought the play tended to drag when she wasn't on stage. Accordingly, her witty, winning performance won her another nod from *Variety* as the year's best actress. The New York Drama Critics agreed, and she received a similar citation from the Barter Theatre in Abingdon, Virginia. The play won the Pulitzer.

Tallulah had great faith in the material, but not in her producer, Michael Myerberg, or director, Elia Kazan. She fought with them bitterly, and also wouldn't speak to Fredric March or Florence Eldridge off stage. She did manage to remain on speaking terms with cast member Florence Reed, and Dick Van Patten, who had a small part in the play, still remembers her fondly. "I was 14 then," he wrote in a 1990 letter to the author, "and Miss Bankhead said I was the only child actor she liked because I could read the Racing Form. She was generous to a fault, and used to give money to anyone who needed it. She loved the play even when nobody thought it had a chance. I will never forget her." Tallulah never forgot him either. In 1960, nearly twenty years after they had worked together, Tallulah mentioned him in an interview to promote her newest play, *Midgie Purvis* (in which three children appeared). She said she didn't like sharing the stage with children, but admitted Van Patten "was an exception. He was a 14-year-old who read the Racing Form and gave me tips on horses. He was a dahling, and I still read the racing news."

She left the play on May 29, 1943 (after 229 performances) due to ulcers and exhaustion and was replaced by Miriam Hopkins. Regarding the rumors that Tallulah was an alcoholic at the time, thus explaining her frayed nerves, Van Patten said, "She did not drink and was on the wagon for the run of the play [she had sworn off alcohol until the Allies recaptured Dunkirk]; however she did consume about twenty Coca Colas a day."

Despite the critical success of her performance, *The Skin of Our Teeth* was not a happy experience. She needed a rest. Moving away from the city seemed a good idea so she bought a rambling white brick house in

Bedford Village, a rural community about an hour's drive north of New York City, in Westchester County. With it came nearly twenty acres of hills and trees, giving her plenty of room to romp and play. She named her house "Windows" because it had 75 of them, added several animals to her pet collection, and soon had going a tremendous house party that continued, more or less, as long as she lived there. At Windows, Tallulah was never alone (in fact, the three things she hated most were going to bed, getting up, and being alone) and in addition to the staff, four or more guests were always there. Her friend Estelle Winwood dropped in one afternoon and stayed for two years, and, later in the decade Patsy Kelly moved in. Kelly, who livened many a 1930s film with her wisecracks, had fallen on hard times and Tallulah gave her a home and a job as paid companion. Word has it they were lovers as well as friends. In the early Fifties, Tallulah invited Patsy to be a guest on her television program, *All Star Revue*. She was a hit, and her career was reborn.

Tallulah made several changes at Windows – a new oil burner, a new well, new landscaping (including 5,000 daffodils, 150 rose bushes and large plantings of rhododendron, tulips and lily of the valley) and she had a large swimming pool put in. A visiting reporter being shown the grounds, asked if she grew any vegetables. "Of course I do," she replied. "I grow chives for my vichyssoise and mint for my juleps."

Tallulah molded Windows to suit her tastes, and her tastes were expensive. By the summer of 1943, her bank account was almost depleted and going back to work was a must. Her name was still hot in New York, but it wasn't a Broadway producer who offered her a job; it was Alfred Hitchcock.

It had been eleven years since her last movie (apart from a brief appearance in *Stage Door Canteen* earlier that year), and her films had all been failures. She was also 41 years old, but none of that mattered to Hitchcock, who offered her $75,000 to play the leading role in *Lifeboat*. How could she turn down such an offer?

Using a John Steinbeck story as a basis, Jo Swerling fashioned a screenplay around the fate of nine survivors of a U-boat torpedo, adrift in a 40-foot lifeboat in the middle of the Atlantic. One of the passengers turns out to be the captain of the Nazi submarine responsible for their plight. It was a tense drama and was a remarkable achievement for Hitchcock in that the entire film took place within the small boat. It was shot entirely in a studio tank at 20th Century-Fox and made generous use of fake fog, wind machines and process shots of the open ocean. It was a fifteen week endurance test for the cast, and Tallulah apparently suffered more than the others. "Thanks to the heat, the singeing lights, submersions followed by rapid dryings-out, I came down with pneumonia early in November," she wrote in her autobiography, and before the film was finished, she came down with pneumonia *again* (see B001). Nevertheless, she stuck it out, and when the film was released early the following year, she was richly rewarded. It was the most interesting and accomplished performance of her film career and showed what she could do with the right part. As the reviewer for the *New York Post* wrote, "Tallulah Bankhead comes into her own in this picture... She is supremely assured and appealing." When the New York film critics met to name the best performance of 1944 by an actress, Tallulah Bankhead was the victor, getting fifteen out of eighteen votes. "At last I had licked the screen," Tallulah later wrote, "a screen which had six times betrayed me" (see B001).

The success of *Lifeboat* led to another film offer, from Ernst Lubitsch, who wanted Tallulah to impersonate Catherine the Great in *A Royal Scandal*, a satiric treatment of the Empress, focusing on her flirtations and adulteries. She accepted the $125,000 offer, and again went to Hollywood and reported for duty at 20th Century-Fox, but this time on a different sound stage, one designed to resemble the Czarina's opulent St. Petersburg palace. And for nearly four months in late 1944, Tallulah cavorted in that palace, wearing beautiful costumes by Rene Hubert and sparring with political advisor Charles Coburn, lady in waiting Anne Baxter and young cavalry officer William Eythe.

Lubitsch was set to direct, but ill health forced him to turn over the reins to Otto Preminger. Lubitsch stayed on as producer, but Preminger lacked his "touch." In a 1990 letter to the author, Vincent Price, who had a minor role, wrote: "*A Royal Scandal* would have been a great film if Mr. Lubitsch had directed. He read us all the script before he was taken ill and it was hilarious, but as it turned out, Miss B. and the whole film was rather Germanically flat." The critics tended to agree, and although Tallulah had never looked better and did manage to inject some gaiety into the proceedings, box office receipts were disappointing.

Tallulah got along well with her director. Preminger was particularly fond of her, and grateful for a kindness she had done him (or rather, his Austrian parents) when Hitler had invaded his homeland in 1938. The elderly Premingers fled Austria and tried to immigrate to America, but quota laws would not allow them to become citizens. Tallulah learned of their plight and asked her father, then Speaker of the House, to use his influence to change the law temporarily due to wartime circumstances. He did, and the Premingers (and thousands of other Europeans like them) were able to find a new home in America. The director never forgot that, and in his autobiography (published in 1977), admitted that a few days before filming was to begin on *A Royal Scandal*, Lubitsch wanted to replace Bankhead with Greta Garbo (who had allegedly expressed an interest in doing the film), but he wouldn't agree and insisted that Tallulah remain (see B116).

Back at Windows in time for Christmas, 1944, Tallulah decided it was time for another crack at Broadway. In January 1945, rehearsals began for Philip Barry's *Foolish Notion*, a comedy about a family that imagines the wife's deceased husband is not only still alive, but coming home. The cast included Henry Hull (who had been Tallulah's leading man in *Everyday* in 1921 and also one of the passengers in Hitchcock's *Lifeboat*), Donald Cook and Mildred Dunnock. The play had a successful pre-Broadway tour, but when it opened at the Martin Beck Theatre on March 15, reviews were lukewarm. "Tallulah Bankhead works valiantly to illuminate a murky script," wrote the critic for New York's *Herald*

Tribune. "She is the only really fine thing about *Foolish Notion*" (see S36). It was performed 104 times before Tallulah took it on a brief tour.

As *Foolish Notion* was being readied for Broadway, Tallulah made her singing debut on national radio warbling "I'll Be Seeing You" with Clifton Webb. She had recorded two songs in England and had sung a little in her films, but by 1945, her singing voice (which was never very good) had grown even worse. The program was the popular *Raleigh Room with Hildegarde* (see R49), and Tallulah made several more appearances on the program, even being named the most popular guest by listeners. Anna Sosenko produced the series, and in a 1991 telephone interview with the author, she said she sometimes regretted making Tallulah sing.

"I asked her to be on the show because the material was suitable for her, but singing was something she probably shouldn't have done. Tallulah knew her voice wasn't the best, but I don't think she knew just how bad it really was. I'm sorry now that we asked her to sing." Miss Sosenko added that Tallulah was highly professional when doing the show. "She always knew her lines and everyone elses too."

In 1946, with *Foolish Notion* well behind her, Tallulah dusted off Noël Coward's *Private Lives*, which had been a huge Broadway success in 1930, hand selected a supporting cast (Donald Cook, Alice Pearce, Mary Mason and Alexander Clark) and hit the summer circuit, opening in rural Connecticut and continuing into Canada. Tallulah enjoyed summer theatre, and why not? She had complete control of every detail and audiences were always appreciative. When the tour ended, late in 1946, she was several thousand dollars richer. 1947 brought her back to Broadway in Jean Cocteau's *The Eagle Has Two Heads*, a romantic drama set in a mythical European kingdom. The play opened on March 19 and gave Tallulah the chance to wear some stunning costumes and enact a powerful death scene, tumbling down several stairs, but it flopped, closing after 29 performances. Tallulah's leading man was Austrian-born Helmut Dantine, a young film actor who was a last minute replacement for Marlon Brando. The 23-year-old Brando had lasted through several try-out performances, but according to Richard Maney, Tallulah's press agent, his behavior on-stage was inexcusable. "During Tallulah's soliloquy [22 minutes long], he squirmed. He picked his nose. He adjusted his fly. He leered at the audience. He cased the furniture." (see B003). Bankhead dismissed him and hired Dantine, an actor who did what he was told.

Bankhead liked Dantine but did admit at the time to her friend, Kiernan Tunney, that "getting rid of Marlon Brando was a fatal error. No good moaning about it though... but the impossible bastard had what the play needed" (see B006).

After *Eagle* failed to take flight, Tallulah decided what she needed was a boost to her income (not to mention ego), so back to the summer circuit she went with *Private Lives*, after turning down Orson Welles's offer to play Lady Macbeth in a production of Shakespeare's play. (Jeanette Nolan took the role instead.) Donald Cook was on hand again to co-star, but Phil Arthur and Buff Cobb took the second leads. After a July opening in Westport, Connecticut, the company moved to Chicago and began an

With William Eythe in *A Royal Scandal* (1945). Courtesy of the Hampden-Booth Theatre Library at the Players, New York City.

With Henry Hull in *Foolish Notion* (1945). Courtesy of the Wisconsin Center for Film and Theatre Research.

extensive national tour.   Noël Coward saw it in Chicago and found Tallulah's performance "extraordinarily good. She played some of it quite beautifully and all of it effectively" (see B037).   He wasn't as impressed with Donald Cook, but nonetheless, gave the company his blessing and Tallulah his permission to bring the play to Broadway sometime in 1948. It reached New York on October 4, opening at the Plymouth Theatre, where it remained for some 30-odd weeks. "When Miss Bankhead puts all her power behind it, 'Private Lives' moves closer into the farcical bailiwick," reported the *New York Morning Telegraph*, "for she turns it into an exuberant acting holiday – belowing, strutting, mugging, but also looking very rapturous and coquettish when it suits her to." It went back on the road in the autumn of 1949. The final performance was in Passaic, New Jersey, on June 3, 1950.   During Tallulah's four-year association with the play, she had played every state except Maine, Nevada and Florida, and the company had grossed more than a million and a half dollars. From her dressing room after the last performance, Tallulah announced that she would never tread the boards of Broadway again.

In August of 1949, before *Private Lives* began its final road tour, Tallulah received a call from Warner Bros.   They wanted her to test for the part of Amanda Wingfield in *The Glass Menagerie,* which was scheduled to begin filming soon. She was elated. It was just the kind of role she wanted to re-establish herself as *serious* actress. She learned the role and reported to the New York studio for four day's worth of tests. According to Irving Rapper, who directed the tests, she gave a magnificent performance. "It was the greatest performance I have ever seen," he later said. "Karl Freund photographed the test. He cried. She *was* that woman" (see B124). Tallulah's alcohol-soaked reputation was well known, but she had promised not to drink during the testing, and she kept that promise until the fourth day, when she was merely supposed to feed another actor his lines. She reeled onto the set, cursing and swaggering, and within minutes Jack Warner had been notified and was calling from California. "I've had enough of that stuff from Errol Flynn," Warner told Rapper. "Every picture we make with Errol Flynn costs a fortune because he is always drunk. I won't put up with it from Bankhead. Go to the next girl" (see B124). Rapper defended Tallulah, but to no avail; Gertrude Lawrence got the part instead and, mysteriously, the film of Tallulah's performance was allegedly ordered burned.

Had Tallulah been cast as Amanda Wingfield, it might have halted her tailspin into the depths of camp and caricature, but probably not for long. It seemed destined that Tallulah not be a film star. She became the star of another medium instead – radio. She was already familiar with the airwaves, having made dozens of guest appearances since 1933, but she had never carried a show on her own. By 1950, television was stealing more and more of radio's audience, and in a last-ditch attempt to hang on, NBC launched *The Big Show*, 90 minutes of music, comedy and fun. Tallulah was asked to be the mistress of ceremonies.

Debuting on Sunday, November 4, 1950, at six o'clock in the evening, *The Big Show* was an enormous success, and critics attributed

Tallulah appeared with President and Mrs. Harry Truman at a 1948 political rally in New York City.

much of that success to its hostess. NBC spared no expense, pouring $50,000 into each program ($10,000 of that amount going to Tallulah). Several big-name guest stars were signed to appear (one show alone had Fred Allen, Margaret Truman, Ginger Rogers, George Jessel, Portland Hoffa and Lucienne Boyer), and Meredith Willson was hired to conduct the orchestra and supply some of his own music.

A running gag on the program was an exaggerated feud between Tallulah and Bette Davis. Tales of their intense dislike for each other had been circulating since the 30s, when Davis started getting roles in films that Bankhead had had first on stage (*Dark Victory, The Little Foxes*). The feud peaked when *All About Eve* was released late in 1950. Margo Channing, the actress Davis portrayed, was supposedly modeled on Bankhead. "Just wait til I get my hands on her," Tallulah growled on one episode of *The Big Show*. "I'll pull every hair out of her mustache." And she said on another, "If they ever make a film *All About Me*, I'll play it myself!" (Tallulah did star in a radio broadcast of *All About Eve* in November 1952.) Despite the alleged feud, both Bankhead and Davis denied the rumors and insisted that, although they were not good friends, there was no animosity between them.

The Big Show became a Sunday evening staple in millions of American homes, and Tallulah was voted 1951's Woman of the Year by the Radio Editors of America. In late 1951, when Tallulah was in London to kick off the second season, she received a letter from actress Cathleen Nesbitt which read, in part, "You do know, don't you, that even if all your supporting cast got lost in a fog and you lost your voice, and forgot your lines, and had a broken leg and had to be pushed on in a bath chair, you'd only have to toss that tawny mane and whisper 'bless you, darlings' and the entire audience would be so happy that it would come over the mike." An accurate assessment of her popularity.

Despite the program's success, it had dealt television merely a minor blow from which it quickly recovered. The battle ended on April 20, 1952, when the program signed off for the last time. The glory days of radio were over. That realization must have saddened Tallulah. She liked radio because it did not reveal her age or altering looks, and because she could read directly from a script with little rehearsal.

Radio had made Tallulah a very rich woman, and very famous, but it had also whittled away her reputation as a dramatic actress. On the air she was never serious; she laughed, made fun of herself, and was the butt of many a joke. Take, for example, the conversation Tallulah had with Ethel Merman on the March 4, 1951 episode:

EM: *I like your dress very much.*
TB: *Now, what do mean by that crack?*
EM: *Nothing. I just said I like your dress.*
TB: *Ethel, my pet. I've known you long enough to know that*
    when you say you like my dress, you're hiding something.
EM: *That's more than your dress does.*
TB: *Now just a minute, Ethel. I have nothing to hide.*

EM: *You said it; I didn't!*

By 1952 she was considered camp, and instead of combatting the image, she gave into it, embellished it and, like John Barrymore before her, became a caricature of herself. Fans expected her to behave outrageously, and they were rarely disappointed.

A month into *The Big Show*, Tallulah went on a lecture tour, getting $1,500 per appearance. Her first booking (on December 5, 1950) was in Dallas, Texas, on the campus of Southern Methodist University. She knocked 'em dead. "It was 90 minutes of what Tallulah laughingly labeled a lecture," reported the Dallas *Times Herald* the next day. "In actuality, the throaty star... danced the Charleston, sang (?), mimicked Katharine Hepburn, mugged, clowned, emoted, recited, chain-smoked; and, oh yes, talked and talked and talked." From Dallas, she flew to Chicago, then Wilmington, Delaware, then back to New York for rehearsals of *The Big Show*. It was a hectic week, and despite the money, an exhausted Tallulah decided the lecture circuit could do without her.

During the early months of 1952, as *The Big Show* waned, Tallulah was learning how to operate a Dictaphone. Harper & Brothers had guaranteed her $30,000 for her autobiography, and when she couldn't sleep, she would turn on the machine and ramble on about her life. Richard Maney, who had been her press agent since *The Little Foxes*, and who had a penchant for purple prose, untangled her random recordings and wrote the titillating memoirs himself.

Published later that year, *Tallulah* became an immediate best seller, was serialized in thirty American newspapers and remained in print for seven years. It was pretty "hot stuff" for 1952. Tallulah (via Maney) discussed her experiences with sex, drugs and drinking and wittily reminisced about the ups and downs of her career, but according to biographer Lee Israel, the book was "filled with half-truths and untruths" (see B004). Ten years before Miss Israel made that accusation, and ten years after *Tallulah* was published, John Kobal interviewed the actress and asked how honest the book had been. "I tried to be completely honest," was her answer. "Of course, one has to protect people who are dead and can't answer back." (see B083).

When her career in radio fizzled, Tallulah, ever eager to try something new, switched to television. Dee Englebach, who had produced *The Big Show*, tried to repeat that program's success with *All-Star Revue*, a variety show for NBC. Tallulah had virtually the same role she had had on radio – hostess – and her contract allowed her to appear on one episode per month, alternating with three other hosts. Her first show aired on the night of October 11, 1952, and appearing with her were Ethel Barrymore, Ben Grauer, Meredith Willson and Groucho Marx. Although well liked, *All-Star Revue* did not top the ratings chart, and the final episode with Tallulah was aired on April 18, 1953. It was time for another career move and Tallulah wasn't one to waste time.

The Sands Hotel in Las Vegas offered her $20,000 a week (more money than she had ever earned in her life) to appear in their nightclub for

Tallulah was a fanatical rooter for the New York Giants, although she didn't thoroughly understand the game of baseball. Courtesy of the Billy Rose Theatre Collection, New York Public Library at Lincoln Center, Astor, Lenox and Tilden Foundations.

three weeks, beginning May 20, 1953. Tallulah was a natural for the nightclub atmosphere, and her stint at The Sands was so successful that she was invited back the following year. The audience loved her from the moment she walked on stage (wearing a long, white gown, very décolleté, and long black gloves) and casually remarked, "now, listen dahlings. I want to correct the impression that this is my first time in a nightclub. I've spent half my life in saloons. But this is the first time I've actually been *paid* for it" (see B004). Her performance was true to her reputation. She was no longer famous as an actress, but as a personality. Later in '53, she lent that personality to *Main Street to Broadway*, a film in which she had an extended cameo. Several other Broadway stars were persuaded by director Tay Garnett to give "guest performances," but Tallulah stole their thunder by giving a bravura impersonation of herself.

Despite her "retirement" from the stage, Tallulah was persuaded by Robert Aldrich and Richard Myers to star in their 1954 production of *Dear Charles*. They had first approached Bankhead in 1953, but she had turned down their offer. Annabella was signed instead, but she was replaced by Lili Darvas during rehearsals. Darvas, too, was found unsuitable, and the producers were convinced that only Bankhead could successfully portray Dolores Darvell, a wealthy middle-aged novelist who faces a serious dilemma: finding a man to pose as father to her three illegitimate children. After a successful summer tour, it opened at New York's Morosco Theatre on September 15, 1954. Reviewers weren't especially kind – "there are many dead spots in the action that even this gifted lady fails to enliven," reported the *Newark Evening News* – yet Tallulah's clowning kept the show going for 155 performances. Dismayed critics concluded that she alone was responsible for its success.

After a handful of guest appearances on television and radio in 1955, she sold her country house and moved back the city in 1956, into a four-story town house on East 62nd Street. And she decided to change her image.

"If I have to go out on a stage once more and say 'Hello, Dahlings,' I shall go stark raving mad," she told her friend Jean Dalrymple, then director of New York's City Center. "Please, dahling, find me something *serious* to do!" What Miss Dalrymple found was Tennessee Williams's *A Streetcar Named Desire*, that emotional powerhouse of a play that had first mesmerized Broadway in 1947, with Jessica Tandy and Marlon Brando. The revival was due to open at the City Center on February 15, and run through the 26, but a trial run at Miami's Coconut Grove Playhouse was disastrous. Tallulah's mannerisms, her basso voice, her throaty laugh, caused the audience to giggle, destroying the play's delicate emotional balance. Tallulah worked hard to remove herself from the part, to actually *be* Blanche DuBois, but she was not altogether successful. The play opened in New York as scheduled, but the audience still laughed, and critics thought she had been miscast, that she was too old, that she lacked the required emotional depth. "Miss Bankhead misses altogether the softer nebulous quality essential to make the neurotic ex-schoolteacher sympathetic," noted *Variety*. "There are some fine moments... but she's never secure or successful." When the first reviews appeared, a party was being given in Tallulah's honor at her townhouse. Among the guests were John Emery and his new wife, Tamara Geva, who ran into Tallulah in an upstairs bedroom. "I walked in and saw her on a chaise lounge weeping. It was a rather frightening picture to see her weep, sobbing very quietly, trying not to be heard" (see B004).

She went directly from *Streetcar* into *Ziegfeld Follies*, an expensively staged revue which was supposed to recapture the beauty and extravagance of the original *Follies*. It didn't and closed before reaching Broadway. By this time, 35 years of smoking, drinking and partying were taking their toll on the 54-year-old Tallulah. She suffered from shortness of breath and was easily fatigued. Her *Follies* contract had even stipulated that she was to have a stage level dressing room and a twenty minute rest between numbers. Despite her slowly failing health, she extracted a few scenes and numbers from *Follies*, titled the creation *Welcome, Darlings*, and took it into summer stock with a cast including Don McKay and James Kirkwood. It opened in Westport on July 16, 1956, and played up and down the the Eastern seaboard until September (see S52).

On January 30, 1957, the day before her 55th birthday, she opened on Broadway in yet another play. She had the title role in *Eugenia*, a mediocre adaptation of Henry James's novel, *The Europeans*. She was attracted to the material, no doubt, because of the name – Eugenia was the name of her sister, her dearest friend, and had been her mother's middle name – but the critics weren't attracted to the play or her performance, and *Eugenia* closed before completing its second week. She spent the remainder of the year guesting on such television programs as *The Steve Allen Show*, *Joe Franklin's Memory Lane*, and *The Schlitz Playhouse of Stars*. She was seen to good advantage in an hour-long episode of *The Lucille Ball-Desi Arnaz Show* (entitled "The Celebrity Next Door"). Bette Davis was supposed to have done it, but she injured her back and – for a change – Bankhead replaced *her*. Tallulah was also engaged by London's famed nightclub the Cafe de Paris for six weeks. She opened there on May 27 – Adlai Stevenson was in the audience – performing a series of songs and sketches, and critics were unanimous in their praise.

Always on the lookout for new material, she took the lead in a dubious comedy/mystery titled *House on the Rocks*. It played a few theatres on the summer circuit in mid-1958, but was abandoned before it could reach Broadway. Instead she went back on the road in *Crazy October*, a black comedy by James Leo Herlihy. It must have been fun for Tallulah to play Daisy, the proprietress of a West Virginia wayside inn, especially since Joan Blondell was on hand to play an earthy prostitute, and her friend Estelle Winwood had the part of Miz Cotten, an aged widow. The play opened in New Haven, then moved to the west coast, stopping along the way in Washington and Detroit. Tallulah hoped to bring the play to Broadway in the spring of '59, but it closed in San Francisco just as the new year was beginning.

Tallulah was occasionally seen on television talk shows during 1959, but it was a relatively inactive year for her. In 1960 she starred in a summer stock revival of *Craig's Wife*, but it was not especially successful, and reports from those who were close to her at the time reveal an ill, pill-addicted woman. Her spirits lifted after reading Mary Chase's new play *Midgie Purvis*. Chase was responsible for *Harvey*, that adorable Pulitzer prize-winning play about Elwood P. Dowd and his invisible rabbit friend. It had set Broadway records in 1944, and Bankhead hoped the Chase name still had magic. She signed the contract and decided to pull herself together; she swore off booze, began eating regularly, and even sought medical aid in easing her addiction to opiates and amphetamines. Vitamin B12 shots were substituted.

The title character of Chase's play is a middle-aged woman who has the heart of a child. As a lark, she disguises herself as a woman of 80 and hires herself out as a baby-sitter to three precocious children. (Five-year-old Pia Zadora was one of them.) The part required Tallulah to slide down a bannister and cavort with the children on a rooftop. It was a physically demanding role, but she insisted on going through with it. On August 14, 1960, the day before rehearsals started, she told the New York *Times* that "*Midgie Purvis* is my second love [the porpoise was her first love at the time]. She's the most adorable woman who ever lived – just a dahling." She also remarked on the rarity of her appearances with children, calling them "terrible scene stealers."

The play opened on February 1, 1961, but failed to catch on and closed after 21 performances. The critics placed most of the blame on the material, which they found disjointed and confusing. Apparently Mary Chase had lost a bit of her magic, but reviewers were generally in agreement that Tallulah had lost none of hers; she was even nominated for a Tony award (her first such nomination), but Joan Plowright won instead for *A Taste of Honey*.

In the summer of '62, Tallulah moved again, to a condominium in a large building on East 57th Street. She also began her two-year association with *Here Today*, a comedy by George Oppenheimer. With Estelle Winwood co-starring, the play made the usual summer and winter stock rounds, continuing off and on until the spring of 1964. She took time off occasionally to appear on television, most notably in a critically acclaimed episode of *The US Steel Hour*, with Nancy Carroll, and even attempted a Broadway "comeback" in January of 1964. Tennessee Williams has said that when he wrote *The Milk Train Doesn't Stop Here Anymore*, he had Tallulah Bankhead in mind as Flora Goforth, the aging has-been actress, weak from a life of drugs and sexual excess, who hopes to dictate her salty memoirs before dying of a terminal illness. Tallulah had expressed an interest in doing the play in 1962, but the role had already been promised to Hermione Baddeley, who opened on Broadway as Flora in 1963. Critics disliked the play and it closed after 69 performances. Williams did some re-writing, scheduled another Broadway opening, and gave the part to Tallulah. It was a wasted effort for both of them. Critics disliked the play even more than before. "Tallulah Bankhead lacks the range, the variety and the subtle development which Hermione Baddeley brought to the first Mrs. Goforth," said the *New York World Telegram and Sun*. The play opened

With Joan Blondell and Estelle Winwood in *Crazy October* (1958).

on January 1, 1964, with Tab Hunter opposite Tallulah, and closed four days later. Broadway would not see Tallulah Bankhead again.

After another brief foray into summer stock as the star of *Glad Tidings* in 1964, Tallulah had a final fling with movie stardom. Since the huge success of *Whatever Happened to Baby Jane?* in 1962 – Tallulah had first been offered the role that eventually went to Joan Crawford – older actresses were being sought for horror films, and Tallulah was no exception. She was paid $50,000 to star in *Fanatic*, the macabre story of a religion-obsessed widow who imprisons and tortures the former fiancée of her dead son. A young Stefanie Powers was the victim and other roles went to Donald Sutherland, Peter Vaughan and Yootha Joyce. The film was shot entirely in England and released in America as *Die! Die! My Darling!* through Columbia Pictures in the spring of 1965. It was a mediocre contribution to the genre, but Tallulah, devoid of flattering make-up, used her baritone voice to great advantage, and was able to imbue a few scenes with her familiar style, magnetism and authority.

As Tallulah entered her sixties, her health began failing again. The shortness of breath was diagnosed as emphysema – she smoked from 80 to 120 cigarettes a day, Craven A's only – and she began to rely more and more on her "caddies," a network of young homosexual men, as companions. They took turns staying in her apartment, keeping her supplied with cigarettes and booze, running errands and making her laugh. But she still found the strength to make several television appearances. In 1965, she was seen on *The Andy Williams Show*, *What's My Line?*, *The Red Skelton Show*, *The Tonight Show* and for a week in October, she co-hosted *The Mike Douglas Show*. She took a respite from television in 1966, but did lend her voice (as the Sea Witch) to *The Daydreamer*, a part live-action/part animated film based on three Hans Christian Andersen stories. The film also utilized the voices of Boris Karloff, Burl Ives, Hayley Mills, Victor Borge, Ed Wynn, Patty Duke, Cyril Ritchard and Sessue Hayakawa.

She was back on television in 1967, as a guest villain on *Batman*, the popular series starring Adam West as the caped crusader. As the "Black Widow," she robbed several of Gotham City's wealthiest banks, disguised herself as Robin at one point to elude the police, and was paid $20,000 for her services. West said he enjoyed working with the legendary actress. "Tallulah was not well when she did our show," he said in a 1990 interview, "but I remember how courageous she was in the face of it all, and what a pro she was. Her sense of humor was outrageous and we got along famously. I enjoyed and admired her."

The *Batman* assignment was her last professional appearance as an actress, but she continued to appear as an occasional television guest of the Smothers Brothers and Merv Griffin. On May 14, 1968, she chit-chatted with other guests, among them Paul McCartney and John Lennon, on *The Tonight Show*. It was her last appearance.

After spending the summer in Rock Hall, Maryland, with her sister (at 67, Eugenia was plump and in fine health), Tallulah returned to New York where, in late November, she came down with the Asian flu. Alarmed by her ever-weakening condition, her latest companion notified

As Mrs. Trefoile in *Die! Die! My Darling!* (1965). Courtesy of Jerry Vermilye.

her personal physician and the actress was hospitalized. She grew worse each day and was finally placed in intensive care. When pneumonia set in, a respirator was needed to breathe for her. She tried to talk once, but the only discernible words were "codeine... bourbon" (see B004). On December 12, 1968, Tallulah Bankhead died at the age of 66. The official cause of death was listed as pneumonia complicated by emphysema.

She was buried in Rock Hall on December 14, in the churchyard of Old St. Paul's. The simple tombstone bears only her name and the dates of her birth and death.

At a memorial service at St. Bartholomew's Church in New York City on December 16, many celebrities, including Marc Connelly and Anita Loos, eulogized Tallulah. A telegram arrived from Alfred Hitchcock and was read to the capacity crowd. "My warmest and most vivid memory of Tallulah is laughter," said Tallulah's former director. "To be with her was a time of fun and enjoyment. When the laughter subsided, there always remained my good friend, a strong and courageous woman."

As Elsa Carlyle in *The Cheat* (1931). Courtesy of the American Museum of the Moving Image, New York.

2

Chronology

1902   **January 31** -- Tallulah Brockman Bankhead born in Huntsville, Alabama, to William and Adelaide Bankhead.

                February 20 (?) -- Adelaide Bankhead dies.

1912   **Christmas** -- sees first play, *The Whip*, at the Manhattan Opera House.

1916   **Autumn** -- father remarries, and is elected to the U.S. House of Representatives.

1917   **September** -- wins "screen opportunity" contest sponsored by *Picture Play Magazine*. The prize, a part in a movie in New York.

1918   Appears in three theatrical films:*Who Loved Him Best? When Men Betray* and *Thirty a Week*. Reviews of her work are encouraging, but she prefers a career on the stage.

                March 18 -- makes Broadway debut (mute walk-on) in *The Squab Farm*.

1919   **Summer** -- allegedly makes summer stock debut.

                July -- appears in *39 East* six times before actors strike closes play.

                August -- the motion picture *The Trap* is released.

1920   **February** -- is assigned lead in play *The Hottentot* but is dismissed during rehearsals.

May 10 -- *Foot-Loose* opens at the Greenwich Theatre. (32 performances.)

1921   **March 2** -- opens in *Nice People* at the Klaw Theatre. (120 performances.)

November 16 -- *Everyday* opens at the Bijou Theatre. (30 performances.)

December (?) -- briefly replaces Kathlene MacDonnell in *Danger.*

1922   **May** -- stars in the pre-Broadway tour of *Her Temporary Husband,* but leaves the cast before reaching New York.

June -- stars opposite Chester Morris in two summer stock plays at Baltimore's New Lyceum Theatre.

September 22 -- *The Exciters* opens at the Times Square Theatre. (43 performances.)

November 1 -- fortune teller tells her success lies "across the water."

1923   **January** -- sails for England.

February 15 -- *The Dancers* opens at Wyndham's Theatre. (344 performances.)

1924   **March 19** -- Stars in *Conchita* at the Queen's Theatre. (37 performances.)

May 7 -- opens in *This Marriage* at the Comedy Theatre. (53 performances.)

July 22 -- appears in *The Creaking Chair* at the Comedy Theatre. (235 performances.)

1925   **February** -- is signed to play Sadie Thompson in *Rain,* but is dismissed by Somerset Maugham in April after second day of rehearsals.

April 21 -- opens in Noël Coward's *Fallen Angels* at the Globe Theatre after learning role in four days. (158 performances.)

September 2 -- *The Green Hat* debuts at the Adelphi Theatre. (128 performances.)

1926   **January 26** -- *Scotch Mist* opens at St. Martin's Theatre. (117 performances.)

            May 18 -- opens in *They Knew What They Wanted* at St. Martin's Theatre. (108 performances.)

            December 14 -- stars in *The Gold Diggers* at the Lyric Theatre. (180 performances.)

1927   **April 5** -- performs in a sketch at the Cafe de Paris in London to benefit the King's College Hospital.

            May 6 -- to benefit the Leicestershire Nursing Home, she appears as Cleopatra during one performance of *Great Lovers of Romance*.

            May 30 -- *The Garden of Eden* opens at the Lyric Theatre. (232 performances.)

            October 17 -- signs contract with Ideal Films and begins work in silent film. *His House in Order.*

1928   **February 28** -- stars in *Blackmail* at the Globe Theatre. (42 performances.)

            May 9 -- opens in *Mud and Treacle* at the Globe Theatre. (46 performances.)

            August 21 -- *Her Cardboard Lover* opens at the Lyric Theatre. (173 performances)

            November -- announces engagement to Count Anthony de Bosdari.

1929   **April** -- announces that engagement is off.

            Summer -- tours provinces in *Her Cardboard Lover.*

            October 29 -- appears in *He's Mine* at the Lyric Theatre. (98 performances)

1930   **March 5** -- opens in *The Lady of the Camellias* at the Garrick Theatre. (136 performances.)

            June 11 -- sings "Don't Tell Him," and "What Do I Care?" for professional recording.

            August 18 -- opens in *Let Us Be Gay* at the Lyric Theatre.

September -- signs contract with Paramount Pictures.

1931   **January** -- sails for New York and begins filming *Tarnished Lady* at Paramount's Astoria Studio. Two other films follow.

April 29 -- *Tarnished Lady* opens.

September 11 -- *My Sin* premieres.

December 11 -- *The Cheat* opens.

1932   **January** -- arrives in Hollywood to begin filming *Thunder Below*.

June 17 -- *Thunder Below* premieres.

July 1 -- *Make Me a Star* is released. Tallulah has cameo as herself.

August 19 -- *The Devil and the Deep* opens.

November 18 -- *Faithless* premieres.

December -- walks away from Hollywood and returns to New York.

1933   **March 1** -- opens in *Forsaking All Others* at the Times Square Theatre. (110 performances.)

August -- signs to star in *Jezebel*, but illness forces her leave the cast soon after rehearsals begin.

1934   **February 15** -- makes national radio debut on *The Rudy Vallee Show*.

May -- returns to England, hoping to resume theatre career.

June -- is persuaded to come back to New York and star in the Broadway production of *Dark Victory*.

November 9 -- *Dark Victory* Opens at the Plymouth Theatre. (51 performances.)

1935   **February 12** -- opens as Sadie Thompson in *Rain* at the Music Box Theatre. (47 performances.)

April 29 -- *Something Gay* opens at the Morosco

Theatre. (56 performances.)

1936   **September 21** -- curtain goes up on *Reflected Glory* at the Morosco Theatre. (127 performances.)

December 21 -- makes three photographic tests in Hollywood for the role of Scarlett O'Hara in *Gone With the Wind.*

1937   **August 31** -- marries John Emery.

November 10 -- opens in *Antony and Cleopatra* at the Mansfield Theatre. (5 performances.)

1938   **April 18** -- *The Circle* opens at the Playhouse Theatre. (72 performances.)

August -- opens in Chicago in *I Am Different*, but show closes before reaching Broadway.

1939   **February 15** -- *The Little Foxes* opens at the National Theatre. (408 performances.)

1940   **February 5** -- *The Little Foxes* begins tour in Washington.

April 15 -- *The Little Foxes* tour ends for the summer in Detroit.

June 15 -- "Tallulah Bankhead Day" declared at the World's Fair, New York City.

July 1 -- opens in *The Second Mrs. Tanqueray* in Maplewood, N.J., and takes the play on summer circuit tour.

September 14 -- the national tour of *The Little Foxes* reopens in Princeton, N.J.

September 15 --Tallulah's father, Speaker of the House William Bankhead, dies in Washington at age 66.

1941   **April 15** -- the national tour of *The Little Foxes* ends in Philadelphia after appearing in 104 cities.

Summer -- appears in the summer stock production of *Her Cardboard Lover.*

June 13 -- divorces John Emery.

December 27 -- opens in Broadway production of *Clash By Night* at the Belasco Theatre. (49 performances.)

1942   **February 3** -- was scheduled to have begun her own radio series on NBC. Plans aborted.

November 18 -- opens as Sabina in *The Skin of Our Teeth* at the Plymouth Theatre. (She leaves the play after 229 performances.)

1943   **April 1** -- moves into "Windows," a country house in Bedford Village, New York.

June 24 -- motion picture *Stage Door Canteen* released. Tallulah appears briefly as herself.

August -- begins filming *Lifeboat* in Hollywood. Finishes 16 weeks later.

1944   **January 12** -- *Lifeboat* released.

October -- begins filming *A Royal Scandal* in Hollywood for 20th Century-Fox.

1945   **January 2** --makes singing debut on radio (*The Raleigh Room With Hildegarde*) with a rendition of "I'll Be Seeing You" with Clifton Webb.

March 13 -- opens in *Foolish Notion* at the Martin Beck Theatre. (104 performances.)

April 11 -- *A Royal Scandal* premieres.

1946   **Summer** -- Stars in the summer stock production of *Private Lives*.

October 27 -- as a guest on radio's *The Fred Allen Show*, she and Allen perform a skit, "The Mr. and Mrs. Breakfast Broadcasting Satire," which became a radio classic.

1947   **March 19** -- opens in the Broadway production of *The Eagle Has Two Heads* at the Plymouth Theatre. (29 performances.)

Summer -- begins extensive tour of *Private Lives*.

1948   **October 4** -- opens in Noël Coward's *Private Lives* at the Plymouth Theatre. (248 performances.) A lengthy road tour followed.

October 21 -- from her dressing room at the Plymouth Theatre, Tallulah introduces President Harry S Truman on the ABC radio network before his campaign address.

October 31 -- addresses crowd of 20,000 at Madison Square Garden, following speech by President Truman.

1949 **August 22** -- begins three days of screen tests for role of Amanda Wingfield in film version of *The Glass Menagerie*. (Gertrude Lawrence got the part instead.)

1950 **June 3** -- the tour of *Private Lives* ends in Passaic, New Jersey, and Tallulah announces that she is retiring from the stage.

November 5 -- *The Big Show* debuts on NBC radio with Tallulah as mistress of ceremonies.

1951 **May 6** -- in a theatrical tribute to ANTA, Tallulah serves as mistress of ceremonies for a series of sketches titled *ANTA Album* at the Ziegfeld Theatre.

September 30 -- launches the second season of *The Big Show* by broadcasting from the London Palladium.

October 7 -- *The Big Show* broadcast originates from the Empire Theatre, Paris.

1952 **January 7** -- named radio's "Woman of the Year" (1951) by the radio editors of America.

April 20 -- final broadcast of *The Big Show*.

September 29 -- *Tallulah* (335 pages, 48 photographs, $3.95) is published by Harper & Brothers, New York.

October 11 -- Tallulah makes television debut as hostess of *All-Star Revue*, on NBC.

1953 **April 18** -- Tallulah makes final appearance on *All-Star Revue*.

May 20 -- makes American nightclub debut at The Sands Hotel, Las Vegas, and begins three-week engagement.

October 13 -- *Main Street to Broadway* released, an MGM film in which Tallulah appears as herself.

1954   **January 5** -- in her first full-length television drama, Tallulah plays the title role of Hedda Gabler in an episode of *The U.S. Steel Hour.*

     August 6 -- begins a four-week return engagement at The Sands, Las Vegas.

     September 15 -- returns to Broadway in *Dear Charles* at the Morosco Theatre. (155 performances.)

1956   **February 15** -- opens as Blanche DuBois in *A Streetcar Named Desire* at the City Center in a limited engagement.

     April 16 -- opens in Baltimore in *Ziegfeld Follies*, a musical revue. It closed before reaching Broadway.

     July 16 -- opens in *Welcome, Darlings*, a musical revue in two acts, with 26 sketches. Played at various summer stock theatres.

1957   **January 30** -- opens in *Eugenia* at the Ambassador Theatre. (12 performances.)

     May 27 -- begins a six-week engagement at the Cafe de Paris, London

     December 3 -- guest stars on an episode of *The Lucille Ball-Desi Arnaz Show.*

1958   **Summer** -- goes on tour with *House on the Rocks*, a play by George Batson.

     Autumn -- tours in *Crazy October* with Joan Blondell and Estelle Winwood.

1959   **October 6** -- *The Boy Who Owned a Melephant* opens at the Palace Theatre, New York. Tallulah narrated the children's film which starred her godson, Brockman Seawell.

1960   **Summer** -- stars in the summer stock production of *Craig's Wife.*

1961   **February 1** -- opens in *Midgie Purvis* at the Martin Beck Theatre. (21 performances.)

1962   **May 5** -- makes second appearance on *The U.S. Steel*

Hour in an episode entitled "A Man for Oona." Nancy
Carroll co-stars.

Summer -- begins two-year summer stock association
with *Here Today*, a comedy in which she co-stars with
Estelle Winwood.

1964   **January 1** -- makes final Broadway appearance in *The
Milk Train Doesn't Stop Here Anymore*. (5 performances.)

Summer -- appears in the summer stock production of *Glad
Tidings*.

Late summer -- films *Die! Die! My Darling!* in England
with Stefanie Powers and Donald Sutherland.

October 11 -- begins a week of co-hosting *The Mike
Douglas Show* on television.

November 16 -- John Emery dies at age 59.

1966   **July 1** -- The film *The Daydreamer* is released. Tallulah
supplied the voice of the Sea Witch.

1967   **March 15** -- first of two episodes of *Batman* airs with
Tallulah as the "Black Widow." (The second episode aired the
next day.)

1968   **May 14** -- Tallulah makes last televised appearance as a guest
on *The Tonight Show*.

December 12 -- succumbs to pneumonia at the age of 66.

December 14 -- is buried in Rock Hall, Maryland.

1972   Four biographies of Tallulah Bankhead published.

1979   **March 11** -- Eugenia Bankhead, Tallulah's sister, dies
in a Maryland hospital at age 78.

As the Queen in *The Eagle Has Two Heads* (1947). Courtesy of the Wisconsin Center for Film and Theatre Research.

3

Stage Work

Tallulah Bankhead's theatrical career is a long and impressive one. Her projects varied greatly in quality, but critics praised her ability to bring even dull plays to life with her vivid style of acting. She was something of a sex symbol in London during the 20s, starring on stage in a string of risqué comedies (her occasional forays into drama at that time were not successsful), but her greatest achievement was on Broadway in Lillian Hellman's *The Little Foxes* (1939), a serious drama in which a more mature and accomplished Tallulah portrayed one of the vilest women in theatre history. She followed that with another hit, Thornton Wilder's allegorical *The Skin of Our Teeth* (1942), but her following plays were not as impressive and she slipped into a habit of caricature and self parody. Her frequent appearances in summer stock were hugely successful, often setting new records, but she was playing to audiences who had come not to see a great actress, but to witness an outrageous performance.

The following list of her theatre work is divided into four sections: Broadway Beginnings (1918-1922), London Acclaim (1923-1930), Broadway Stardom (1933-1964) and Summer Stock. There are four plays included here which don't technically fit into any of the categories: *Her Temporary Husband* (1922), *I am Different* (1938), *Ziegfeld Follies* (1956) and *Crazy October* (1958). They are listed where they fall chronologically. The latter three closed before reaching Broadway, and although the first, *Her Temporary Husband*, did reach New York, Tallulah had left the cast before it opened there.

BROADWAY BEGINNINGS (1918-1922)

S1 THE SQUAB FARM

Opened: March 13, 1918 (Bijou Theatre)   45 performances

Credits

Director, J.C. Huffman; Producers, The Messrs. Shubert;
Playwrights, Frederic and Fanny Hatton

Cast

Lowell Sherman (Bruce Sanford); Alma Tell (Virginia Leslie);
William L. Gibson (Jack Logan); Harry Davenport (Gus "Gloom"
Johnson); Charles M. Seay (Harry Fox); Bert Angeles (Jed Burns);
Fred Kaufman ("Pinkie" Florshein); Alfred Dayton (Eddie James);
Raymond Bloomer (Duke Kenyon); G. Oliver Smith (Randolph
Travers); Julia Bruns (Dixie DeVere); Vivian Rushmore (Mary
Martin); Ann Austin (Cleo deMontigmy); Susanne Willa ("Pop"
Tracy); Florence Doyle (Babette LaMar); Dorothy Klewer (Rea St.
John); Marie Centlivre (Peggy Rogers); Tallulah Bankhead (Gladys
Sinclair); Helen Barnes (Hortense Hogan); Jeannette Horton (Jane
Sanford)

Review Summary

"There are several young and comely cuties who represent the director's
troupe of hussies." (*New York Globe*, March 14, 1918)

Commentary

The Squab Farm was Tallulah's first Broadway appearance, but the sixteen-
year-old was seen on stage only once, and had nothing to say. The play was
an episodic comedy set in a motion picture studio in Southern California,
and revolved around a director and his leading lady, who gave the play its
climax when she refused to wear a fig leaf costume in a movie about Adam
and Eve. Her modesty suddenly made moral men of heretofore *im*moral
Sanford and his crew, and the implausibility of the situation turned off
reviewers, and the audience. The dialogue, however, with its naughty
allusions and hints at bacchanalian goings-on, was highly complimented.

Frederic and Fanny Hatton, a Chicago-based husband and wife
writing team, had few superiors in the late teens when it came to penning
bright lines, witty dialogue and novel situations, but *The Squab Farm* was
an uncharacteristic disappointment.

S2 39 EAST

Opened March 31, 1919 (Broadhurst Theatre)   160 performances

Credits

Director/playwright, Rachel Crothers; Producer, Mary Kirkpatrick

Cast

Luis Albertini (Count Gibitti); John Kirkpatrick (Washington);
Gertrude Clemens (Rosa); Jessie Graham (Evania); Victor

Sutherland (Timothy O'Brien); Blanche Frederici (Miss McMasters); Alison Skipworth (Miss deMailly); Albert Carroll (Dr. Hubbard); Lucia Moore (Mrs. Smith); Mildred Arden (Myrtle Clarence); Henry Hull/Sidney Blackmer (Napoleon Gibbs); Constance Binney/Tallulah Bankhead (Penelope Penn); John Morris (Park Policman)

Commentary

Constance Binney and Henry Hull, the stars of the successful Rachel Crothers play, announced that they would be taking weekend vacations during the summer months of 1919 and would need replacements. Tallulah read for the part and was hired. Sidney Blackmer replaced Henry Hull. He and Tallulah appeared in *39 East* for the first time on July 25, and had appeared in the play six times when it was forced to close due to a city-wide actor's strike.

The play was set in a New York boarding house and offered a glimpse into the lives of its boarders during one spring day. The story was inocuous and simple, but it was that very simplicity that endeared the play to its audience. The lack of the review summary is not an accidental ommission: Tallulah's performance in *39 East* was apparently not officially reviewed, although an unidentified review (badly crumpled and torn) is filed at the Shubert Archive in New York City. Most of it is missing, but one surviving paragraph clearly reads, "Tallulah Bankhead gave to her performance of Penelope Penn the idyllic beauty which it demands."

Although the play had opened at the Broadhurst Theatre, it had moved to Maxine Elliott's Theatre by the time Tallulah and Blackmer made their first appearance.

S3   FOOT-LOOSE

Opened: May 10, 1920 (Greenwich Village Theatre)   32 performances

Credits

Director/Producer, George C. Tyler; Playwright, Zoë Akins (adapted from *Forget-Me-Not* by H.C. Merivale and F.C. Grove); Staging, O.P. Heggie

Cast

Robert Casadesus (Prince Malleotti); Elisabeth Risdon (Alice Verney); Tallulah Bankhead (Rose de Brissac); John Webster (Pietro); O.P. Heggie (Barrato); Norman Trevor (Sir Horace Welby); Emily Stevens (Stephanie); Lillian Brennard (Lady Phillis Nelson)

Review Summary

"Tallulah Bankhead, as Stephanie's high-strung, grief-striken daughter-in-law, showed that she is a promising young actress." (*New York Evening Sun*, May 11, 1920)

"Tallulah Bankhead [is] a most promising ingenue who, with only a year's stage experience, was able to inject a telling realism into a difficult emotional role." (*New York Evening Mail*, May 11, 1920)

Commentary

Rose de Brissac was Tallulah Bankhead's first substantial Broadway role (not including her brief stint as Constance Binney's replacement in *39 East*) and indeed she often referred to *Foot-Loose* as her first play. Emily Stevens starred as Stephanie, Marquise de Mohrivant, an evil woman who forces Alice Verney, head of an exclusive English family, to accept her as a house guest. Her hold upon the Verneys is gained through her threat to prove that her late son was under age when he married Alice's sister, Rose (Tallulah). The Marquise's conspiracy is successful until a Corsican named Barrato arrives. A few years before, the Marquise had had this Barrato thrown out of her husband's gambling parlor in Paris. The presence of Barrato so frightens Stephanie that she leaves the Verneys in peace and scampers back to London.

S4   NICE PEOPLE

Opened: March 2, 1921 (Klaw Theatre)   120 performances

Credits

Director/Playwright, Rachel Crothers; Producer, Sam H. Harris

Cast

Tallulah Bankhead (Hallie Livingston); Katharine Cornell (Eileen Baxter-Jones); Edwin Hensley (Trevor Leeds); Francine Larrimore (Theodora Gloucester); Guy Milham (Oliver Comstock); Hugh Huntley (Scottie Wilbur); Merle Maddern (Margaret Rainsford); Frederick Perry (Hugh Gloucester); Robert Ames (Billy Wade); Frederick Maynard (Mr. Heyfer).

Review Summary

"Miss Tallulah Bankhead is a delight as the catty, over-indulging friend." (*Zits Weekly Newspaper*, March 12, 1921)

"There should be a special word of appreciation for the comely and competent Tallulah Bankhead who luxuriates in a feline role." (*New York Times*, March 3, 1921)

Commentary

Tallulah and Katharine Cornell (in their only appearance on stage together) were two of several fun-loving young people in the play who, in their small minds, can think only bad of a good girl (Francine Larrimore) who is caught in a compromising situation. (She and her beau are caught in a storm and must spend the night together.)

Tallulah left the cast of *Nice People* before the end of its run to appear in a play written expressly for her by Rachel Crothers.

S5   EVERYDAY

Opened: November 16, 1921 (Bijou Theatre)   30 Performances

Credits

Director/Playwright, Rachel Crothers; Producer, Mary Kirkpatrick

Cast

Frank Sheridan (Judge Nolan); Minnie Dupree (Fannie Nolan); Tallulah Bankhead (Phyllis Nolan); Lucile Watson (Mrs. Raymond); Mary Donnelly (May Raymond); Don Burroughs (T.D. Raymond); Henry Hull (John McFarlane)

Review Summary

"Tallulah Bankhead has an agreeable manner, a good diction and a certain sincerity." (*New York American*, November 17, 1921)

"Tallulah Bankhead, though suffering from hoarseness, was a clean-cut and effective Phyllis." (*New York World*, November 17, 1921)

"Tallulah Bankhead is showing encouraging growth, and barring a mannerism of speech or two, she appears to have before her no obstacles to achieving finer parts." (*Christian Science Monitor*, December 12, 1921)

Commentary

Rachel Crothers wrote *Everyday* especially for Tallulah, and it is a pity that the play wasn't better received. Critics found it talky and inactive, but they were unamimous in their praise for its star. The reviewer for *Christian Science Monitor* (see review summary) was especially perceptive in his critique, and it is interesting to note that the mannerisms that later came to define a Bankhead performance, were already much in evidence by 1921.

Tallulah starred as Phyllis Nolan, a nineteen-year-old girl who spends two years in Europe and returns to her small-town home in Missouri with an entirely new outlook on life. She is shocked to find it ugly and cheap. The discovery that her politician father is domineering and bigoted and that her mother is a pathetic brow-beaten woman is also disturbing. Phyllis also discovers that she is expected to marry the state's political boss and, for a time, she tries to readjust herself to the old conditions, but finally revolts and marries the son of the local butcher, a wounded warrior back from France who is the only honest idealist among the townspeople.

Henry Hull played the young man Tallulah married, and he married her again twenty-six years later in *Foolish Notion* (see S36).

S6   DANGER

Opened: Dec. 22, 1921 (39th Street Theatre)   79 Performances

Credits
Producer, Carle Carleton; Playwright, Cosmo Hamilton

Cast
Gilda Leary (Mrs. Sturgess); Leslie Howard (Percy Sturgess); Marie Goff (Mrs. Scorrier); Ruth Hammond (Elizabeth); Kathlene MacDonnel (Mary Hubbard); H.B. Warner (John Fitzroy Scorrier); Stapleton Kent (Albert); Knox Orde (Hon. Algernon Menkin, M.P.)

Commentary
Tallulah Bankhead briefly replaced one of the female cast members, but there is some confusion as to which female cast member she replaced. Some sources list Marie Goff, while others insist it was Kathlene MacDonnell. Tallulah said in her autobiography that it was MacDonnell, so let's leave it at that. It is also hard to say exactly when the replacement took place – either December 1921, or January 1922. Suffice it to say that it was only for a short time, approximately two weeks. No reviews of Tallulah's performance in *Danger* have been found. A pity, for they would settle both arguments.

S7   HER TEMPORARY HUSBAND

Opened: May 9, 1922 (Stamford Theatre, Stamford, Conn.)

Credits
Director, H.H. Frazee; Produced by, Players and Patrons Associated, Inc.; Playwright, Edward Paulton; Settings, Oscar Eagle.

Cast
George Drury Hart (Dr. Gordon Spencer); Aileen Poe (Kate Tanner); Harry R. Allen (Judd); Tallulah Bankhead (Blanche Ingram); Robert Elliott (Tom Burton); Thomas A. Braidon (Clarence Topping)

Review Summary
"Tallulah Bankhead does splendidly... She has poise, a good voice and exceedingly good looks... and [she] makes the most of all this equipment." (*New York Times*, May 12, 1922)

Commentary
Several sources list *Her Temporary Husband* as one of Tallulah Bankhead's Broadway plays. It was not. She was supposed to have starred in the

Broadway production, but for unknown reasons, she left the cast before it reached New York. When it opened in Stamford, it was scheduled to reach Broadway on May 22, but it didn't get there until August 31, by which time Ann Andrews had replaced Tallulah.

Paulton's story concerned Blanche Ingram, a young attractive woman who, because of her eccentric father's will, must marry an old man before getting her inheritance. She goes to a sanatorium to find a husband who she hopes will soon die and leave her free to marry the man she truly loves. Tom Burton, secretly in love with Blanche and aware of her plan, sneaks into the sanatorium and disguises himself as an 80-year-old man. He woos the girl and convinces her to marry him. When Blanche falls into a lake and is rescued byTom, he reveals his true identity and confesses his love for her. He also tells her that the man she wants to marry is a fortune hunter, merely interested in her inheritance. A grateful Blanche decides to stick with Tom.

After a week in Stamford, Tallulah accompanied the play to New Haven, Waterbury and Hartford, before leaving the cast to join the George Marshall Players in a summer stock production in Baltimore (see S46, 47). According to some publicity stories published before its Stamford opening, the motion picture star Mitchell Harris was also in the cast, but his name does not appear in any printed cast list.

S8   THE EXCITERS

Opened: Sept. 22, 1922 (Times Square Theatre)   43 Performances

Credits

Director, Edgar Selwyn; Producers, Arch and Edgar Selwyn; Playwright, Martin Brown; Art Direction/Scenic Production, Clifford Pember; Gowns, Madame Francis

Cast

Enid Markey (Ermintrude Marilley); Chester Morris (Lexington Dalrymple); Thais Lawton (Mrs. Hillard Rand); Tallulah Bankhead ("Rufus" Rand); Marsh Allen (Hillard Rand); Frederick Karr (Mr. Rackham); Robert Hyman (Sumter Dalrymple); Florence Flinn (Vaughn); Allan Dinehart (Dan McGee); Albert Marsh (Chauffeur); Echlin Gayer (Joselyn Basset-Brown); Wright Kramer (Seymour Katz); Aline MacMahon (Miss Files); Roy Gordon (Flash Fagan); Edwin Walter (St. Joe); Jerry Hart (First Man); Sidney Dudley (Second Man)

Review Summary

"[Tallulah Bankhead] is a gifted young woman upon whose shoulders we fear success is weighing a little heavily. She looks tired and a bit fed up with her work." (*New York Mail*, Sept. 23, 1922)

"[Tallulah Bankhead] fitted into the part very well indeed [but] she should do something about her voice, which has entirely too much huskiness to be pleasing." (*New York Sun*, Sept. 23, 1922)

"Tallulah Bankhead was charming. She was beautifully dictioned. She had a fine sense of comedy. She had chic, allure and dominancy. But she had been too much applauded before the play had started." (*New York American*, Sept. 23, 1922)

Commentary

After a less-than-exciting career in the theatre, this fast-paced comedy by Martin Brown was expected to make a star of Tallulah. She played "Rufus" Rand, eighteen, beautiful, restless and bored with life in general. She is one of a group of equally blasé young people who have banded themselves together in club called "the exciters," agreeing to take every opportunity to start anything that will furnish a thrill. On the way to a party, "Rufus" unintentionally skids her car into a ditch and suffers a temporary paralysis of the spine. She is brought home but there is a possibility she will die before morning, and if she dies without marrying, the family will lose a fortune. The only available man is a burglar, who has been trapped in the house by the sudden return of the family. In her semi-conscious state, "Rufus" insists on marrying him. She recovers, and months later, discovers that her burglar-husband is good-looking and interesting. Much to the consternation of the family, but to the great joy of the other "exciters," she refuses to get a divorce. A way is eventually found to give "Rufus" the thrill of her young life: he wasn't a burglar after all.

Although critics were impressed with Tallulah's performance, they found the play tiring. Alexander Woollcott, writing for the *New York Times*, complained that it couldn't decide what it wanted to be, farce or melodrama, and the the *New York Post* headlined its review, "'The Exciters' is not so Exciting."

Chester Morris (1901-1970), who played one of the young "exciters," is best known for his work in motion pictures, especially as the star of the Boston Blackie series for Columbia. He did his best work, however, in a trio of films for Roland West: *Alibi* (1929), *The Bat Whispers* (1930) and *Corsair* (1931).

LONDON ACCLAIM (1923-1930)

S9 THE DANCERS

Opened: Feb. 15, 1923 (Wyndham's Theatre)　　344 Performances

Credits

Director/Producer, Sir Gerald Du Maurier; Playwright, Hubert Parsons [Sir Gerald Du Maurier and Viola Tree]

Cast

Gerald Du Maurier (Tony/The Earl of Chively); H.W. Furniss (Billy); Tallulah Bankhead (Maxine/Tawara); Nigel Bruce (Mack); Noel Barker (Mrs. Mack); Ward McAllister (Nat); Lyn Perring (Wal); Juliette Compton (Nellie); J. Phillips-Roberts (A Settler); Frank Esmond (An Entertainer); Ernest Bucalossi (Buke); Basil Foster (John Carruthers); Edwin Underhill (Hon. Charlie Paxton); William G. Fay (Station Agent); Henrietta Watson (Mrs. Mayne); Una Venning (Miss Pringle); Norman Forbes (James Fothering); Jack Hobbs (Evan Carruthers); Audry Carten (Una Lewry); Doris Cooper (Day); Dino Galvani (French Waiter/French Stage Manager); Joan Pereira (Jeanne); A. Scott-Gatty (The Duke of Winfield)

Review Summary

"Miss Tallulah Bankhead in a less spectacular part was extraordinarily effective, avoiding false and strained notes with a ready skill." (*Punch*, Feb. 28, 1923)

"The dancer Maxine is played by an American lady with the singular name of Tallulah Bankhead, and could not, we think, be better played." (*The Times*, February 16, 1923)

Commentary

Hubert Parsons, listed as the playwright, was really a pseudonym used by Gerald Du Maurier and Viola Tree, the real authors of *The Dancers*. Their story concerned Tony, a bartender in a saloon somewhere in the western provinces of Canada. Maxine, who dances at the saloon, loves him, but he loves Una Lewry, a London society girl whom he left behind when he ventured to Canada. When he learns a relative has died, making him the Earl of Chively, he returns to his homeland, and makes an attempt to renew the romance with Una. But she has been unfaithful and is in a difficult situation – pregnant and unmarried. She intends to marry Tony and take advantage of his position so her child will have a proper home, but when she sees him, she cannot go through with her plan and poisons herself instead. Maxine, meanwhile, has also come to England and is dancing professionally under the name Tawara. Tony finds her, is finally able to return her love, and they are married.

Critics weren't too happy with the play, but accurately predicted its good production values and superior acting would make it popular.

S10   CONCHITA

Opened: March 19, 1924 (Queen's Theatre)   37 Performances

Credits

Director, Alfred Butt; Playwright, Edward Knoblock; Producer, Basil Dean; Scenery and Costumes, George W. Harris

Cast

Miles Malleson (Lorenzo); Charles Groves (Tio Mignel); Tristan Rawson (Ben); Barbara Gott (Affrodita); Lyn Harding (Don Pablo); Tallulah Bankhead (Conchita); Mary Clare (La Rubia); Clifford Mollison (Pepito)

Review Summary

"Miss Tallulah Bankhead – whose first name is in itself a melodious romance – was a lithe and lively Conchita, a good dancer, and what her compatriots call a 'good-looker' into the bargain." (*The Times*, March 20, 1924)

Commentary

"Tallulah Bankhead in Conchita" announced the marquee of the Queen's Theatre, marking the first time Tallulah was the star. And a star she remained the rest of her professional life. Unfortunately the play was a poor choice to launch a starring career. Set in a Cuban inn, Tallulah, the maid who is descended from a famous Spanish dancer (and who has inherited the talent), becomes involved with a hot-blooded American sailor who kills anyone who annoys his lady love. Before the sailor can be tried for the crimes, he and Conchita sail away into the night. It was a conspicuous failure, but merely a minor stumbling block for Tallulah. Her career recovered quickly and she continued her ascent.

S11   THIS MARRIAGE

Opened: May 5, 1924 (Comedy Theatre)   53 Performances

Credits

Director, J.E. Vedrenne; Producer, E. Holman Clark; Playwright, Eliot Crawshay Williams; Assistant Director, Jose G. Levy

Cast

Cathleen Nesbitt (Vera Farington); Herbert Marshall (Christopher Maitland); A. Bromley Davenport (James Farington); Tallulah Bankhead (Yvonne Taylor); Auriol Lee (Nan Courtfield); Tom Reynolds (Goodson)

Review Summary

"Miss Tallulah Bankhead was the vulgar lady, and succeeded in blacking the chimney." (*The Times*, May 8, 1924)

Commentary

This Marriage involved a young married man (Marshall) who has tea with a young adventuress (Bankhead) in order to explain to her the monotony of married life and the cussedness of things in general. Bored by his talk, the woman seduces him and becomes his mistress. When the wife (Nesbitt) finds out about the affair, she goes to the other woman and tells her to go right on being her husband's mistress, that she has made him very happy, but she must also be an ideal mistress. The woman recoils and leaves hurridly. The couple are reunited.

In her autobiography (*A Little Love and Good Company*, 1973), Cathleen Nesbitt fondly remembers the play, and Tallulah Bankhead. She and Tallulah received equal billing as the stars, but the theatre had only one star dressing room. It was stage level while the others were upstairs. There was some debate as to who would occupy the dressing room, Cathleen insisting it be Tallulah, she being a visitor to England, and Tallulah insisting it be Cathleen. Apparently it was decided that Tallulah would get the room and all was well until she realized that Cathleen would be breastfeeding her baby son between acts. "I will not have that lovely baby going upstairs," Tallulah said. "This is your room. No arguments!"

S12 THE CREAKING CHAIR

Opened: July 22, 1924 (Comedy Theatre)   235 Performances

Credits

Director, C. Aubrey Smith; Producer, Martin Sabine; Playwright, Allene Tupper Wilkes, revised by Roland Pertwee

Cast

J. Phillips Roberts (Essaie Aissa); Nigel Bruce (Angus Holly); C. Disney Roebuck (Sir John Prestich, M.D., F.R.C.S.); Tallulah Bankhead (Anita Latter); Olga Slade (Rose Emily Winch); C. Aubrey Smith (Edwin Latter); Fabia Drake (Sylvia Latter); Rita John (Mrs. Carruthers); Eric Maturin (John Cutting); Reginald Dance (Philip Speed); Sam Livesey (Oliver Hart); Matthew Boulton (Henley); Joseph French (Jim Bates)

Review Summary

"Miss Tallulah Bankhead has a part so enigmatic as to be a perpetual irritation." (*The Times*, July 23, 1924)

Commentary

The Creaking Chair had the audience guessing who killed Mrs. Carruthers. Was it the Anglo-Egyptian wife of the invalid? Or the man in a fez? Is it the invalid's beautiful daughter (everyone knows she has a gambling problem). Or the detective? Or the invalid who, it turns out, doesn't need a wheelchair? Or is it the strange man off stage who plays the tom-tom? The ending was said to be quite good, and the identity of the villain a genuine surprise.

The cast played it straight at first, but when the audience was less than thrilled, the tone was changed and it was played for laughs.

C. Aubrey Smith (1863-1948) is best known as a jutty-eyebrowed character actor in numerous Hollywood films of the 30s and 40s.

S13   FALLEN ANGELS

Opened: April 21, 1925 (Globe Theatre)   158 Performances

Credits

Director, Anthony Prinsep; Producer, Stanley Bell; Playwright, Noël Coward; Scenery, Joseph & Phil Harker

Cast

Tallulah Bankhead (Julia Sterroll); Arthur Wellesley (Frederick Sterroll); Mona Harrison (Saunders); Gerald Ames (William Banbury); Edna Best (Jane Banbury); Austin Trevor (Maurice Duclos)

Review Summary

"Mr. Coward writes brilliant dialogue; but he owes much to his two clever actresses, Miss Tallulah Bankhead and Miss Edna Best." (*The Times*, April 23, 1925)

Commentary

Coward's play had a simple story (two married women reminisce about a former lover while their husbands are away, and try to decide how to act when he comes for a visit) but the performances of the two leads and the dialogue made it seem much more substantial.

Margaret Bannerman had first been cast as Julie Sterroll, but illness forced her to withdraw from the play four days before it was scheduled to open. Noël Coward called on Tallulah, who had just been dismissed from the cast of *Rain*. (Olga Lindo was hired in her place.) She took the role, the play opened as scheduled, and she literally saved the day. Coward never forgot it. In his autobiography (see B037) he describes the first day Tallulah arrived to rehearse: "She came flying into the theatre with vitality a little short of fantastic... She tore off her hat, flipped her furs into a corner and embarked on the first act. On the first night she gave a brilliant and completely assured performance. It was a tour de force of vitality, magnetism and spontaneous combustion." Critics agreed with Coward's assessment of Bankhead, but found the play too risqué for comfort.

Fallen Angels had its American debut on December 1, 1927, when it opened on Broadway with Fay Bainter and Estelle Winwood.

S14   THE GREEN HAT

Opened: September 2, 1925 (Adelphi Theatre)   128 Performances

Credits

Playwright, Michael Arlen, adapted from his novel; Producer, Nigel
Playfair; Orchestral Direction, J.H. Squire; Scenery, Hamzeh Carr

Cast

Beatrix Lehman (A Lady's Maid); Ronald Sinclair (An English
Reporter); Herman De Lange (Manager of the Hotel Vendomme,
Deauville/A French Doctor); Frederick Leister (Dr. Conrad
Masters); Eric Maturin (Gerald Haveleur March); Leonard Upton
(Napier Harpenden); Norman McKinnel (Major-General Sir Maurice
Harpenden); Julian Royce (Hilary Townsend); Tallulah Bankhead
(Iris Fenwick, *née* March); Barbara Dillon (Venice Pollon);
Geoffrey Wincott (Turner, a servant); Harold Anstruther (Lord de
Travest); Beryl Freeman (Mrs. Wallace/Clothilde); Mignon
O'Doherty (Mrs. Armitage/Sister Virginia); J.W. Mason (Convent
Porter); Cyril Nash (Truble, a Butler)

Review Summary

"Miss Tallulah Bankhead... has tears in a voice often husky with the
monotony of anguish and a lightning-like quickness of emotional response."
(*The Illustrated Sporting and Dramatic News*, September 7, 1925)

"Tallulah Bankhead... has a strange, hoarse voice and a strange breathless
deliverly (is too often, indeed, breathlessly inaudible.)" (*The Times*,
September 3, 1925)

Commentary

While *The Green Hat* was doing so-so in London, it was doing record
business on Broadway where Katharine Cornell had the lead. Metro-
Goldwyn-Mayer later used the play as a basis for two films: *A Woman of
Affairs* (1928) with Greta Garbo; and *Outcast Lady* (1934) with Constance
Bennett. For a while, Irving Thalberg considered remaking it as a vehicle
for his wife, Norma Shearer, but nothing came of the idea.

   Gladys Cooper was the first actress considered for the lead in the
London production, and she even signed a contract. But she changed her
mind and withdrew from the production before rehearsals began (see
B133). When Cooper showed up for the opening night performance, the
two actresses were expected to get into a fight, but Cooper disappointed the
crowd by being poised and pleasant.

S15   THE SCOTCH MIST

Opened: January 26, 1926 (St. Martin's Theatre)   117 Performances

Credits

Producer, Basil Dean; Playwright, Sir Patrick Hastings; Scenery,
George W. Harris; Orchestral Direction, Morton Stephenson

Cast

Edmund Breon (Freddie Lansing); Tallulah Bankhead (Mary
Denvers); Beatrix Lehman (Betty); Lumena Edwardes (Alice);
Abraham Sofaer (Claude Montague); Marcus Barron (Merton);
Brember Wills (Jonathan Waterhouse); Robert Horton (Sir Lawson
Denvers); Godfrey Tearle (David Campbell); Frances Ross-Campbell
(Elizabeth)

Review Summary

"This absurdly fascinating actress [Bankhead] defies the fact that the
character she plays is so exaggerated. She seems to dart and flit around the
three tall, stiff men with whom she is concerned like lightning among three
monoliths, giving form, character and reaction to things by nature
irresponsive." (*The Illustrated Sporting and Dramatic News*, Feb. 27,
1926)

"[Tallulah Bankhead] was quite adequate to the emotional demands of the
part. Her hoarseness, her very breathlessness, suggests fathomless depths of
passion." (*The Times*, January 27, 1926)

Commentary

This particular story (which received some criticism for its raciness)
concerned Mary Denvers, the young wife of a middle-aged cabinet
minister, Sir Lawson Denvers. The marriage is hardly a good match; the
husband is cold and boring while the young wife is an incorrigible
excitement hunter who is always risking her reputation on the tight-rope of
adventure. David Campbell, a friend of Sir Lawson, invites his friend on a
fishing expedition to the highlands. Mary invites herself, and flirts
shamelessly with David behind her husband's back. David at first resists the
temptation, but finally gives in and they plan to spend the rest of their lives
together, regardless of her reputation or her husband's career.

S16   THEY KNEW WHAT THEY WANTED

Opened: May 18, 1926 (St. Martin's Theatre)   108 Performances

Credits

Director/Producer, Basil Dean; Playwright, Sidney Howard;
Scenery, George W. Harris, adapted from the original designs of
Carolyn Hancock; Orchestral Direction, Morton Stephenson

Cast

Glenn Anders (Joe); Wilfred E. Shine (Father McKee); Guy Pelham
Boulton (Ah Gee); Sam Livesey (Tony); Leonard Loan (The RFD);
Tallulah Bankhead (Amy); Mario Mariani (Angelo); Enrico Gangi
(Giorgio); James Dyrenforth (The Doctor); Giuseppina Pessione
(First Italian Mother); Master Mario Borlenghi (Her Son); Rena

Pessione (Second Italian Mother); Livgina Massara (Her Daughter); Charles Lennars, Gnoci Adamo, Jenny Giusti, Beatrix Lehman, Eileen Raven (Italian Farm Hands)

Review Summary

"Miss Bankhead, tested at last for restraint and some subtlety, passes the test with honour." (*The Times*, May 19, 1926)

"It is impossible not to feel rather tired of the perpetual motion and nervous excitability of Miss Tallulah Bankhead." (*The Illustrated Sporting and Dramatic News*, June 12, 1926)

Commentary

In Sidney Howard's popular play, Tallulah was Amy, a young woman who arrives at Tony's farm in Napa Valley because she was tired of waiting tables at a San Francisco spaghetti joint. Tony is of Italian blood and had courted Amy through the mail. But Tony is old, and it was the photograph of Joe, the young farmhand, that had persuaded Amy to come to Napa Valley and marry the man. When she arrives at the house, finding a party in progress, it is young Joe who welcomes her, not Tony. She assumes he is her husband and begins to flirt, but Joe, a gentle and shy man, doesn't tell her she's made a mistake. Not until Tony is carried in on a stretcher (he was injured in an auto accident) does she realize who her true husband-to-be is. But she wants a husband more than a dreary job, so she goes through with the wedding, eventually learning to appreciate Tony's merits, and to love him for them. She and Joe have an affair first, but Tony has also learned to appreciate her, and after an outburst of wrath, decides to keep her and to father Joe's child.

Tallulah was perhaps proudest of her performance in *They Knew What They Wanted* as she was of any of her London plays. A testimony to her effectiveness in the role can be found in Cathleen Nesbitt's autobiography (see B109) in which she writes about a love scene with Tallulah and Glenn Anders. "They generated between them so much intensity of passion that when he finally put his hands on her shoulders and a little shiver went through her, the entire audience shivered too as the curtain went down."

Tallulah had been typecast by London audiences as a naughty but glamorous woman who, by turns, chases and is chased by men, and the role of Amy was an attempt to break free of that image. To a degree she was successful – critics praised her performance more than any other to date – but her fans were disappointed and preferred the other Tallulah.

Pauline Lord had been Amy in the original Broadway production (1924), and Hollywood used the play as a basis for three films: *The Secret Hour* (Paramount, 1928) with Pola Negri and Jean Hersholt; *A Lady to Love* (Metro-Goldwyn-Mayer, 1929) with Vilma Banky and Edward G. Robinson; and RKO used the original title for their 1940 adaptation starring Carole Lombard and Charles Laughton.

It reappeared on Broadway in 1956 as the basis for the musical, *The Most Happy Fella*, which was performed 678 times.

S17   THE GOLD DIGGERS

Opened: December 14, 1926 (Lyric Theatre)   180 Performances

Credits

Producer, William Mollison, in association with Jack Waller and Herbert Clayton; Playwright, Avery Hopwood; Scenery, F.L. Lyndhurst; Orchestral Direction, David Bor

Cast

Jobyna Howland (Mabel Munroe); Joan Barry (Violet Dayne); Dorothy St. Elmo (Sadie); Madge Aubrey; (Trixie Andrews); Dorothy Field (Dolly Baxter); Marjorie Brooks (Gypsy Montrose); Tallulah Bankhead (Jerry Lamar); Betty Shale (Cissie Gray); Hugh Williams (Wally Saunders); Ruth Terry (Topsy St. John); Joan Clarkson (Eleanor Montgomery); Ian Hunter (Stephen Lee); Fred Kerr (James Blake); David Wilton (Tom Newman); John Perry (Fenton Jessup); Charles Carson (Barney Barnett); Sydney Seaward (Freddie Turner); Jessie Bateman (Mrs. Lamar)

Review Summary

"[Tallulah Bankhead] is as spontaneous and attractive as ever." (*The Illustrated Sporting and Dramatic News*, January 1, 1926)

"Miss Bankhead plays her part with unflagging energy." (*The Times*, December 15, 1926)

Commentary

The Gold Diggers, about a group of chorus girls and their efforts to snare rich men, first opened on Broadway in 1919 with Ina Claire as Jerry Lamar and stayed there for two years. Although the story was often changed, the gold digging theme remained popular in plays and films throughout the 1930s.

The London production, which followed the Broadway opening by seven years, was much less successful by comparison, lasting barely six months. And if it were up to the critics, it would not have lasted that long. The costumes impressed reviewers more than the material did. In one scene Tallulah wore gold pajamas which drew cheers from her fans, and that scene alone probably helped the production remain open as long as it did.

S18   THE GARDEN OF EDEN

Opened: May 30, 1927 (Lyric Theatre)   232 Performances

Credits

Directors, Herbert Clayton, Jack Waller; Producer, William
Mollison; Playwrights, R. Bernauer and R. Oesterreicher, adapted
by Avery Hopwood

Cast

Gladys Falk (Liane); Marcelle Roche (Adele); Diana Caird (Cleo);
Arthur Holman (Call Boy); Eva Moore (Rosa); George Bellamy
(Revard, a waiter); Tallulah Bankhead (Toni Lebrun); Edward Irwin
(Durand, A Police Inspector); Barbara Gott (Madame Grand); Eric
Maturin (Henri Glessing); Herman De Lange (Count De L'esterel);
Ivo Dawson (Count De Mauban); Robert English (Baron Lapereau);
Robert Mawdsley (Richard Lamont); Murri Moncrieff (Maitre
d'Hotel); Arthur Ross (Waiter); Dino Galvani (Professor Roasio);
Rex Caldwell (General Deval); Annie Esmond (Aunt Mathilde);
Frederick Volpe (Uncle Herbert); Arthur Bond (The Prime
Minister); George Bellamy (Prince Miguel De Santa Rocca); Roy
Emerton (Servant to the Prince)

Review Summary

"Miss Bankhead's voice is quite prettily husky. She makes the most of it,
and there is the proper suggestion of emotion too deep for words in every
phrase which sticks in her throat." (*The Times*, May 31, 1927)

Commentary

The Garden of Eden was the story of a virtuous cabaret girl. Toni Lebrun,
a dancer at a disreputatable Parisian night club, violently resists the
advances M. Glessing, hits him over the head with a champagne bottle and
loses her job because of the incident. Rosa, her dressing room maid, is
actually a reduced Russian Baroness who saves up her tips every year until
she has enough to take a short holiday in Monte Carlo and live in her
accustomed style. Instead of letting Toni be thrown out into the street, Rosa
takes her along to Monte Carlo and passes her off as her daughter. While in
Monte Carlo, Toni meets and decides to marry a young man of social
standing. As the wedding is about to be performed, the truth of Toni's past
is revealed and the husband-to-be rejects his bride. Toni does not deny the
story, but tears off her lace wedding gown in front of the assembled guests,
stripping to her underwear. This gesture so fascinates the prime minister
that he falls at her feet and Toni decides to marry the seventy-five-year-old
man despite his age.

In her 1972 biography of Bankhead, Lee Israel briefly describes the
plot of *The Garden of Eden* and insists that Toni loses her job at the
cabaret because she resists the advances of a lesbian, but the various plot
summaries in papers at the time do not support that claim.

London critics were critical of the play; they said it clumsily,
stupidly and ineptly tried to glorify the romantic dream of success.
Nevertheless, it was a hit with Tallulah's fans, and they liked her best in the
scene where the wedding didn't come off, but the dress did! It was the first

of two plays in which Tallulah appeared in her underwear (the second was *Her Cardboard Lover* the following year).

The Garden of Eden was made into a film in 1928 by United Artists with Corinne Griffith as Toni.

S19 BLACKMAIL

Opened: February 28, 1928 (Globe Theatre)   42 Performances

Credits

Director, A.H. Woods; Producer, Raymond Massey, in association with Alfred Butt and A.H. Woods; Playwright, Charles Bennett

Cast

Frank Vosper (Ian Tracy); Amy Veness (Mrs. Cook); Alexander Onslow (Peter Hewitt); Tallulah Bankhead (Daphne Manning); Alfred Clark (Mr. Manning); Henrietta Watson (Mrs. Manning); Reginald Gardner (Jimmy Manning); James Rennie (David Webster); Julian Hamilton (A Detective Sergeant)

Review Summary

"[The climax] of the play is made entirely plausible by Miss Bankhead's skill in carrying an emotional crisis into downright hysteria." (*The Times*, February 29, 1928)

Commentary

Blackmail was infinitely more popular when made into a motion picture in 1929, especially one directed by Alfred Hitchcock. It was his first talking picture, and the German actress Anny Ondra starred as Daphne. According to Charles Bennett, the playwright (who adapted his work for the screen), Tallulah was never considered for the film.

"My original play was about a shopgirl," Bennett said in a 1991 telephone interview, "but Tallulah was not the type to play a shopgirl; her image demanded a more glamorous occupation, so the setting of the play was moved from one end of Chelsea to the other, so Tallulah's character wouldn't have to be a shopgirl. When Hitch decided to make the film, he went back to the original play, so Tallulah was never considered. She wouldn't have been right for the part."

Blackmail was Bennett's second play after a disappointing career as an actor, and when A.H. Woods optioned it and went after Tallulah to star in it, the responsibility of reading the play to Tallulah fell on Bennett.

"Mr. Woods and I went to her apartment on Farm Street, and I read the entire thing to her," said Bennett. "When I was finished, she said she would do it, and A.H. pulled two hundred one pound notes out of his pocket and tossed them into the air. 'These are for you, Tallulah!' he said, and being rather poor at the time, I couldn't help wishing that one of those pound notes was for me!" Bennett soon had plenty of pound notes, and when he migrated to California in 1940, he quickly became one of Hollywood's most noted screen writers.

S20   MUD AND TREACLE

Opened: May 9, 1928 (Globe Theatre)   46 Performances

Credits

Director, Albert Butt; Producer, Basil Dean; Playwright, Benn W. Levy

Cast

Tallulah Bankhead (Polly Andrews); Douglas Burbridge (Lafayette); Eric Maturin (Hector Wilson); Robert Harris (Archie Pretty); Mabel Terry Lewis (Daisy Andrews); Ursula Jeans (Pearl Pretty); Lamont Dickson (Roland Pretty); Nicholas Hannen (Solomon Jack); Ivor Barnard (Alfred Turner)

Review Summary

"Miss Tallulah Bankhead is emotionally adequate to Polly on about half her acting power." (*The Times*, May 11, 1928)

Commentary

Mud and Treacle began with a prologue in which the body of Polly Andrews is discovered lying strangled on a couch, and the rest of the play showed how Miss Andrews came to meet such a dreary end. It was a novel idea and required the audience not to *anticipate* the climax, but to realize its inevitability. That is where critics had a problem; after watching Polly Andrews for three acts, her murder seemed inappropriate. As one critic said, "she seems hardly important enough to call down the lightning."

S21   HER CARDBOARD LOVER

Opened: August 21, 1928 (Lyric Theatre)   173 Performances

Credits

Director, Gilbert Miller; Producer, Leslie Howard; Playwrights, Valerie Wyngate and P.G. Wodehouse (adapted from *Dans sa Candeur Naive* by Jacques Deval); Musical Director, David Bor

Cast

Barbara Tallerman (A Lady); Phillip Clowes (A Gentleman); Herman De Lange (Monsieur Bonnevant); Edward Mervyn (Charly); Robert Newton (Paul Guisard); Leslie Howard (Andre Sallicel); Arthur Hammond (A Croupier); Tallulah Bankhead (Simone); Jack

Melford (Tony Lagorce); Tom Woods (Cloak Room Attendant);
Elizabeth Arkell (Albine)

Review Summary

"[The role] gives Miss Tallulah Bankhead an opportunity for an exhibition
of talent which, if it had more breadth and vigour than subtlety, seemed to
be what was expected of her by the audience whose hystertical enthusiasm
has become an uncomfortable rule at these festivals of lingerie." (*The
Times*, August 22, 1928)

Commentary

Wyngate and Wodehouse adapted Jacques Deval's French play into English,
and, according to a few critics, left some of the wit and characterization
behind. Nevertheless it was a hit and caused Tallulah's gallery fans to cheer
and applaud wildly.

The simple yet pleasing story concerned Simone, a young, rich and
beautiful woman, recently divorced from Tony Lagorce, whose open
infidelities she can no longer endure, yet whose physical attributes still
arrouse her passions. To protect herself from re-marriage, which she
knows would be disastrous, she persuades Andre Sallicel to pose as her
lover and to protect her from the advances of her former husband. This
cardboard lover performs his duties admirably, and before the third act
ends, Simone realizes she loves the man and is no longer afraid of falling
victim to Tony's physical charms.

Tallulah took the play on a tour of the provinces the following year,
opening in Liverpool on May 6, and reprised her role thirteen years later
(1941) in American summer stock (see S49). Metro-Goldwyn-Mayer
filmed the play twice, in 1928 with Marion Davies, and in 1942, with
Norma Shearer making her last film appearance after twenty years of
stardom. The material had also been the basis for MGM's *The Passionate
Plumber*, a 1932 Buster Keaton vehicle. The original Broadway production
(1927) had starred Jeanne Eagels.

Leslie Howard (1893-1943), who played the cardboard lover, is best
known as Ashley Wilkes, the object of Scarlett O'Hara's desire in *Gone
With the Wind*. He and Tallulah had acted together before, albeit briefly,
when she replaced Kathlene MacDonnel in *Danger* on Broadway in 1921
(see S6).

S22   HE'S MINE

Opened: October 29, 1929 (Lyric Theatre)   98 Performances

Credits

Directors, Herbert Clayton, Jack Waller; Producer, Herbert
Chown; Playwright, Louis Verneuil, adapted by Arthur Wimperis;
Scenery, Joseph & Phil Harker; Orchestral Direction, Roger
Jalowicz

Cast

Allan Aynesworth (The Duc de Bellencontre); Frederick Volpe (The Marquis de Chantalard); Helen Haye (The Duchesse de Bellencontre); George Howe (Etienne de Bellencontre); Isabel Wilford (Victorine); Clarkston Blakiston (Hector); Sunday Wilshin (Simone de Chantalard); Tallulah Bankhead (Wanda Myro); Rex De Vigne (Footman); Owen Reynolds (Eugene); Henry Kendall (Maxime de Bellencontre)

Review Summary

"Miss Tallulah Bankhead goes through it all with unceasing animation." (*The Times*, October 30, 1929)

Commentary

Louis Verneuil's rather complicated story had Tallulah making her way into the Chateau Bellencontre by a subterfuge, declaring herself to be a Serbian Princesse, in an attempt to win back her lover, Maxime de Bellencontre, now betrothed to Simone, daughter of the Marquis de Chantalard. The elaborate sets received more attention and praise from the critics than the play itself, which was found to be rather dull, and much too long.

S23 THE LADY OF THE CAMELLIAS

Opened: March 5, 1930 (Garrick Theatre)   136 Performances

Credits

Director, Nigel Playfair; Produced By The Daniel Mayer Company and Nigel Playfair; Playwright, Alexandre Dumas, translated from the French by Edith Reynolds and Nigel Playfair; Sets, George Sheringham; Incidental Music, Alfred Reynolds; Costumes, Mrs. Gordon Craig, Mrs. Lovat Fraser and George Sheringham

Cast

D.A. Clarke-Smith (Le Baron de Varville); Winifred Evans (Nanine); Joan Matheson (Nichette); Tallulah Bankhead (Marguerite); Violet Marquesita (Olympe); Richard Goolden (Saint-Gaudens); Renée de Vaux (Prudence); Harold Warrender (Gaston); Glen Byam Shaw (Armand); Cecil Humphreys (Le Comte de Giray); Terence de Marney (Gustave); C.V. France (Duval); Angus L. MacLeod (Arthur); H. Scott Russell (A Messenger); Marcus Barron (Doctor); Joan Sutherland (Anais); Ellen Pollack (Esther); and Andree Tourneur, Natalie Denny, Pat O'Flynn, Jane Connard, Gabrielle Brune, Monica Morrice, Norman Arlett, Antony Eustrel, Anthony Hawtrey, Terence Ransom, Richard Turner, Gerald Kent (Guests)

Review Summary

"Tallulah was very very attractive, of course, and she does all there is to be done in a part that belongs to another age." (*The Times*, March 6, 1930)

"There are no flashes of genius in her performance. There are no amazing and unforgettable moments. There are no lines spoken with the sudden effect that reveals a world of feeling and experience..." (*The Graphic*, March 15, 1930.)

"Miss Bankhead's monotony of delivery and a certain pervasive modernity of manner and style tell against her. In a part such as this, something more than vitality and a willing spirit is needed. But she is worth seeing." (*The Sunday Times*, March 8, 1930)

Commentary

Dumas's *La Dame aux Camelias* is rarely referred to by its proper name. It has been nicknamed "Camille," and it is by that title the story is best known, perhaps because the many film versions have all been titled *Camille*. It was first filmed in 1912 with Sarah Bernhardt, again in 1915 with Clara Kimball Young, and in 1917 with Theda Bara. The Russian actress Nazimova remade it in 1921 (with Rudolph Valentino as Armand), and Norma Talmadge starred in still another version in 1927, but the definitive *Camille* would have to be Metro-Goldwyn-Mayer's lavish 1936 production starring Greta Garbo and Robert Taylor. There has only been one film adaptation since: a 1974 made-for-TV film in England with Greta Scacchi, however, *Camille 2,000*, a soft-core porn film from 1969, was loosly based on the story..

To attempt a stage revival of *Camille* was, as Tallulah has remarked, a "risky do." She was following in the footsteps of legendary actresses Sarah Bernhardt and Eleanora Duse, both of whom had starred in successful stage productions of the story earlier in the century. And as was feared, Tallulah's *Camille* was not well received by many critics. However, Tallulah's gallery fans loved the play, making it a modest success.

In the opening night audience was Olga Nethersole who had played Camille many years earlier.

S24   LET US BE GAY

Opened: August 18, 1930 (Lyric Theatre)   128 Performances

Credits

Director, Gilbert Miller; Producer/Playwright, Rachel Crothers;
Scenery, Joseph & Phil Harker; Orchestral Direction, Louis Rose

Cast

Tallulah Bankhead (Kitty Brown); Arthur Margetson (Bob Brown);
Sybil Carlisle (Perkins); Bellenden Powell (Whitman); Ernest Haines

(Williams); Helen Haye (Mrs. Boucicault); Walter Fitzgerald (Struthers); Joan Matheson (Dierdre Lessing); Francis Lister (Townley Town); Ronald Ward (Bruce Dean); Cecily Byrne (Madge Livingston); Eric Cowley (Wallace Grainger)

Review Summary

"Miss Bankhead, though her heart was breaking, was gay." (*The Times.* August 10, 1930)

Commentary

Let Us Be Gay had starred Francine Larrimore when it opened on Broadway in February 1929, and Metro-Goldwyn-Mayer bought the rights as a vehicle for Norma Shearer. Their film version was released just as Tallulah's London production was opening, and for a while, Londoners had a choice of seeing *Let us Be Gay* as a play at the Lyric Theatre, or as a film a few blocks away at the Empire. Some critics compared the two versions as well as the two lead performances. Edith Shackleton, writing for *The Times*, preferred the play because the film performers "had to sit more closely together than they did on the stage, and there was a loss of elegance all around." As far as Tallulah versus Norma, Tallulah won. "Miss Norma Shearer... could not give her Kitty Brown the same inconsequent charm the character got from Miss Bankhead," was Miss Shackleton's conclusion.

The story is set in a rich strata of American society. Old Mrs. Boucicault invites the young and pretty Mrs. Brown to entice away a Mr. Brown, for whom her granddaughter, Dierdre Lessing, has developed an "appetite," and which is likely to spoil the grandmother's plan for the girl to marry a decent young man. But Mrs. Brown turns out to be the former wife of Mr. Brown (their divorce is shown in a brief prologue). The Browns try to keep their ex-relationship from becoming known. They meet in secret places, but the granddaughter gets drunk, tells everyone of her passion and makes her way toward Mr. Brown's bedroom, only to find Mrs. Brown already there. It creates an embarassing situation, but the divorced couple must explain, the air is cleared, and they decide to remarry.

BROADWAY STARDOM (1933-1964)

S25 FORSAKING ALL OTHERS

Opened: March 1, 1933 (Times Square Theatre)   110 performances

Credits

Director, Thomas Mitchell; Producer, Arch Selwyn; Playwrights, Edward Barry Roberts, Frank Morgan Cavett; Sets, Donald Oenslager; Costumes, Hattie Carnegie

Cast

Harlan Briggs (Dent); Cora Witherspoon (Mrs. Paula La Salle); Fred Keating (Jefferson Tingle); Donald MacDonald (Shepherd Perry); Tallulah Bankhead (Mary Clay); Nancy Ryan (Dottie Winters); Roger Sterns (Arthur Smith); Anderson Lawlor (Dillon Todd); Millicent Hanley (Constance Barnes); Ilka Chase (Elinor Branch); Barbara O'Neil (Susan Thomas); Ethel Remey (Maid); George Lessey (Hooker Mason); Robert Hudson (Rev. Duncan); Delancey Cleveland (Mr. Martin); Georgette Spelvin (A Lady); Henry Fonda (A Gentleman)

Review Summary

"Miss Bankhead is likeably brisk and tomboyish, excitingly agile at swinging from mood to mood, tone to tone, and knows how to keep her [audience] guessing as well as grinning." (*New York American*, March 2, 1933)

"In the face of her human, plastic and intelligent performance, it is difficult to understand how Hollywood could have done her wrong." (*New York World Telegram*, March 2, 1933)

Commentary

Despite the glowing critical reception to Tallulah's performance, the play failed, and the cause was bad timing. *Forsaking All Others* opened the very day that President Roosevelt declared a bank holiday. All the banks across America were closed and no one had access to their money. Theatre tickets were suddenly an unaffordable luxury and despite Tallulah's efforts to keep the show afloat (she was the producer), it finally closed, and she reported a loss of forty thousand dollars.

She was Mary Clay, a young woman who is deserted at the altar on her wedding day, forgives the man, is about to go through the ceremony again, but realizes she loves someone else and marries the other man instead.

A young Henry Fonda made one of his earliest Broadway appearances as a surprised wedding guest, and Thomas Mitchell (1892-1962), later to become an Oscar-winning character actor in films, chalked up one of his several theatre directing credits. Tallulah and Mitchell got along, and she would call on him twice more.

Metro-Goldwyn-Mayer acquired the screen rights and released a film version the following year starring Joan Crawford as Mary, Clark Gable as the man she really loves and Robert Montgomery as the indecisive would-be groom.

S26   DARK VICTORY

Opened: November 9, 1934 (Plymouth Theatre)   51 performances

Credits

Director, Robert Milton; Producer, Alexander McKaig; Playwrights, George Brewer, Jr. and Bertram Bloch; Sets, Robert Edmond Jones

Cast

Earle Larrimore (Dr. Frederick Steele); Mildred Wall (Miss Wainwright); Frederick Leister (Dr. Parsons); Tallulah Bankhead (Judith Traherne); Ann Andrews (Alden Blaine); Myra Hampton (Josie); Edgar Norfolk (Michael); Dwight Fiske (Leslie Clark); Helen Strickland (Miss Jenny); Lewis Dayton (Postman)

Review Summary

"Miss Bankhead infuses [the play] with the odd sort of vitality that distinguishes her acting, and she plays with intuitive stage intelligence." (*New York Times*, November 10, 1934)

"Miss Bankhead's performance was fluent, a work worthy of the daughter and the niece of two of America's most important statesmen." (*New York Herald Tribune*, November 10, 1934)

"At odd moments, even in the later difficult moments, [Tallulah Bankhead] brings into her playing a note of tense feeling which cuts through the theatricalism." (*New York Sun*, November 10, 1934)

Commentary

After the failure of *Forsaking All Others* in 1933 and weakened from a near-fatal illness, Tallulah was relunctant to try another Broadway play in 1934, but *Dark Victory* was an exciting proposition, and she proved equally capable in heavy drama as she was in comedy. Critics were complimentary of her performance, but didn't especially like the play, and when another serious illness forced Tallulah to leave the cast, it closed after 51 performances.

David O. Selznick paid $50,000 for the screenrights as a possible vehicle for Janet Gaynor or Carole Lombard. He also tried unsuccessfully to talk Greta Garbo into doing it. (She wanted to do *Anna Karenina* instead.) Samuel Goldwyn was also interested in the material as a vehicle for Merle Oberon, but it was Warner Bros. who finally filmed the story in 1939. The material fared much better as a film and Bette Davis received an Oscar nomination for her portrayal of Judith Traherne, the Long Island socialite slowly dying from a brain tumor. George Brent was the doctor/husband, Geraldine Fitzgerald was the long-suffering friend (called "Ann King"), and other roles went to Humphrey Bogart and Ronald Reagan.

S27   RAIN

Opened: Feb. 12, 1935 (Music Box Theatre)   47 performances

Credits

Director, Sam Forrest; Producer, Sam H. Harris; Playwrights, John Colton and Clemence Randolph (from W. Somerset Maugham's *Miss Thompson*); Sets, W. Oden Waller.

Cast

Elizabeth Dewing (Native Girl); K.A. Fernando (Native Policeman); John Walker, Frank DeSilva (Two Natives); Emma Wilcox (Ameena); Kent Thurber (Private Griggs, USMC); Jack McKee (Corporal Hodgson, USMC); Walter Gilbert (Sergeant O'Hara, USMC); Granville Bates (Joe Horn); Ethel Wilson (Mrs. Alfred Davidson); Nicholas Joy (Dr. McPhail); Ethel Intropidi (Mrs. McPhail); Tallulah Bankhead (Sadie Thompson); Herbert Ransom (Rev. Alfred Davidson)

Review Summary

"Being an actress of extraordinary range, [Tallulah Bankhead] has the proper equipment for every situation the play invents – fear, remorse, pathos, contempt and pity for the misery of the world." (*New York Times*, February 13, 1935)

"I must be blunt and call Miss Bankhead's Sadie better even than the late Miss Eagels'. For hers is a sturdier Sadie, fleshier, meatier, and less of a prey to the neuroses." (*New York American*, February 13, 1935)

"Miss Bankhead overworks and overacts." (*New York Evening Journal*, February 13, 1935)

Commentary

Sadie Thompson is perhaps Somerset Maugham's most famous character; certainly his most colorful. Jeanne Eagels mesmerized Broadway with her 1922 portrayal of the salty South Seas trollop, and Gloria Swanson's 1928 film interpretation was also critically acclaimed. Joan Crawford took the role in the 1932 remake, and Rita Hayworth had a 1953 hit with still another version, in 3-D!

Tallulah's association with Sadie went back to 1925, when she was hired by producer Basil Dean to star in the London production, only to be fired by Maugham three days into rehearsals. It was a devastating blow and even led to a suicide attempt. It was a half-hearted attempt (swallowing twenty aspirin tablets could hardly be called a *serious* attempt to end one's life) but her despondency was genuine. Finally getting her chance to tackle the role, Tallulah was sure that it would not only prove to Maugham that firing her had been a mistake, but would also be her great American success. It failed on both counts. Tallulah had matured considerably in a decade and instead of weeping and swallowing another twenty aspirin, she moved on to the next project, albeit hastily and without much serious thought.

S28   SOMETHING GAY

Opened: April 29, 1935 (Morosco Theatre)   56 performances

Credits
Director, Thomas Mitchell; Producers, The Shuberts; Playwright, Adelaide Heilbron; Settings, Donald Oenslager

Cast
Percy Ames (Hatters); Kent Thurber (Nick); Walter Pidgeon (Herbert Grey); Nancy Ryan (Julie Freyne); Hugh Sinclair (Jay Cochran); Tallulah Bankhead (Monica Grey); Elizabeth Dewing (Marie); Roy Gordon (Dick Matthews)

Review Summary
"The adventurous Miss Bankhead is adrift again in an untrustworthy drama, and the usual condolences are in order." (*New York Herald Tribune*, April 30, 1935)

"Miss Bankhead has never been in better mood or in finer fettle. She plays with a real humor that skips blithely over the defects of the script and almost succeeds in shaking the life into Miss Heilbron's comedy." (*New York Evening Journal*, April 30, 1935)

Commentary
Tallulah referred to *Something Gay* "as misleading a title as ever was hung on two hours of plot and dialogue" (see B001), and the reviews bear her out. The plot sounded promising (wife returns from a long visit to discover that her husband has been having an affair with the young widow upstairs, tries to win him back by making him jealous, but ends up falling in love with her "hired" escort and running away with him, leaving the husband at home, alone) but the material was found old-fashioned and empty.

The play closed on June 29, 1935, exactly two months after it had opened.

S29   REFLECTED GLORY

Opened: Sept. 21, 1936 (Morosco Theatre)   127 performances

Credits
Director/Playwright, George Kelly; Producer, Lee Shubert; Settings, Norman Rock.

Cast
Clay Clement (Mr. Hanlon); Elizabeth Dunne (Hattie); Ann Andrews (Miss Sloane); Tallulah Bankhead (Miss Flood); Philip Reed (Mr.

Well); Alden Chase (Mr. Howard); Robert Bordoni (Bruno);
William H. Turner (Stage Door Man); Chester Miller (A Waiter);
Madeline Holmes (Mrs. Howard); William Brisbane (Mr.
Omansetter); S.T. Bratton (Irene)

Review Summary

"It is my sad duty to report that Miss Bankhead has not yet been able to
escape from the ill luck that has been hers ever since she returned from
London... She was invariably worthy of attention and regard, while her
vehicle was not." (*New York Herald Tribune*, September 22, 1936)

"Miss Bankhead gives one of her best performances. She is happier under
the Kelly direction than she has been for some time." (*New York Daily
News*, September 22, 1936)

"Miss Bankhead has converted all her recklessness, all her careless,
scattered talents, all her undeveloped aptitudes into something that appears
very simple, something that has an uncommon naturalness and a high
polish. This is the play she needed." (*Brooklyn Daily Eagle*, September 22,
1936)

Commentary

Craig's Wife is perhaps the best known of George Kelly's many plays, but
Reflected Glory ranks among his least known.
    Tallulah played a gifted emotional actress of the theatre named Miss
Flood who, despite her success, yearns for a simpler life. She is tempted to
marry an early love from Baltimore and try for a home and children, but
she can't find the courage to leave her work. Next comes an actress-chaser
from Chicago. Again she is tempted to marry, but it turns out he is more
attracted to her earning capacity than to her as a woman. Besides, he's
already married. Her wise stage manager, who has known her for a very
long time, tells her to remain in the theatre, for it is only there she can find
true happiness. She takes his advice and sticks to the footlights.

S30 ANTONY AND CLEOPATRA

Opened: Nov. 10, 1937 (Mansfield Theatre)   5 performances

Credits

Director, Reginald Bach; Producer, Lawrence Rivers, Inc.;
Playwright, William Shakespeare, adapted by Professor William
Strunk, Jr., Cornell University; Settings, Jo Mielziner; Music, Virgil
Thompson; Costumes, Jo Mielziner and Cecil Beaton

Cast

Conway Tearle (Mark Antony); John Emery (Octavius Caesar); E.
Malcolm Dunn (M. Aemilius Lepidus); Averell Harris (Sextus

Pompeius); Thomas Chalmers (Domitius Errobarbus); Wilfrid
Seagram (Eros); Frederic Voight (Scarus); Richard Ross (Dercetus);
Charles Bowden (Demetrius); Henry Adrian (Philo); Stephen Fox
(Thyreus); Ralph Chambers (Agrippa); Henry Saunders (Dolabella);
Wilton Graf (Proculeius); John Parrish (Menas); George V. Dill
(Canidius); William Barwald (Alexas); Robert Williamson
(Mardian); Fred Hanschi (Dionedes); Lawrence Fletcher (A
Messenger); Tallulah Bankhead (Cleopatra); Regina Wallace
(Octavia); Fania Marinoff (Charmian); Georgia Harvey (Iras);
Kamila Staneska (A Dancer)

Review Summary

"Although Miss Bankhead is an actress as well as an interesting personality,
the Queen of the Nile is definitely not her dish. There is no suggestion of
majesty in this Cleopatra and, curiously enough, not much sensuousness or
passion." (*New York Times*, November 11, 1937)

"Tallulah Bankhead barged down the Nile last night as Cleopatra – and
sank. Miss Bankhead can be a brilliant performer. She has many exciting
gifts... but as the serpent of the Nile, she proves no more dangerous than a
garter snake." (*New York Post*, November 11, 1937)

"Tallulah Bankhead is glamorous and magnetic in her scenes, but otherwise
this Shakespearean revival is long, windy and dull." (*Variety*, November
17, 1937)

Commentary

For the rest of her life, Tallulah would refer to *Antony and Cleopatra* as
the lowest point in her theatrical career. It may have been (although *The
Milk Train Doesn't Stop Here Anymore*, 1964, came pretty close), and she
invariably faulted herself for the play's failure. Her performance *was*
harshly criticized, but the failure of the play cannot be placed squarely on
her shoulders. If any one person must be singled out, it would have to be
William Strunk, the professor from Cornell who adapted the play for its
revival. He altered scenes, changed a few lines, and reduced the role of
Errobarbus, for which he was severely criticized. Next in the line of fire
was Conway Tearle, whose portrayal of Mark Antony was liked even less
than Tallulah's Cleopatra. The entire cast (with the exception of John
Emery, Tallulah's husband) was said to be inadequate. Only Emery, said
the critics, understood how to read Shakespeare's poetic lines.

Shakespeare's play had previously been presented by the Selwyns and
Adolph Klauber in 1924 with Rollo Peters and Jane Cowl. Before that, it
was the opening attraction at the New Theatre which a group of
millionaires built for New York in 1909. E.H. Sothern and Julia Marlowe
starred. The play has been revived many times by Shakespearean stock
companies, and has reappeared on Broadway twice since the 1937 fiasco: in
1947 with Katharine Cornell and Godfrey Tearle; and in 1951 with
Laurence Olivier and Vivien Leigh. Both productions were successful.

S31   THE CIRCLE

Opened: April 18, 1938 (Playhouse Theatre)   72 performances

Credits

Director, Bretaigne Windust; Producer, William A. Brady;
Playwright, W. Somerset Maugham; Settings: Donald Oenslager;
Costumes, Hattie Carnegie.

Cast

May Marshall (Spaulding); Bramwell Fletcher (Arnold Champion-
Cheney, M.P.); Audrey Ridgwell (Mrs. Shenstone); Tallulah
Bankhead (Elizabeth); John Emery (Edward Luton); Cecil
Humphreys (Clive Champion-Cheney); James E. Corbett (Benson);
Grace George (Lady Catherine "Kitty" Champion-Cheney); Denis
Hoey (Lord Porteous)

Review Summary

"It cannot be easy for an actress of Miss Bankhead's temperament to sit still
and let the action come to her, but she does it and does it so well that it is
another demonstration not only of her dynamic personality but of her
theatrical intelligence." (*New York World Telegram*, April 19, 1938)

"Miss Bankhead, after having experimented with many differing roles,
finds herself back playing the sort of part that made her a ten-year London
favorite." (*New York Daily News*, April 19, 1938)

"Tallulah Bankhead gives the best performance of her American career.
Without sacrificing the animation of her personality, she plays the part
with respect for its meaning." (*New York Times*, April 19, 1938)

Commentary

In Maugham's light comedy, Tallulah was Elizabeth Champion-Cheney, a
young English matron who is considering running away from her dull
husband, Arnold, to live with Edward Luton, a dashing young lover.
Thirty-five years before, her husband's mother, Lady Kitty, had left her
husband and run off with the handsome and debonaire Lord Porteous.
Elizabeth has always thought of their romance as glamorous and
fascinating, but just as she is about to join her lover, Lady Kitty and Lord
Porteous arrive. They are now old, weary, disillusioned and unhappy.
They, along with the father who was left alone so many years before, try to
persuade Elizabeth to stay with her husband. She considers their advice,
but leaves anyway.
    The Circle was an interesting change of pace for Tallulah, and she
did well with the part. She had excellent support from Grace George who
came close to stealing the play with her delightful performance as Lady
Kitty. The production was well received and would probably have enjoyed

a long run had a summer heat wave not forced it to close prematurely. (Air conditioning was not yet commonplace.)

The play had first appeared on Broadway in September 1921, with Estelle Winwood as Elizabeth, Mrs. Leslie Carter as Lady Kitty, John Drew as Lord Porteous and Ernest Lawford as Clive. It was most recently revived in 1989, with Rex Harrison as Lord Porteous, Glynis Johns as Lady Kitty and Stewart Granger as Clive. Elizabeth was played by Roma Downey and received billing as a minor character.

It was Rex Harrison's last Broadway appearance before his death in the summer of 1990.

S32 I AM DIFFERENT

Opened: August 18, 1938 (Savoy Theatre, San Diego, Cal.)

Credits

Director, Thomas Mitchell; Producer, Lee Shubert (in association with Joseph M. Gaites); Playwright, Zoë Akins (adapted from the Hungarian by Lili Hatvany); Settings, Kay Nielsen.

Cast

Walter Holbrooke (Jimmy); Fritzi Scheff (Baroness Stephanie Torff); Hala Linda (Mrs. Lou Hoeffler); Elizabeth Valentine (Miss Yanni); Charlotte Cooper (Olga); Shirley Cooper (Sari); Glenn Anders (Dr. Thomas Held); John Emery (Alex Thoersen); Ara Gerald (Vera Nitzish); Chester Miller (Pista, the Butler); Herschel Bentley (Conrad, Another Servent); Tallulah Bankhead (Judith Held); Thomas Loudon (Otto); Dorothy Adams (Wilma Bernd); Francesca Rotoil (Polyluko); Margaret Seddon ("Provincial Penelope")

Review Summary

"Gives Tallulah Bankhead an opportunity to exercise her singular talents and familiar gestures and mannerisms that always please her followers." (*Cincinnatti Enquirer*, November 1, 1938)

"Miss Bankhead's pert and sparkling performance at times creates the deception that here is something more than a conversation piece. But it is not." (*Washington Evening Star*, November 22, 1938)

Commentary

With the moderate success of *The Circle*, Tallulah decided she and her husband, John Emery, would try for another hit, and Lily Hatvany's comedy seemed the perfect vehicle. Zoë Akins adapted the play into English and Thomas Mitchell was plucked from Hollywood to direct (after George Cukor decided not to take the job).

Hatvany's play was a battle of the sexes, and Akins changed the setting to a charasterically Akinesque background of baronial hall, old family retainers and vintage champagne. It centers around Judith Held, a wise and beautiful woman who, from the safe haven of a comfortable marriage to a complacent doctor, writes volumes on the proper regulation of the adult sex life. She is especially averse to feminine jealousy and implores her readers to control their emotions. Into her life leaps Alex Thoersen, a hedonistic young man who has just been shot by a jealous mistress for merely expressing his wish to meet the authoress. Judith soon discovers that it isn't so easy to control the emotions when faced with love with a capital L, and when she finds her lover in the arms of a designing minx, she too succumbs to jealousy and attempts to kill him. Fortunately, her aim is poor.

A Broadway opening was tentatively scheduled for the late fall 1938, but a west coast try-out was thought necessary since additional script revisions would be likely. It opened in San Diego on August 18, and made a brief stop at the Biltmore Theatre in Los Angeles before moving to San Francisco's Curran Theatre on September 5. Reviews were poor and it was obvious that it would take more than script revisions to save *I am Different*. Nevertheless, before its Chicago opening on September 28 (at the Selwyn Theatre), the first and third acts were re-written and speeded up. Reviews were no better, but it made money in Chicago and remained there for two weeks. It closed temporarily for additional changes, then re-opened in St. Louis on October 24 and moved to Cincinnatti on October 31. Plans for a Broadway opening were scrapped, but the play hobbled along through the South making one night stands, until arriving at Washington's National Theatre on November 21. It closed permanently on November 26.

The play was a failure, but it is memorable for a classic faux pas. In one scene Glenn Anders was supposed to run on stage following the sound of gunfire, shouting, "I heard a shot," find John Emery lying on the floor, examine him, and say, "It's only a flesh wound." One night he was chatting in the wings with Tallulah and missed his cue. He was so discombobulated that when he finally did rush on, a few seconds late, he shouted, "I heard a flesh wound," looked at the body and announced, "It's only a shot."

S33 THE LITTLE FOXES

Opened: Feb. 15, 1939 (National Theatre)   408 performances

Credits

Director/Producer, Herman Shumlin; Playwright, Lillian Hellman; Settings, Howard Bay; Costumes, Aline Bernstein

Cast

Abbie Mitchell (Addie); John Marriott (Cal); Patricia Collinge (Birdie Hubbard); Carl Benton Reid (Oscar Hubbard); Dan Duryea (Leo Hubbard); Tallulah Bankhead (Regina Giddens); Lee Baker

(William Marshall); Charles Dingle (Benjamin Hubbard); Florence
Williams (Alexandra Giddens); Frank Conroy (Horace Giddens)

Review Summary

"As the malevolent lady of 'The Little Foxes,' [Tallulah] plays with a
superb command of the entire character." (*New York Times*, February 16,
1939)

"Miss Tallulah Bankhead offers the finest performance of her local career,
a portrayal that is honest, merciless and completely understanding." (*New
York Herald Tribune*, February 16, 1939)

"Regina, as played by Miss Bankhead, is a splendid portrayal, rating among
her best stage performances... Her acting is a personal triumph." (*Variety*,
February 22, 1939)

Commentary

The Little Foxes would be Tallulah's greatest success ever. For the first
time in her career, every needed element fell into place – a strong director,
a powerful play, a meaty part and supporting players who were
accomplished and effective.

   She began rehearsals under the direction of Herman Shumlin, but as
had been her habit in the past, she merely walked through the role,
prefering to save her "performance" for opening night. Shumlin did not
approve of the technique, and told her so.   He wanted her to really
rehearse, which led to an argument. A raging Tallulah fled to her dressing
room with Shumlin right behind. According to Maurice Zolotow in *No
People Like Show People* (1951), Shumlin closed the door behind him and
said to his temperamental star, "Listen, Tallulah... if I don't criticize you
any more I know that on opening night you'll give a sensational
performance. But you'll do it on instinct and nerve. I want you to bury
Tallulah in Regina Giddens. Then you'll know *why* you do the things you
do and you'll be sensational on opening night and every other night" (see
B146). Tallulah had to admit he was right, and from then on she
disciplined herself and worked. And she was richly rewarded. For her
performance as Regina Giddens, she was cited by *Variety* as the best actress
of the 1938/39 Broadway season. Not only did the play establish her as a
great actress, it also made her financially secure. (In addition to her salary,
she also received ten percent of the nightly box-office receipts.)

   Tallulah's respect for Shumlin and Lillian Hellman did not endure as
long as the play did; she grew to loath them, and the reason was politics.
Tallulah had never been politically minded, despite having a grandfather,
father and uncle in Washington, but the ever-worsening war in Europe had
altered her way of thinking, and when Russia invaded Finland in November
of 1939, she immediately volunteered to aid the victim. She wanted to give
a benefit performance of *The Little Foxes*, the receipts to be used for
Finnish relief, but Shumlin and Hellman vetoed her proposition. "I don't
believe in that fine, lovable little Republic of Finland that everybody gets

so weepy about," Bankhead quotes Hellman as saying. "I've been there and it looks like a pro-Nazi little republic to me" (see B001). Bankhead was outraged, and refused to speak to either of them. Undeterred, she instead donated her salary to the cause for six months.

After the play closed on Broadway, *The Little Foxes* (with most of the cast intact, although Eugenia Rawls had replaced Florence Williams) went on the road, opening on Feb. 5, 1940, and closing two months later. It re-opened on September 14, 1940, and closed on April 15, 1941. Tallulah did not miss a single performance. She played when she was sick, when she was tired, and when a Minnesota blizzard kept all but thirteen people at home.

When Hollywood made a film of Lillian Hellman's play in 1941, Tallulah was passed over for the lead. She was not considered box office, and when Bette Davis got the part instead, Tallulah was angry. According to John Emery, her husband at the time, she picked up every piece of bric-a-brac she could find and smashed it against the wall, cursing the name of Bette Davis with every crash (see B118). Carl Benton Reid, Charles Dingle, Dan Duryea and Patricia Collinge repeated their roles in the film (replacements included Teresa Wright as Alexandra and Herbert Marshall as Horace), and Davis received an Oscar nomination for her performance. And that performance was remarkably similar to Bankhead's. Davis admitted many times that the resemblence was deliberate, that there was no other way to play Regina Giddens. As she said to Ramon Romero in a 1952 *Theatre Arts* interview, "Miss Bankhead's characterization of Regina Giddens is unequalled. It made no concessions to sympathy, Legions of Decency or accounting departments. It was flesh-and-blood realization of what Miss Hellman had written" (see B258).

S34   CLASH BY NIGHT

Opened: Dec. 27, 1941 (Belasco Theatre)   49 performances

Credits

Director, Lee Strasberg; Producer, Billy Rose; Playwright, Clifford Odets; Scenery, Boris Aronson.

Cast

Lee J. Cobb (Jerry Wilenski); Robert Ryan (Joe W. Doyle); Tallulah Bankhead (Mae Wilenski); Katharine Locke (Peggy Coffey); Joseph Schildkraut (Earl Pfeiffer); John F. Hamilton (Jerry's Father); Seth Arnold (Vincent Kress); Ralph Chambers (Mr. Potter); Art Smith (Tom); William Nunn (A Waiter); Harold Gran (A Man); Joseph Shatluck (Abe Harowitz); Stephan Eugene Cole (An Usher)

Review Summary

"Miss Bankhead gives the best performance of her theatrical career. In a lesser actress, Mae would have been a routine wife who cheated her husband, but our Tallulah is made of sterner stuff." (*New York Morning Telegram*, December 30, 1941)

"Tallulah Bankhead... is mannered when at loose ends. But when she has a mood or an idea to catch hold of, she can bite into it like a tigress." (*New York Times*, December 30, 1941)

"Although Tallulah Bankhead hardly manages to seem the rebellious Staten Island housewife, she plays with that vibrant air of excitement which always makes her so satisfying to watch." (*New York Herald Tribune*, December 29, 1941)

Commentary

In this Clifford Odets drama, Mae Wilenski (Bankhead) is a bored Staten Island housewife with a young child and a "hulking nitwit" of a husband. Into their life comes Earl Pfeiffer, a handsome young man who is a WPA buddy of her husband's, and although Mae realizes the danger of the situation and tries to dissuade Earl from hanging around, he moves into their spare bedroom and the inevitable affair begins. The husband catches on, and when Mae attempts to leave him, he stalks Earl and brutally kills him in the half-darkness of a movie projection booth, where Earl had found work.

It was a stark drama and although the performances were praised, the play was found too grim. The United States had entered World War II less than two weeks before the play opened and the already uncertain and worried public didn't want to see a disturbing play. It closed less than a month after opening.

A film version starring Barbara Stanwyck was made in 1952. The location was changed to a California fishing village, where Mae shows up to live with her brother, Joe Doyle (Keith Andes) and his wife (Marilyn Monroe). She marries a thick-headed and hot-tempered fisherman, Jerry Wilenski (Paul Douglas), and bears him a child, but has an affair with movie projectionist Earl Pfeiffer (Robert Ryan, who had played Mae's brother on stage). The denouement is the same in both versions.

S35 THE SKIN OF OUR TEETH

Opened: November 18, 1942 (National Theatre)   359 performances

Credits

Director, Elia Kazan; Producer, Michael Myerberg; Playwright, Thornton Wilder; Settings, Albert Johnson; Costumes, Mary Percy Schenck

Cast

Harry Clark (Usher); Florence Reed (Fortune Teller); Eulabelle Moore (Hester); Stanley Praeger (Fred Bailey); Tallulah Bankhead

(Lily Sabina); Florence Eldridge (Mrs. Antrobus); Andrew
Ratousheff (Mammouth); Frances Heflin (Gladys); Fredric March
(Mr. Antrobus); Ralph Kellard (Professor/Mr. Tremayne); Ralph
Cullinan (Homer); Viola Dean (Ivy); E.G. Marshall (Mr.
Fitzpatrick); Morton DaCosta (Announcer); Remo Buffano
(Dinosaur); Dickie Van Patten (Telegraph Boy); Montgomery Clift
(Henry); Arthur Griffin (Doctor); Joseph Smiley (Judge); Emily
Lorraine (Miss T. Muse); Edith Faversham (Miss E. Muse); Eva
Mudge Nelson (Miss M. Muse); Elizabeth Scott, Patricia Riordan
(Girl Drum Majorettes)

Review Summary

"[Tallulah Bankhead] is irresistibly comic and endlessly entertaining, but
when she is out of sight, the play sags badly." (*New York Journal
American*, November 19, 1942)

"It is Tallulah Bankhead as Sabina... who provides the merriest
moments...." (*New York Post*, November 19, 1942)

"Tallulah Bankhead plays... with verve and vivacity. So much so, that one
does not so much follow the play at times, as wait for Sabina to come back
on the stage." (*PM*, November 19, 1942)

Commentary

Thornton Wilder's allegorical play revolves around the Antrobus family of
Excelsior, New Jersey – father, mother, two children, and the maid, Lily
Sabina. As the play opens, Mr. Antrobus sends a telegraph to his wife (by
smoke signal) that he will be home late because he has been busy at the
office fixing up the alphabet, bringing the multiplication table to the masses
and inventing the wheel. A few scenes later the weather turns cold, unusual
for August, and it is announced that the ice age is coming! Moses, Homer
and other neighbors seek shelter in the Antrobus home, and the family pets
(a dinosaur and mammouth), are put outside to become extinct. Mr. and
Mrs. Antrobus cram their children with knowledge, so if they survive, they
can keep civilization going.

The second act jumps ahead several thousand years to Atlantic City
and the convention of the Ancient and Honorable Order of Mammals. Mr.
Antrobus is elected head of the Human Subdivision. Sabina's character is
now a beauty contest winner who tries to seduce Mr. Antrobus, but her
machinations are interrupted by the Great Flood. Mr. Antrobus, his wife
and Sabina climb into the ark with the animals and are saved.

The third act jumps ahead to a war, any war. Sabina is now a camp
follower, which she has been for seven years. Mr. Antrobus leads an army
into battle, but his forces are beaten. He doesn't give up, but decides to go
back into the battle, but this time he intends to listen to the "voice of the
people, their confusion and need" as well as his wife and children. Mankind
has survived, but only by the skin of its teeth.

The Little Foxes was the apex of Tallulah's theatrical career, but

Wilder's play was a close second. She did not get along with director Kazan or producer Myerberg (she considered them incompetent, penny-pinching and vulgar), but she was professional enough to keep backstage arguments backstage. Her performance continued to be fresh and vibrant, but so violent was her temper that other cast members were afraid to show up before curtain time. By the time she left the show on May 29, 1943 (after 229 performances), she had stopped speaking entirely to Fredric March and his wife, Florence Eldridge. Several members of the cast had also stopped speaking to *her*. In his autobiography, *A Life* (1988), Elia Kazan says that Bankhead is one of only two people in his life whom he has hated. He often refers to her as "the bitch," and presents her as demanding, vulgar and trouble-making. (He does compliment her performance, however, and admits that she "made a director out of me" see B080.)

Tallulah got along splendidly with child actor Dickie Van Patten. She normally didn't want to appear on stage with children, but as Van Patten admitted in a 1990 letter to the author, "She said I was the only child actor she liked because I could read the racing form."

When Tallulah left *The Skin of Our Teeth* due to health problems (exhaustion and ulcers), she was replaced by Miriam Hopkins, but she remained the definitive Sabina. Her performance so impressed the New York Drama Critics that they deemed it the best of 1942 (by an actress). She received a similar citation from *Variety*, and from the Barter Theatre in Abingdon, Virginia.

S36 FOOLISH NOTION

Opened: March 13, 1945 (Martin Beck Theatre)   104 performances

Credits

Director, John C. Wilson; Producer, The Theatre Guild (Theresa Helburn, Lawrence Langor); Playwright, Philip Barry; Production Supervisor, Armina Marshall; Sets/Lighting, Jo Mielziner; Music, Arthur Norris; Costumes, Mainbocher.

Cast

Tallulah Bankhead (Sophie Wing); Joan Shepherd (Happy Hapgood); Barbara Kent (Florence Denny/Flora); Donald Cook (Gordon Roark); Mildred Dunnock (Rose/Flora); Aubrey Mather (Horatio Wing); Maria Manton (Elsie/Flora); Henry Hull (Jim Hapgood)

Review Summary

"'Foolish Notion' presents Tallulah Bankhead with the role of her life. She runs the gamut of style of acting and has a glorious time." (*New York Morning Telegraph*, March 15, 1945)

"Held down by a script which permitted her to be herself only part of the time, Miss Bankhead, the rest of the time was not herself." (*New York Times*, March 14, 1945)

"Tallulah Bankhead works valiantly to illuminate a murky script. Never has she been more assured, versatile and properly exhibitionistic." (*New York Herald Tribune*, March 14, 1945)

Commentary

Bankhead biographer Brendan Gill says that Philip Barry should have been the ideal playwright for Tallulah. "They had minds similar in acuteness and irony." Perhaps so, but those similarites worked no charms on *Foolish Notion*. It was a critical failure, although Tallulah's flamboyant performance kept the theatre filled for over three months.

In the play she starred as Sophie Wing, a celebrated stage actress whose husband, Jim Hapgood, has been missing for five years, presumably killed in the war. In the meantime she has fallen in love with her co-star, Gordon Roark, and decides to have her husband declared legally dead. Her father-in-law and adopted daughter grieve for the missing Jim more than Sophie does, and when a series of strange messages indicate that Jim is not only alive but is on his way home, each member of the family takes turns imagining the homecoming in a different way.

Following its run on Broadway, Tallulah took the play on tour from late 1945 into the spring of 1946. Donald Cook remained in the cast as Roark, but John Emery replaced Henry Hull as the missing husband. No longer husband and wife, Bankhead and Emery apparently had no hard feelings and worked well together.

It's interesting to note that Henry Hull (1890-1977) had first played Tallulah's husband in the 1921 production of *Everyday*. He had also been a passenger in Alfred Hitchcock's 1944 motion picture, *Lifeboat* and was the star of *39 East* (1919), the first play in which Tallulah had a speaking part. They did not appear together in the play, however, as he had been replaced by Sidney Blackmer by the time Tallulah joined the cast.

S37   THE EAGLE HAS TWO HEADS

Opened: March 19, 1947 (Plymouth Theatre)   29 performances

Credits

Director/Producer, John C. Wilson; Playwright, Jean Cocteau (adapted by Ronald Duncan from *La Mort Ecoute aux Portes*); Settings, Donald Oenslager; Costumes, Aline Bernstein.

Cast

Eleanor Wilson (Edith De Berg); Kendall Clark (Maxim, Duke of Willenstein); Tallulah Bankhead (The Queen); Helmut Dantine (Stanislas); Cherokee Thornton (Tony); Clarence Derwent (Baron Foen)

Review Summary

"Tallulah, let it not be mistaken, is an actress with a great deal of natural ability, but, like some others, she seems to be under the delusion that if an actress doesn't act all over the stage... she isn't an actress and may just as well go back to Connecticut and commune with the chickens." (*New York Journal-American*, March 24, 1947)

"Tallulah Bankhead never looked lovelier, and her gowns are magnificent. Her performance is one of the finest ever given by an American actress." (*Women's Wear Daily*, March 20, 1947)

"[Tallulah Bankhead] played with a chip on her shoulder, and a determination not to be heard beyond the eleventh row." (*New York Journal-American*, March 20, 1947)

Commentary

Jean Cocteau (1889-1963) is known today primarily because of his strangely poetic films from post-war France, most of them starring the actor Jean Marais – *La Belle et La Bête* (*Beauty and the Beast*), from 1945, is probably the best known – but in his day he was a highly regarded poet, artist, novelist, essayist, painter, screenwriter, set designer and actor. Amazingly, he was also the leading French playwright of the period and *The Eagle Has Two Heads* was one of his most successful plays. Under its original title, *La Mort Ecoute aux Portes*, it fared well in Europe, but it either lost something in the translation or the taste of Americans was far removed from the taste of the French. It failed miserably on Broadway.

Simply told, the play opened with the Queen of a mythical European country mourning the death of her mate, the victim of an assassin's bullet. Into her bedroom chamber bursts Stanislas, a loutish revolutionary with intentions of murder. In a 20,000 word monologue, the Queen persuades the young hot-head to abandon his mission. Come to slay, Stanlislas remains to love. But the Queen does not feel as he does and crazed by her taunts, Stanislas shoots the Queen, then drinks poison.

The role interested Bankhead greatly. The first act monologue was a particular challange. To hold an audience's attention for nearly half an hour was a feat of acting which critics were quick to compliment. She also had the chance to wear several stunning costumes and the climatic death scene required her to tumble head first down several stairs, a stunt which she performed every night, majestically and realistically, without a single injury. Donald Oenslager, who designed the palace sets, told Brendan Gill that he had padded the carpet on the stairs, but was still amazed at the chances Tallulah took (see B003).

Helmut Dantine made a dashing Stanislas, but Marlon Brando had first been assigned the role. His on-stage behavior during try-outs, however, greatly annoyed the cast, particularly Tallulah, and he was replaced two weeks into rehearsals. He fidgetted during Tallulah's monologue and stretched out his death scene for more than a minute while he staggered about, moaning, looking for a place to collapse. The scene was meant to be serious, but the audience roared with laughter! This behavior does not befit the accomplished actor Brando later became, but according to Charles Higham's 1987 biography of the actor, Brando despised Bankhead and wanted out so badly that he deliberately misbehaved, hoping to be fired (see B072).

S38   PRIVATE LIVES

Opened: October 4, 1948 (Plymouth Theatre)   248 performances

Credits
Director, Martin Manulis; Producer, John C. Wilson; Playwright, Noël Coward; Settings, Charles Elson; Costumes, Mainbocher.

Cast
Barbara Baxley (Sibyl Chase); Donald Cook (Elyot Chase); William Langford (Victor Prynne); Tallulah Bankhead (Amanda Prynne); Therese Quadri (Louise)

Review Summary
"Tallulah Bankhead is hugely funny as Amanda... She may burst the play apart at its seams, so gusty is her performance, but she satisfies her fans..." (*New York Morning Telegraph*, October 6, 1948)

"Coward's romantic witticisms might or might not stand up in the glare of the post war theatre, but Miss Bankhead's demonstration is very definitely a striking and amusing display of fireworks." (*New York Herald Tribune*, October 5, 1948)

"When Miss Bankhead puts all her power behind it, 'Private Lives' moves closer into the farcical bailiwick." (*New York Times*, October 5, 1948)

Commentary
Noël Coward's *Private Lives* first opened on Broadway on September 4, 1930, with Gertrude Lawerence and Noël Coward himself starring. It was performed 101 times, and Metro-Goldwyn-Mayer filmed it the following year with Robert Montgomery and Norma Shearer.

The story centers around Elyot Chase and Amanda Prynne. Once married, they now have different spouses. By an amazing coincidence they are both honeymooning in the same hotel in France, and even more amazing, have adjoining suites. Amanda and Elyot are still enormously attracted to each other and eventually give in to their sex drives and run off with each other, leaving their respective mates to their own devices. Back in Amanda's Paris flat, she and Elyot start to fight all over again.

Amanda Prynne was one of Bankhead's favorite roles, and the longer she played it (nearly four years, including several summer circuit tours) the more she altered it to fit her personality. By the time the Bankhead company reached Broadway, the character of Amanda bore little resemblance to the one Coward had written. On the subsequent tour, she changed it even more, and added several southern expressions when performing in her native south. She even waved a small Confederate flag in one scene. She had made *Private Lives* her own, and although some theatre purists balked, the audience had as much fun as she did.

S39   DEAR CHARLES

Opened: Sept. 15, 1954 (Morosco Theatre)   155 performances

Credits

Director, Edmund Baylies; Producers, Richard Aldrich and Richard Myers (in association with Julius Fleischman); Playwright, Alan Melville (adapted from *Les Enfants d'Edouard* by Marc-Gilbert Sauvajon, who adapted it from *Slightly Scandalous* by Frederick Jackson); Settings/Lighting, Donald Oenslager; Costumes, Gene Cofin; Miss Bankhead's Gowns, Madame Bertha.

Cast

Norah Howard (Martha); Larry Robinson (Walter); Tom Raynor (Bruno); Fred Keating (Edward); Tallulah Bankhead (Dolores); Grace Raynor (Martine); Robert Coote (Sir Michael Anstruther); Werner Klemperer (Jan Letzaresco); Hugh Reilly (Jeffrey); Alice Pearce (Madame Bouchemin); Mary Webster (Lucienne); Peter Pell (Jean-Pierre).

Review Summary

"Miss Bankhead shows her teeth, works her shoulders, bellows the Bankhead laugh, spins like a 50-cent maple top, exhibits undeniably attractive gams, uses her eyes like wheel bearings, fans her fingers, and uses every voice register ever known to man or woman." (*New York Morning Telegraph*, September 17, 1954)

"If not entirely ingenue looking, [Tallulah Bankhead] has slimmed down a bit and gives the old impression of animal grace, dynamic drive and the familiar style, racous humor, magnetism and authority. She makes the transparent tinsel of 'Dear Charles' diverting theatre." (*Variety*, September 22, 1954)

"Tallulah can sometimes seem to imbue a dull part with her typical styling and make it glow, but there are many dead spots in the action that even this gifted lady fails to enliven." (*Newark Evening News*, September 16, 1954)

Commentary

On June 3, 1950, from her dressing room at the Central Theatre in Passaic, New Jersey, Tallulah announced that the final performance of *Private*

Lives would be her last theatrical appearance. She was true to her word for three years but Tallulah was not one to be idle. When *The Big Show* folded and her television series failed to catch on, she was ready to tread the boards again.

She turned down *Dear Charles* when it was first offered to her in 1953. Annabella was signed, but she was replaced during rehearsals with Lili Darvas. A try-out tour during the winter of 1953/54 was disastrous, so Darvas was also let go and the producers were right back where they had started – knocking on Tallulah's door. This time she accepted their offer and took the play on a successful summer tour (see S51) before the Broadway opening.

In *Dear Charles*, Tallulah portrayed Dolores Darvell, a Parisian novelist/lecturer who has enjoyed a rather promiscuous life. She has three young adult children, all illegitimate, and all sired by different men. Dolores has not told the children the truth, but has lead them to believe that their father is dead, that his name was Charles, and that the large portrait in the hall is his likeness. When the eldest two of her children announce their engagements, Dolores decides to make their heritage seem more respectable. She gathers them together, tells them the whole sordid truth, and unveils her plan – to invite her three former lovers to her home and let the children meet them. She will marry the one they like best and will pass him off as their father. The men (a staid Britisher, a Polish pianist and an unscrupulous American) arrive, but the children can't decide who they like best. So back on the wall goes the portrait of "Charles" and Dolores continues to pass herself off as a widow.

Originally entitled *Slightly Scandalous*, Frederick Jackson's play premiered in 1944 with Janet Beecher. It flopped but the script was adapted into French by Marc-Gilbert Sauvajon. As *Les Enfants d'Edouard*, it was a mild success in Paris before the British playwright Alan Melville adapted the material back into English. The title was changed to *Dear Charles* and it was a hit in London with the French-born actress Yvonne Arnaud. Critics were hardpressed to find something complimentary to say about the second American production of *Dear Charles*, but were kind to its star. It's impressive run was attributed entirely to Tallulah's blustery performance.

The play closed on January 29, 1955, and began a cross-country tour on February 1. Theodore Newton replaced Fred Keating as Edward, William Roerick replaced Hugh Reilly as Jeffrey, and Patsy Kelly replaced Alice Pearce and received prominent billing as Madame Bouchemin.

S40   A STREETCAR NAMED DESIRE

Opened: February 15, 1956 (City Center)   16 performances

Credits

Director, Herbert Machiz; Produced by, New York City Center Company; Playwright, Tennessee Williams; Settings, Watson Barratt (based on original designs by Jo Mielziner)

Cast

Vinnette Carroll (Negro Woman); Jean Ellyn (Eunice Hubbell); Frances Heflin (Stella Kowalski); Gerald O'Laughlin (Stanley Kowalski); Rudy Bond (Mitch); Bruno Damon (Steve Hubbell); David Anthony (Sailor); Tallulah Bankhead (Blanche DuBois); Lou Gilbert (Pablo Gonzales); Sandy Campbell (A Young Collector); Edna Thomas (Mexican Woman); Dorrit Kelton (A Strange Woman); Bert Bertram (A Strange Man)

Review Summary

"It is a plain fact that [Tallulah Bankhead] is miscast – not because she is notoriously a comedienne, but because she is, as a person and as a performer, notoriously indestructible. Blance DuBois is a girl who deceives herself. There is no self-deceit anywhere in Miss Bankhead." (*New York Herald Tribune*, February 16, 1956)

"Tallulah gives this one a Sunday try. She is not always capable of being anything but Tallulah, but she has rolled up her sleeves and plunged into the part with both fists." (*New York Journal-American*, February 16, 1956)

"Miss Bankhead misses altogether the softer nebulous quality essential to make the neurotic ex-schoolteacher sympathetic. There are some fine moments... but she's never secure or successful." (*Variety*, February 22, 1956)

Commentary

Tennessee Williams's *A Streetcar Named Desire* made its Broadway debut in 1947. It was the most talked about play of the season and won critical acclaim for its stars, Marlon Brando and Jessica Tandy, who was awarded a Tony for her performance. It has been revived many times and has been filmed twice, in 1951 with Vivien Leigh (who received a Best Actress Oscar for her interpretation of Blanche), and as a made-for-TV film in 1984 with Ann-Margaret.

At 54, Tallulah Bankhead was perhaps the oldest actress to attempt Blanche, and for that reason, critics had a hard time accepting her in the role. Tennessee Williams, apparently, had no such reservations about her age, and was pleased that Miss Bankhead would star in a revival of his play. In fact, he had suggested Tallulah to Irene Selznick when his play was first optioned in 1947. Miss Selznick vetoed his suggestion because Tallulah, she feared, would destroy the "moth-like side of Blanche" (see B145). As it turned out, she was right.

Tallulah's personality was much too strong to ever properly convey the fragility of Blanche, and despite a concerted effort to control her mannerisms, she was ultimately unsuccessful. The audience laughed in places where they shouldn't, completely shattering the delicate emotional balance. Tallulah knew her personality interfered with her performance, but as she remarked to the director, "That's me. I'm Tallulah Bankhead.

What can I do?" (See B002).

It is impossible to say how Tennessee Williams truly felt about Tallulah's performance. He was often asked, but he gave a different answer each time. Writing for the *New York Times* shortly after *Streetcar* closed, he said "I doubt any actress has ever worked harder... To me, she brought to mind the return of some great matador to the bull ring... after having been almost fatally gored... I am not ashamed to say that I shed tears almost all the way through and that when the play was finished I rushed up to her and fell to my knees at her feet" (see B250). But in 1971, when interviewed by Rex Reed for *Esquire,* the playwright admitted the "*worst* Blanche DuBois in the world was poor Tallulah, although I must say she was amusing."

S41   ZIEGFELD FOLLIES

Opened: April 16, 1956 (Shubert Theatre, Boston, Mass.)

Credits

Producers, Richard Kollmer and James Gardiner; Director of Dances and Musical Numbers, Jack Cole; Director of Sketches, Christopher Hewett; Lighting, Peggy Clark.

Review Summary

"Apart from some moments of Tallulah Bankhead's performance (she could not fail to arrest attention!)... this 'Follies' was plain dull." (*Boston Globe*, April 29, 1956.)

"Tallulah Bankhead... uses all her range tones in several skits of doubtful humor, talks one song and actually attempts to sing another, but the total result will hardly add to her artistic reputation." (*Philadelphia Evening Bulletin*, May 3, 1956)

Commentary

In this extravagant revue, budgeted at half a million dollars ($90,000 worth of scenery alone, including a $10,000 curtain made of ostriche feathers), Tallulah headed a cast of 61, including Carol Haney, Julie Newmar and Beatrice Arthur. It was intended to recapture the beauty of the original, but fell far short of its goal. Reviews in Boston were terrible, so after sixteen performances, the company moved to Philadelphia, opening on May 1 at the Shubert Theatre. Reviews were no better. It was booked to run for three weeks, but it closed there on May 12, and plans to open at New York's Winter Garden Theatre on May 26 were dropped, marking the first time that an edition of the *Ziegfeld Follies* closed before reaching its destination. The expensive scenery was disposed of.

Tallulah salvaged a few of the numbers and sketches, and with a few of the original cast members, took the new revue (titled *Welcome, Darlings*) on a summer stock tour of the northeast the same year (see S52).

Before *Follies* opened in Boston, Tallulah was asked why she was starring in a revue for the first time in her life. "Somerset Maugham once said that a play should have a beginning, a middle and an end," she answered. "A revue doesn't. A revue is the queen of non-sequiturs – which is what I am anyway."

S42 EUGENIA

Opened: January 30, 1957 (Ambassador Theatre)   12 performances

Credits

Director, Herbert Machiz; Producer, John C. Wilson (in association with the Theatre Corporation of America); Playwright, Randolph Carter (adapted from *The Europeans*, by Henry James); Scenery, Oliver Smith; Lighting, Peggy Clark; Costumes, Miles White.

Cast

Reynolds Evans (Mr. Wentworth); Anna Meacham (Gertrude Wentworth); Irma Hurley (Charlotte Wentworth); Robert Duke (Rev. Alfred Brand); Scott Merrill (Felix de Costa); Tallulah Bankhead (Eugenia); Jay Barney (Robert Acton); June Hunt (Elizabeth Acton); Therese Quadri (Marie)

Review Summary

"Miss Bankhead is done in by her own play which sets her up as a vain, shallow, pretentious, talkative phoney bore. It never has been my experience that an astute star would choose a vehicle encompassing all these defects... but she has." (*New York Morning Telegraph*, February 1, 1957)

"Miss Bankhead is mightier than the cast, the director, the adaptor and Henry James... [She] gives a bold and booming performance." (*New York Times*, January 31, 1957)

Commentary

Tallulah agreed to star in this production, no doubt, because of the title. Eugenia was the name of her sister, was her mother's middle name and was the first name of one of her dearest friends, Eugenia Rawls. She should not have allowed sentiment to influence her career decisions.

In this adaptation of James's novel, Tallulah was Eugenia, the Baroness Munster. She and her dilettante brother, Felix, are a couple of threadbare opportunists who arrive at an uncle's estate in Boston with the hope of marrying into wealth and shoring up their fading fortunes. There is an immediate clash between the European hedonists and the yankees, to whom life is a discipline. Felix romances one of the Wentworth heiresses while an affluent widower courts Eugenia, but before she can dissolve her union with the Baron, Felix accidentally blurts out his sister's intentions toward the widower and he leaves. Felix wins his girl, but Eugenia is left to face a bleak future spent in shabby hotels.

S43   CRAZY OCTOBER

Opened: October 8, 1958 (Shubert Theatre, New Haven, Conn.)

Credits
Director/Plawright, James Leo Herlihy; Producer, Walter Starke; Costumes, Alvin Colt.

Cast
Colin Wilcox (Dorrie Cotton); Tallulah Bankhead (Daisy Filbertson); Jack Weston (Rudy "Baby" Filbertson); Joan Blondell (Thelma); Fred Beir (Boyd); J. Frank Lucas (Charlie); Estelle Winwood (Miz Annabel Cotton)

Reviews
"Tallulah Bankhead's delivery – even her manner of sauntering around the stage – can be side-splitting. But this is nothing new; it is merely the inimitable Tallulah in another role..." (*Yale Daily News*, October 9, 1958)

"The role of the inn proprietress could be interesting when it is developed, but its potentialities have not yet been fully realized. However, the actress [Bankhead] does okay with what she has." (*Variety*, October 15, 1958)

"The fans of Tallulah Bankhead are a loyal lot and it's a good thing they are because her new play will demand their last full measure of devotion... [she] does not attempt to play her role straight, and perhaps it's just as well." (*Detroit Times*, November 10, 1958)

Commentary
Herlihy's play was set in a West Virginia coal mining ghost town near the Kentucky line where Daisy Filbertson runs a roadside inn called the Blue Note. In addition to Baby, her 23-year-old, dim-witted, calypso-crazed son, her three permanent guests are Thelma, an aging prostitute with a heart of gold, Miz Annabel Cotton and her daughter, Dorrie. Miz Annabel is an elderly widow who had instructed Daisy to have her husband's body cremated, but Daisy, the greedy woman that she is, buried the man in the parking lot instead and gave the old woman some fireplace ashes. (When the highway came through, she had to dig up the skeleton and stash it in the attic.) Since Miz Annabel had no money, Daisy decided that Dorrie could work for her as perpetual repayment of the debt. Daisy's scheme had gone unnoticed for years, but when Boyd, a stranger just passing through, stops by for a cup of coffee and stays long enough to fall in love with Dorrie, he suspects the former identity of the skeleton and its connection with the girl's financial bondage. Daisy tries to conceal her secret, but doesn't count on the resourcefulness of her son. He wins a $500 honeymoon trip for the

young couple and a vacation in Trinidad for himself. Her friends desert her and Daisy is left alone with the skeleton.

When the play opened in New Haven, the usual pre-Broadway tour began. It moved on to Washington, D.C. opening there on October 13 (with Mary Doyle replacing Colin Wilcox), and was scheduled to open at New York's Alvin Theatre on November 3. But reviews were poor to bad, and the production shuttered on October 25 for revisions. The Broadway opening was postponed indefinitely, but the play re-opened in Detroit on November 10, then moved to Hollywood's Huntington Hartford Theatre on November 20. It was booked for three weeks at San Francisco's Geary Theatre, where it opened on December 15, but reviews had not improved and the play closed for good on January 3, 1959.

Herlihy based the play on his own short story, *The Sleep of Baby Filbertson.*

S44 MIDGIE PURVIS

Opened: Feb. 1, 1961 (Martin Beck Theatre)   21 performances

Credits

Director, Burgess Meredith; Producer, Robert Whitehead and Roger L. Stevens; Playwright, Mary Chase; Scenery/Lighting, Ben Edwards; Costumes, Guy Kent

Cast

Mary Farrell (Mrs. Durkee); William Redfield (Canfield Purvis); Russell Hardie (Edwin Gilroy Purvis); Tallulah Bankhead (Midgie Purvis); Alice Pearce (Dorothy Plunkett); John Cecil Holm (Luther Plunkett); Janice Mars (Vivian Stubbs); Richard Prahl (Louis Kronfeldt); Nydia Westman (Althea Malone); Jane Van Duser (Emma Pasternak); Kip McArdle (Mother); Pia Zadora (Cleo June); Paul Mace (Wesley); Joseph Grassi (Harry); Clinton Sundberg (Dr. Monroe Sidensticker); William Callan (Jack Fedderson); Red Grange (Bill Lomax); Jean Brun (Babe Jensen)

Review Summary

"[Tallulah Bankhead] tries anything and everything, works hard and long and shamelessly to evoke much more of tottering baby-sitter Purvis than the author gave her as tools..." (*New York Morning Telegraph*, February 3, 1961)

"Despite an unusual restraint in Miss Bankhead's behavior as compared with the display of personality which often marks her performances, she is still too strong an individual to be merged into Midgie Purvis." (*The Wall Street Journal*, February 3, 1961)

"Miss Bankhead's performance is delightfully expert... She gives not only a good show, but also a characterization of depth and strength." (*New York Post*, February 2, 1961)

Commentary

Mary Chase won a Pulitzer prize for *Harvey*, a delightful play about Elwood P. Dowd and his imaginary friend, a six-foot tall rabbit. (Miss Chase's first draft of the play concerned a woman and a four-foot canary named Daisy, and Tallulah would have been her choice to play the woman.) It was a Broadway smash in 1944 with Frank Fay and was a money-making film in 1950 with James Stewart, but her subsequent plays were not as successful. *Mrs. McThing* (1952) was offered to Tallulah but she turned it down, allowing Helen Hayes to take the role. The Chase play Tallulah *did* accept turned out to be another in a long list of career mistakes.

Tallulah was Midgie Purvis, the middle-aged wife of a raw-food tycoon, and the mother of a rather stuffy son, Canfield, who is president of the Junior Chamber of Commerce. Midgie has retained the heart of a child and enjoys playing pranks, although her humor is not appreciated at home. When the son brings home the girl he intends to marry, Midgie makes her entrance by sliding down a bannister. The embarrassed son tells his mother he is ashamed of her and accuses her of ruining his life. Her heart broken, Midgie leaves. She disguises herself as an 80-year-old woman and goes about having the time of her life, even forming a Mother Machree Club. She hires herself out as a babysitter and creates an enchanting little hideaway in an old candystore for herself and her three charges. There is a swing on the roof and a fireman's pole to slide down. Canfield finds her, confesses that he was wrong, that he really enjoys having a fun mother. Midgie's faith in her family is restored and she bids a touching farewell to the three youngsters.

Midgie Purvis was a role Tallulah could have fun with, and the fun started on the first day of rehearsals. According to Pia Zadora, who played one of the children, Tallulah arrived at the theatre disguised as a bag lady. "No one knew it was Tallulah," Miss Zadora said in a 1991 telephone interview. "She was walking around in the theatre annoying the director and Miss Chase. They were about to throw the woman out, but she pushed back her hair and said, 'Don't fool yourselves, dahlings. It's me!'"

Pia Zadora was only five years old when she did *Midgie Purvis*, but she said it made an indelible impression. "It was my very first Broadway show, and when I met Tallulah for the first time, she looked down at me, and said, 'How long have you been in show business, young lady?' I looked at my brand new Mickey Mouse wristwatch and said, 'exactly twenty minutes.' Tallulah let out one of her loud throaty laughs, and I was her pet from then on. She wasn't known to be chummy with children, but she took an interest in me, and every day she sent her secretary out to buy a new gift for me."

The young Zadora also took an interest in Tallulah. "I thought she was terrific. And when she ordered a hotdog for lunch, with relish, ketchup, horseradish sauce, mustard and sauerkraut, I had to have one just like it. An hour later, I was at the hospital having my stomach pumped.

Tallulah thought that was funny too!"

Tallulah's role was a strenuous one, and although she was nearing sixty, and was suffering health problems, she insisted on performing the stunts anyway. Miss Zadora remembers only that she had occasional trouble breathing "but it was no wonder. She smoked like a fiend. She was never without a cigarette. It seemed to part of her mouth, always hanging there. And she just let the ashes fall."

Midgie reminded some critics of the Tallulah of old, the energetic young actress who would turn cartwheels to liven up a dull scene. Unfortunately, even Tallulah's antics failed to liven *Midgie Purvis*, and it closed during its third week. Her antics were well-enough liked, however, to warrant a Tony nomination, her first, but she lost the award to Joan Plowright (who won for *A Taste of Honey*).

S45   THE MILK TRAIN DOESN'T STOP HERE ANYMORE

Opened: Jan. 1, 1964 (Brooks Atkinson Theatre)   5 performances

Credits

Director, Tony Richardson; Producer, David Merrick; Playwright, Tennessee Williams; Sets, Rouben Ter-Arutunian; Music, Ned Rorem; Lighting, Martin Aronstein.

Cast

Bobby Dean Hooks, Konrad Matthaei (Stage Assistants); Tallulah Bankhead (Mrs. Goforth); Marian Seldes (Blackie); Ralph Roberts (Rudy); Tab Hunter (Christopher Flanders); Ruth Ford (The Witch of Capri)

Review Summary

"Miss Bankhead gives a vivid but empty portrayal of the dissipated old harpy, but she doesn't create more than the outline of a character... Moreover, her enunciation is so slurred that she's frequently hard to understand." (*Variety*, January 8, 1964)

"Tallulah Bankhead presents a colorful woman, malevolent, shrewd, carnal, selfish, cruel, diseased and terrified. What makes her Flora Goforth vivid, rather than just nasty, is the exuberent, what-the-hell fillip Miss Bankhead gives the role." (*New York World Telegram & Sun*, January 2, 1964)

Commentary

Perhaps the least successful of Tennessee Williams' many plays, *Milk Train* is set on Italy's "Divine Coast," where lives Mrs. Flora Goforth, an aging woman of great wealth and notoriety. Once a celebrated Follies beauty, the ailing woman is writing her lurid memoirs, detailing her numerous marriages and innumerable affairs. Also in the house is Blackie, Flora's wildly neurotic secretary to whom she is dictating her memoirs. Into her home and life comes Christopher Flanders, an itinerant young man, poet and maker of mobiles, who is out of cash and almost starving. Nicknamed the Angel of Death, he has a habit of attaching himself to old wealthy women who haven't long to live. Before Flora dies, the young man offers her real understanding of life, but she merely wants physical pleasure and tries to lure him into her bed. She doesn't accept his offer, and he refuses hers.

In 1962, Tallulah saw an early draft of the play, called Williams and asked for the part. Williams said he had had her in mind as Flora from the begining, but had already agreed to let Hermione Baddeley do it. The play opened on Broadway in 1963 and closed after 69 performances. For the 1964 opening, Williams gave Tallulah the part and revised his play slightly, adding dimension to the poet's chracter, but his efforts were wasted. It lasted four days.

In his autobiography, *Memoirs* (1975), Williams said *Milk Train* might have been a success if Tallulah had been able to play Flora five years earlier. By 1964, at age sixty-two, she "no longer had the physical stamina to put it over. She was too deep into liquor and pills, and she had great difficulty in projecting clearly past the front of the house" (see B145). According to Charles Higham's biography of Katharine Hepburn (see B068), Tony Richardson, the director, wanted Hepburn for the lead role, but was unable to sway Williams from his intention to sign Bankhead.

Milk Train was the last Broadway play in which Tallulah Bankhead appeared, but she wasn't ready to leave the theatre just yet; she continued performing in summer stock for several months.

The play was adapted for the screen in 1968, and released by Universal as *Boom*. Elizabeth Taylor was Flora (too young for the part), Richard Burton was Christopher (too old for the role) and Noël Coward was the Witch of Capri (the only member of the cast to get good reviews). Critics hated the film and thought a better title would have been *Thud*.

SUMMER STOCK

It has often been written that Tallulah Bankhead was introduced to summer stock in 1940, but Brendan Gill mentions in his biography (see B003) that she spent two weeks in 1919 as an apprentice in Somerville, Mass. and another two in Baltimore. Tallulah never referred to the experience. The first *official* record of her involvement in summer theatre dates from 1922, when she spent two weeks in Baltimore with the George Marshall Players. (Chester Morris was also along.)

From 1940 until 1964, she played several seasons of stock, and her contracts involved not only a guaranteed salary plus a percentage (she often cleared as much as $5,000 a week), but footlights. She refused to perform in a theatre without footlights (to lessen the unflattering shadows caused by spots and overhead lights).

S46   SLEEPING PARTNERS

Opened: June 11, 1922 (New Lyceum Theatre, Baltimore, Maryland)

Credits
Playwright, Sacha Guitry

Cast
Harry Minturn (He Is As Others Are); Tallulah Bankhead (She Is Like All Shes, Extraordinary); Horace Braham (The Husband Is Just A Husband With A Beard); Wyrley Birch (The Servant Is A Servant)

Commentary
Tallulah joined the George Marshall Players in the summer of 1922 and was part of their summer stock company for two weeks. *Sleeping Partners* was the first of two plays they did in Baltimore, each lasting a week at the New Lyceum Theatre.

Sacha Guitry's play had been a Broadway success with H.B. Warner and Irene Bordoni in 1918.

S47   GOOD GRACIOUS, ANNABELLE

Opened: June 20, 1922 (New Lyceum Theatre, Baltimore, Maryland)

Credits
Playwright, Clare Kummer

Cast
Tallulah Bankhead starred as Annabelle. Others in the cast were Chester Morris, Langdon Gillett, Wyrley Birch, Paul Henrichs, Audrey Hart, Katharine Atkinson and Lee McLaughlin.

Commentary
This was the second of two summer stock plays put on by the George Marshall Players at Baltimore's New Lyceum Theatre. There was a heat wave at the time, but according to local reviews, the plays were so amusing that no one gave a thought to the heat (except between acts).

Good Gracious, Annabelle was Kummer's first play after a successful career writing songs. The play had first opened in New York on October 31, 1916, with Roland Young, Lola Fisher and Walter Hampden, and was performed 111 times.

S48   THE SECOND MRS. TANQUERAY

Opened: July 1, 1940 (Maplewood Theatre, Maplewood, N.J.)

Credits

Director, William Miles; Playwright, Sir Arthur Wing Pinero; Settings, Albert Ward.

Cast

Colin Keith-Johnston (Aubrey Tanqueray); Ralph Kellard (Gordon Jayne, M.D.); Stephan Eugene Cole (Morse); James MacColl (Cayley Drummle); Tallulah Bankhead (Paula Tanqueray); Eugenia Rawls (Ellean Tanqueray); Leonore Harris (Mrs. Alice Cortelyon); Edmund George (Sir George Orreyed); Madeleine Clive (Lady Orreyed); Jess Barker (Captain Hugh Ardale)

Commentary

Tallulah and her entourage were driven from theatre to theatre in their own bus, stopping wherever they pleased for a picnic, or a swim, or at little cafes for cokes. At once such place somewhere in the Berkshires, an old man walked over to Tallulah's table and asked if she was Edna St. Vincent Millay. "No, but I am somebody very famous," she told him. "I'll write my name on a slip of paper and after I'm gone you must open it and see." A little later, as the company was boarding the bus, the old man ran out of the restaurant and shouted with glee, "Thank you, Ella Wheeler Wilcox!"

From Maplewood, the production moved to Amherst, Mass., then on to Harrison, Maine, Matunuck, Rhode Island, Stockbridge, Mass., White Plains, New York, Dennis and Marblehead, Mass., then finally to Cedarhurst, New York (Long Island), playing a week at each location. The summer tour ended on August 31. It had been a successful tour, and she had given consistently good performances. Harold J. Kennedy (who was then director of a summer stock theatre in Amherst, Mass.) said later that she "gave one of the greatest acting performances I have ever seen. If I had not been such a neophyte in the theatre at the time I would have stolen the money to bring it to Broadway" (see B081).

The Second Mrs. Tanqueray premiered in London, at the St. James Theatre, in May 1893. Mrs. Patrick Campbell starred and became forever associated with the role. She appeared in countless revivals, both in England and the United States, for another fifteen years. Mrs. Leslie Carter, Eleanora Duse and Ethel Barrymore also had success with Pinero's play.

S49 HER CARDBOARD LOVER

Opened: June 30, 1941 (Westport County Playhouse, Westport, Ct.)

Credits

Director, John C. Wilson; Producers, Cheryl Crawford, Dorothy and Julian Olney, Richard Aldrich; Playwight, Jacques Deval (adapted by P.G. Wodehouse); Settings, Raymond Sovey; Tallulah's

Costumes, Hattie Carnegie; Make-up and Coiffure, Elizabeth
Arden.

Cast

Tallulah Bankhead (Simone); Ralph Kellard (Monsieur Bonnevant);
Edwin Gordon (Charly); Stephan Eugene Cole (Paul Guisard); Fred
Keating (Tony Lagorce); Francis Russell (Cloak Room Attendent);
Ish-Ti-Opi (Croupier); Nancy Perkins, John Kishler (Young
Couple); Viola Frayne (Albine)

Commentary

This was Tallulah's second time to star in Deval's play; she had appeared in
the 1928 London production and toured the provinces with it the following
year, with Leslie Howard producing (see S21).

According to Denis Brian's biography of Bankhead (see B002), the
summer tour began in Cedarhurst, New York, on Long Island, and began
rather badly. Brian relates how a furious Bankhead insisted that the actor
playing the Croupier be replaced immediately and enlisted the help of
Lyman Brown, an agent-friend, who sent a young Ricardo Montalban to
see her. Tallulah approved, gave him the part, and told him after his first
performance, "Marvelous darling. It was the way they'd play it in France.
It was done with dignity. You'll be with us for the rest of the tour." Oddly
enough, Montalban's name does not appear in any of the playbills from the
tour.

The company also played White Plains, New York, Maplewood,
N.J., Ivoryton, Conn., Ogunquit, Maine, Stockbridge, Marblehead, Dennis,
and Westboro, Mass.

S50 PRIVATE LIVES

Opened: June 19, 1944 (Strand Theatre, Stamford, Conn.)

Credits

Director, Martin Manulus; Producer, John C. Wilson; Playwright,
Noël Coward; Settings, Charles Elson.

Cast

Barbara Baxley (Sibyl Chase); Donald Cook (Elyot Chase); Phil
Arthur (Victor Prynne); Tallulah Bankhead (Amanda Prynne);
Therese Quadri (Louise)

Commentary

Tallulah Bankhead is almost as closely associated with *Private Lives* as she
is *The Little Foxes*. In the late 40s it was her signature play, and when she
wasn't guesting on a radio show or flopping on Broadway in *The Eagle Has
Two Heads* (in the spring of 1947), she was thrilling back road audiences
with her unique interpretation of Amanda Prynne.

The 1944 performance listed above lasted only a week and was her only appearance in summer theatre that year. Although it was not officially part of the summer and winter stock tours that followed (beginning in 1946 and continuing off and on for four years), it is the earliest substantiated production in which she starred. The cast listed is the one most often seen in the various tours (the 1944 cast included John Hoysradt, Carol Stone, Alexander Clark and Alice Pearce). Tallulah brought *Private Lives* to Broadway for a successful revival in late 1948 (see S38) then went back on the road for another year, finally closing the show in Passaic, New Jersey, on June 3, 1950.

In those four years of touring, it is difficult to determine exactly how many performances were given, but it is a fact that the only states not included in the various tours were Nevada, Maine and Florida. Donald Cook and Tallulah were with the production from beginning to end, but Mary Mason, Buff Cobb and Eugenia Rawls each had a turn as Sibyl (when Barbara Baxley wasn't available), and Alexander Clark and William Langford alternated with Phil Arthur as Victor. Therese Quadri seemed to have exclusive rights to portray the maid, but in the first few engagements, Alice Pearce had the part, and Claudine LeDuc took over for the final performances in 1950.

Summer stock engagements of *Private Lives* include two weeks at the Greenwich Playhouse (Greenwich, Conn.) beginning June 24, 1946; a week at Chicago's Harris Theatre beginning July 27, 1947; two weeks at the Biltmore Theatre (Hollywood, Calif.) ending July 26, 1948; and one week at the Falmouth Playhouse (Coonamessett-on-Cape Cod, Mass.) in July 1949.

S51   DEAR CHARLES

Commentary

Before its Broadway opening in September 1954, *Dear Charles* made the usual summer stock rounds. The play had a checkered past, and the producers wanted to "test" its audience appeal before hitting Broadway. With Tallulah as the star, its audience appeal was much greater than expected, and the producers booked a Broadway opening with confidence. (See S39).

S52   WELCOME, DARLINGS (a revue)

Opened: July 16, 1956 (Westport Country Playhouse, Westport, CT.)

Credits

Director, Jay Harnick; Producers, Philip Langer and Peter Turgeon; Contributing Playwrights, Paul Keyes, Hugh Martin, Timothy Gray, Marshall Barer, Dean Fuller, Jerry Herman, Jerry de Bono and Sheldon Harnick; Musical Direction, Peter Howard and Ted Graham;

Settings, Martin Reiss; Production Associate, Gus Schirmer, Jr.; Pianists, Peter Howard and Ted Graham; Stage Manager, Peter Pell.

Cast

Don Crichton, Timothy Gray, Tallulah Bankhead, Bob Bakanic, Don McKay, James Kirkwood, The Martins, Gwen Harmon, Sheila Smith, Preshy Marker.

Commentary

After the failure of *Ziegfeld Follies* earlier in the year (see S41), Tallulah salvaged a few songs and sketches, christened her creation *Welcome, Darlings*, and persuaded a few of the original cast members to join the production, which consisted of two acts and 26 sketches. Tallulah sang *I've Heard a Lot About You*, recited Dorothy Parker's *The Waltz*, and even impersonated Peter Pan in a sketch titled "Love and Thimbles, Peter." In the Peter Pan skit, Tallulah had some especially good lines. When Wendy introduced herself as Wendy Moira Angela Darling, Tallulah replied, "I am Peter Pan, darling." It brought the house down every time.

After a few rehearsals, a summer stock tour began at Westport and continued on to Ivoryton, Conn., Dennis, Mass., Matunuck, Rhode Island and other theatres on the Eastern Seaboard.

S53 HOUSE ON THE ROCKS

Opened: June 1958

Credits

Director, Arthur Sircom; Producer, Charles R. Wood; Playwright, George Batson; Set Designer, John Raymond Freiman.

Cast

Joseph Campanella (Morena); Ruth Hammond (Louise Cortland); Leona Maricle (Martha Brand); Carlton Colyer (David Granger); Mirianne Marshall (Kathy); Tallulah Bankhead (Alexandra); Madeleine Morka (Mrs. Hamilton); Warren Kemmerling (Carlin); Marian Russell (Nora Taylor); Gerald M. Makuch (Brent)

Commentary

House on the Rocks, a tale of murder at a lonely upper Hudson River valley estate, was a revision of Batson's own *Celia*, a play which premiered in 1953 with Jessie Royce Landis. It wasn't especially liked, and it was hoped the revised version would be liked well enough to warrant a Broadway opening. It wasn't and the play was abandoned after the summer tour ended.

Joseph Campanella, in a 1991 telephone interview from his home in California, said he remembers the experience vividly. "It was not my first experience in summer stock, or my first time to support a star, but

Tallulah Bankhead was the first larger than life personality I encountered. She was intimidating to many of the players, but we got along great."

Campanella was appearing in the daytime soap opera *The Guiding Light* at the time, and he said when he read for the part, "Tallulah rushed up to the stage, grabbed my face, looked me over and said she had loved my work on television. She also said I was the right size for the part – I'm six foot two, and I weighed 185 pounds at the time – so I thought my chances for getting the role were pretty good. And, sure enough!"

About *House on the Rocks*, Campanella said he had forgotten much of the plot ("It was an out and out melodrama"), but he remembered one scene quite well: when Tallulah (whose character was supposed to have been a former society singer) put on a recording she had made years ago. "It was one of those great torch songs, very bluesy, and Tallulah had recorded it as a lark one night late at a party. It sounded like a professional recording, and the song was perfectly suited to her deep voice. The sound of that lovely torch song and Tallulah's reaction while listening to it combined to make one of those magical moments. It was the best moment in the show."

The play was presented in Detroit, Kennebunkport, Maine, Harrisburg, Penn., Warren and Columbus, Ohio, Binghampton, New York, Laconia-Gilford, New Hampshire and Nyack, New York.

S54   CRAIG'S WIFE

Opened: June 30, 1960 (Tappan Zee Playhouse, Nyack, New York)

Credits

Director, Ron Winston; Playwright, George Kelly; Settings and Lighting, Thomas Barnes and David Johnston.

Cast

Dorothy Sands (Miss Austen); Dorothy Blackburn (Mrs. Harold); Martha Orrick (Mazie); Tallulah Bankhead (Harriet Craig); Rosalyn Newport (Ethel Landreth); Frank Schofield (Walter Craig); Dortha Duckworth (Mrs. Frazier); Ronald Gary (Delivery Boy); John Dutra (Billy Berkmire); Richard Hamilton (Joseph Catelle); Ray Barron (Harry); John Lyden (Expressman); Nicholas Pryor (Eugene Fredericks); Layton Ferol (Western Union Messenger)

Commentary

Craig's Wife was the second George Kelly play in which Tallulah starred; she had a moderate success in 1936 with *Reflected Glory*, but *Craig's Wife* is certainly Kelly's best-known play. It has been filmed three times: in 1928 with Irene Rich, in 1936 with Rosalind Russell, and in 1950 (as *Harriet Craig*) with Joan Crawford.

The play opened the 1960 summer stock season in Nyack, and the opening night performance attracted several celebrities, including Helen Hayes, Horton Foote, Nancy Kelly, Carson McCullers and Sylvia Sidney.

From Nyack, the company traveled to Chicago for a week, then to Maine before ending the tour in Vineland Station, Ontario.

S55   HERE TODAY

Opened: June 1962

Credits

Director, Jack Sydow; Playwright, George Oppenheimer; Settings, Pat Belew.

Cast

Bill Story (Jeffrey Windrew); Fran Bennett (Gertrude); Peter Hobbs (Philip Graves); Jill Kraft (Claire Windrew); Estelle Winwood (Mrs. Windrew); Richard Kendrick (Stanley Dale); Tallulah Bankhead (Mary Hilliard); Donald Symington (Spencer Grant)

Commentary

Oppenheimer's play opened in 1932 with Ruth Gordon and has been a summer stock favorite ever since. Tallulah's version did not limit itself to summer stock of 1962, but also continued (off and on) in the west through the winter of 62/63, and made its final stand in early 1964. It had been on the road for nearly two years.

S56   GLAD TIDINGS

Opened: June 1964

Credits

Director, Christopher Hewett; Playwright, Edward Mabley; Sets, Herbert Senn; Tallulah's Wardrobe, Guy Kent.

Cast

Evelyn Russell (Ethel Nash); Fay Sappington (Mrs. MacDonald); George Hyland (Henry); William Roerick (Steve Whitney); Jacquelyn Hyde (Agnes Bell); Pamela Raymond (Claire Abbott); Tallulah Bankhead (Dolaura Abbott); Emory Bass (Gus Kramer); David Dowe (Terry Abbott)

Commentary

In her last summer stock appearance, Tallulah was Dolaura Abbott, a temperamental film star who once had an affair with Steve Whitney, now about to marry Ethel Nash, a wealthy magazine publisher. Dolaura causes

Steve to change his mind, however, when she tells him about his 19-year-old illigitimate daughter. He marries Dolaura instead.

The production opened in early June and played in several theatres in Massachusettes, Connecticut and Maine.

PROFESSIONAL APPEARANCES

This section includes Tallulah Bankhead's work in night clubs and on the lecture circuit. Several of her appearances at benefit shows and theatrical pageants are also listed.

NIGHT CLUBS

S57 **Cafe de Paris** (London) April 5, 1927. To benefit the Kings College Hospital, Tallulah produced a "special cabaret and gala night of entertainment," and performed a sketch entitled "Always Apologize."

S58 **The Sands** (Las Vegas) May 20, 1953. (Tallulah made her American night club debut performing a 32-minute routine of jokes, songs and dramatic monologues. She was engaged for three weeks.)

S59 **The Sands** (Las Vegas) August 6, 1954. (Opened in a return engagment which lasted for four weeks.)

S60 **Cafe de Paris** (London) May 27, 1957. (Was engaged for six weeks, and her act included songs and sketches, including Dorothy Parker's monologue *The Waltz*.)

THE LECTURE CIRCUIT

S61 **Dallas, Texas** December 5, 1950. (Tallulah made her debut on the Lyceum circuit when she addressed an audience of 2,800 in the McFarlin Auditorium on the campus of Southern Methodist University. She was paid $1,500 for each appearance.)

S62 **Chicago, Illinois** December 6, 1950. (Continued with her lecture tour.)

S63 **Wilmington, Delaware** December 7, 1950. (Gave her third and final lecture; she decided the schedule was too exhausting. The audience was as appreciative as ever, but the pressure was too great.)

OTHER APPEARANCES

S64 Actors Fund Benefit (Baltimore, Maryland) November 4, 1922. (Tallulah participated in this "huge matinee" to raise money for the Actors Fund of America. Also on hand were Elsie Janis, Ruth Chatterton, Conway Tearle, Ralph Morgan and Hope Hampton. Tallulah acted in a comedy skit with Robert Warwick. The benefit was successful in raising over $5,000.)

S65 Great Lovers of Romance (New Theatre, London) May 6, 1927. (Replacing the Baroness Ravensdale, Tallulah posed as Cleopatra for one performance in a tableau, presented during a matinee of Marie Tempests's *London Pride* to benefit the Leicestershire Nursing Association.)

S66 The Snob (Palladium, London) December 1929. (Tallulah played in her first variety show.)

S67 Military Entertainment (Camp Langdon, New Hampshire) August 17, 1941. (Tallulah entertained soldiers with songs and sketches.)

S68 Navy Relief Show (Madison Square Garden, New York) September 2, 1942. (Tallulah was part of a Floradora Sextette act in which the roles were reversed. Appearing as "boys" were Tallulah, Leonora Corbett, Eve Arden, Sophie Tucker, Peggy Wood and Gertrude Lawrence, and as "girls" were Ed Wynn, Vincent Price, Clifton Webb, Danny Kaye, Boris Karloff and Eddie Cantor.)

S69 Political Rally (Madison Square Garden, New York.) October 31, 1948. (Tallulah followed President Truman on the platform and addressed an audience of 20,000.)

S70 Damon Runyon Cancer Fund (New York City) April 1951. (Tallulah participated in this benefit by joining Ed Wynn, Ethel Merman, Bob Hope and Frank Sinatra in a barbershop quintet.)

S71 ANTA Album (Ziegfeld Theatre, New York) May 6, 1951. (In this tribute to the American National Theatre and Academy, Tallulah was mistress of ceremonies. Others participating were Faye Emerson, Margaret Webster, Hedda Hopper and Helen Gallagher.)

S72 Dedication (Huntsville, Alabama) May 18, 1962. (Tallulah traveled to her the town of her birth to dedicate Bankhead Hall, named for her father and uncle, and shared the platform with several relatives.)

As Constance Porter in *Lifeboat* (1944).

4

Film Work

Tallulah Bankhead had two spurts of filmmaking – from 1917 to 1919, and in 1931/32. Her other film appearances were sporadic. Although she was never a star of the medium, her pictures generated a lot of publicity, and her career (such as it was) was exceptionally long: she made her first film in 1917, and her last was released in 1965. Most Bankhead filmographies list *A Woman's Law* as a film she made in 1928. The title is not included here because she didn't make it (see F4). And although other filmographies usually include *The Virtuous Vamp* (1919), a film in which Bankhead allegedly appeared as an extra, that title has also been eliminated because her appearance in the film is purely speculative.

This filmography marks the first appearance of the film *Who Loved Him Best?* (1917, released 1918), and although some may argue that she didn't appear in the movie (the Library of Congress, for instance, where the film is housed, does not include her in their cast list), the American Film Institute recognizes it as Tallulah's first picture, and photos showing Tallulah being directed by Dell Henderson and chatting between scenes with Edna Goodrich were published in a fan magazine at the time.

* * * * *

F1   WHO LOVED HIM BEST? (*Mutual Film Corporation*)

Released: February 1918   Length: 5 reels

Credits

Director, Dell Henderson; Photography, Sol Polito

Cast

Edna Goodrich (Doria Dane); Herbert Evans (George Steele); Miriam Folger (Mrs. Schuyler); Frank Otto (Harry North); Charles Martin (Gilbert Jasper); Burt Busby (C.M. Winton); Nadia Cary

(Amy Winton); Thomas Wallace (Director); Francois Du Barry
(Assistant Director); Tallulah Bankhead (Nell)

Synopsis

A film producer discovers young, pretty Doria Dane working in a sewing
factory. He gives her a job in the movies and falls in love with her. He
wants to marry his discovery, but she loves another: a Greenwich Village
sculptor named George Steele. She abandons her film career, and models
for Steele's statue "American Militant." Doria encourages him to
concentrate on his work and give up his frivolous Greenwich Village
friends. He follows her advice, works hard on the sculpture, and wins a
prestigious award for it. But the limelight dims his ambition and he falls
prey to the fashionable Mrs. Schuyler, a wealthy widow who wants to make
him her second husband. But Doria, however, is determined to win him
back, so she bursts into his studio during a wild party and shatters his
masterpiece, only to explain later that she had destroyed an imitation; the
real statue is intact and at another studio. George realizes his mistakes and
the two are reunited.

Review Summary

"The story is tiresome, without any strength..." (*Variety*, Feb. 15, 1918)

"Is a story that ought to go well in the average neighborhood house. It is
clean and, though somewhat lacking in comedy touches, affords five reels
of well put together entertainment." (*Motion Picture News*, Feb. 16, 1918)

Additional Sources

Reviews: *Exhibitor's Trade Review* (Feb. 2, Feb. 9, 1918); *Motography*
(Feb. 2, 1918); *Moving Picture World* (Feb. 16, 1918).
See Also: *Images in Low Key; Cinematographer Sol Polito, A.S.C.*
(Lazarou), pp. 9, 80.

Commentary

Tallulah Bankhead's role in *Who Loved Him Best?* (known as *Art and the
Woman* during production) was Tallulah's prize for winning *Pictureplay
Magazine's* screen opportunity contest. Since she never referred to the
film, and since her character is not mentioned in any of the review
summaries of the plot, one can only guess what her role in the film was –
perhaps one of the artist's rowdy friends. Mutual filmed the story in late
1917 on locations in Brooklyn and in Greenwich Village, particularly West
12th Street between 5th Avenue and University Place.

The photographer, Sol Polito (1892-1960), graduated to more
important projects, eventually becoming one of Hollywood's most
respected cinematographers, especially noted for his black and white
photography at Warner Bros. in the 1930s and 40s.

Edna Goodrich (1884-1974) was a stage actress before joining the
film industry in 1915, and this was one of many Mutual films of the late
teens in which she was starred. The film still survives and is housed at the

Library of Congress, Washington, D.C.

F2   WHEN MEN BETRAY   (*Graphic Film Corporation*)

Released: June 1918   Length: 6 reels

Credits

Director/Scenario, Ivan Abramson; Assistant Director, William
Abramson; Photography, Marcel Le Picard

Cast

Gail Kane (Marion Edwardes); Robert Elliott (Raymond Edwardes);
Juliet Moore (Vivian Edwardes); Sally Crute (Lucille Stanton);
Gertrude Braun (Florence Edwardes); Tallulah Bankhead (Alice
Edwardes); Jack McLean (Bob Gardner); Reed Hamilton (Dick
Gardner); Dora Mills Adams (Mrs. Gardner); Stuart Holmes
(Frederick Barton)

Synopsis

Raymond Edwardes, husband and father, is infatuated with Lucille Stanton,
and despite the pleadings of his wife, Marion, and daughter, Vivian, he has
an extra-marital affair. His sisters, Florence and Alice, also try to talk him
out of having the affair, but to no avail. He feigns illness and doesn't
accompany his wife to an evening social function, letting his friend, Fred
Barton, take her instead. After she has gone, he goes to see his lover,
leaving his younger sister, Alice, alone in the house. Bob Gardner, a young
scoundrel who is engaged to Raymond's elder sister, Florence, comes to the
house and rapes Alice, then leaves to find pleasure elsewhere. When
Raymond reaches Lucille's apartment, he finds Bob Gardner there, and
realizes what a fool he has been. When his wife returns home from the
reception with Fred Barton, Raymond asks her forgiveness. She forgives
him. When Bob Gardner shows up again he gets into a fight with Fred
Barton and is killed in the struggle. The household finally returns to
normal when Dick Gordon, Bob's brother, marries Alice and Lucille goes
out in search of another boyfriend.

Review Summary

"Risque story not suited to family programs. Gail Kane, Tallulah
Bankhead, Stuart Holmes and Robert Elliott deserve special mention for
their rendition of their parts." (*Exhibitor's Trade Review*, June 8, 1918)

"Tallulah Bankhead, as the foolish girl rudely awakened, plays with
sincerity and feeling." (*Motion Picture News*, June 15, 1918)

Additional Sources

Reviews: *Exhibitor's Trade Review* (June 1, June 15, 1918); *Moving
Picture World* (June 15, June 29, 1918)

Commentary

When Men Betray gave 16-year-old Tallulah Bankhead her first substantial film role. The film has not survived so it is impossible to judge her performance, but reviewers were impressed. And considering that the critics had probably never heard of her before, the very fact that they singled her out in their reviews was a compliment of the highest order.

Gail Kane (1885-1966) was a lovely brunette who left the stage in 1913 for a film career that lasted until the early 20s. She was at her peak in the late teens, especially in films about World War I. Robert Elliott (1879-1963) was also a popular star in the teens. His popularity began to wane in the 20s, but he remained active as a character actor into the 1940s, even showing up in *Gone With the Wind* as Rhett Butler's Yankee Major-jailer.

Many of the exterior scenes of *When Men Betray* were shot on the Gould Estate in Lakewood, New Jersey.

F3   THIRTY A WEEK   *(Goldwyn Pictures Corporation)*

Released: October 1918   Length: 5 reels

Credits

Director, Harry Beaumont; Scenario, J. Clarkson Miller, from the stage success by Thompson Buchanan; Photography, George Webber; Art Direction, Hugo Ballin

Cast

Tom Moore (Dan Murray); Tallulah Bankhead (Barbara Wright); Alec B. Francis (Mr. Wright); Brenda Fowler (Mrs. Wright); Warburton Gamble (Freddy Ruyter); Grace Henderson (Mrs. Murray); Ruth Elder (Minnie Malloy)

Synopsis

Mr. and Mrs. Wright, a very wealthy couple, employ as a chauffeur, young Dan Murray, an Irishman. Their daughter, Barbara, although engaged to wealthy Freddy Ruyter, is really in love with Dan, and one evening when Dan is driving her home, she tampers with the engine. The car won't start again, and the couple have to stay out all night. Barbara declares her love for Dan, but he doesn't dare reciprocate, although he is in love with her as well. When Dan brings her home the next morning, Mr. Wright says angrily that if it had been anyone other than a common chauffeur, he would consider his daughter compromised, whereupon Barbara suddenly insists that she *is* compromised. They are married and Danny takes his new bride to the home of his mother, who does not entirely approve, but is won over when Barbara displays a liking for the recordings of John McCormack. Mr. Wright is not so easily won over, and he tries to break up the marriage by having Dan dismissed from a series of jobs. When a friend of Dan's becomes ill, and must be sent to Arizona, he helps raise the needed money by winning an auto race. When he gives the money to

Minnie, the sick man's wife, she kisses him. Freddy Ruyter, Barbara's spurned lover, was watching, and tells Barbara that he saw Dan giving money to another woman. She runs home to her parents who begin divorce proceedings. When she is asked to sign the divorce complaint, she cries out "I can't! I love him!" and runs upstairs to her room. Mr. Wright decides that his daughter's happiness is important after all, so he phones Dan and asks him to come and pick up his wife. He does, and Barbara says she wants to go back to their little flat and start all over again, even though Dan will only be making thirty-a-week.

Review Summary

"Tallulah Bankhead makes a sweet little ingenue as the young wife, but she should make up the ends of her mouth to turn up instead down, to conceal a slight tendency to 'cattishness'." (*Variety*, Oct. 18, 1918)

"Excellent acting on the part of Tom Moore and his leading woman, Tallulah Bankhead, gives *Thirty a Week* a value far above its merits as a story." (*Moving Picture World*, October 26, 1918)

Additional Sources

Reviews: *Exhibitor's Trade Review* (Oct. 26, Nov. 2, 1918); *Motion Picture News* (Oct. 26, 1918); *Motion Picture World* (Nov. 23, 1918);*The New York Times* (Oct. 14, 1918); *Wids Film Daily* (Nov. 17, 1918)

Commentary

As Barbara Wright, Tallulah Bankhead had her first film lead, and her work was favorably received. Tom Moore, her leading man, was one of three popular actor-brothers: Owen (Mary Pickford's first husband) and Matt, the youngest, who was perhaps the most popular of the three and continued to appear in films through the 30s.

Some scenes of *Thirty A Week* were filmed in New York's shopping district, especially 5th Avenue, and at a automobile racetrack in Sheepshead Bay, near Brooklyn.

F4   THE TRAP   (*Universal*)

Released: August 1919   Length: 6 reels

Credits

Director, Frank Reicher; Scenario, Eve Unsell, from an original story by Richard Harding Davis and Jules Eckert Goodman

Cast

Olive Tell (Jean Carson); Sidney Mason (Bruce Graham); Jere Austin (Ned Fallon); Rod LaRocque (Doc Sloan); Tallulah Bankhead (Helen Carson); Joseph Burke (Henry Carson); Earl Schenck (Steve Fallon)

Synopsis

Jean Carson, an Eastern bred girl who teaches school in the Yukon, marries Steve Fallon, a gambler, after her father and his partner, Ned, who is Steve's brother and who also loves her, go prospecting for gold. Later, when Steve drunkenly boasts of having another wife elsewhere, Jean leaves him. When Ned returns from a prospecting expedition and proposes, Jean confides in him, and then travels to New York to visit with her sister, Helen. News comes that Steve has died, so Jean marries Bruce Graham, a broker. Five years later, with Jean happily married and the mother of two children, Doc Sloan, a former gambling friend of Steve's, tells her that Steve is not dead, but alive, and is pursuing Helen. He will reveal everything about her past if she tries to interfere. Ned, who has also moved to New York, balks at Sloan's story and assures Jean that Steve is dead, that he buried him. Ned later lures Sloan to kill him, planning to claim the murder was done in self defense, but Jean, hiding in an adjoining room, shoots Sloan herself. Ned takes the blame, but is acquitted and marries Helen.

Review Summary

"Direction, star and cast as a whole do not measure up to the possibilities of the story." (*Motion Picture News*, August 30, 1919)

"It is a good enough picture, in its way, but it can't be classed among the big league stuff. It is just a moderately good program offering, having no claim to distinction." (*Wids Daily*, August 24, 1919)

Additional Sources

Reviews: *Exhibitor's Trade Review* (Aug. 30, 1919); *Moving Picture World* (Aug. 30, 1919)
See Also: *Motion Picture News* (Aug. 23, 1919)

Commentary

The Trap was released in England as *A Woman's Law*. Owing to this, the title, *A Woman's Law*, often shows up erroneously in Bankhead filmographies as a British film made in 1928.

Olive Tell was the star of this picture and ads for the film mentioned her name alone. Some advance publicity did mention that Tallulah Bankhead had been cast in a supporting role, but she was definitely not the selling point. In fact, so minor was Tallulah's role in *The Trap* (and so minor was the film, apparently) that reviewers did not bother to mention her name. Somewhat disappointing considering how favorably her film work was received the previous year.

F5   HIS HOUSE IN ORDER   (*Ideal Films,* London)

Released: January 1928   Length: 7,400 feet

Credits

Director, Randle Ayrton; Producer, Mayrick Milton; Scenario, Patrick L. Mannock, from play by Arthur Wing Pinero; Photography, H.M. Wheddon

Cast

Tallulah Bankhead (Nina Graham); Ian Hunter (Hilary Jesson); David Hawthorne (Filmer Jesson); Eric Maturin (Major Maurewarde); Mary Dibley (Geraldine); Windham Guise (Sir Daniel Ridgeley); Nancy Price (Lady Ridgeley); Claude Beerbohm (Pryce Ridgeley); Sheila Courtney (Annabel Jesson); Pat Courtney (Derek Jesson)

Synopsis

Nina Graham, the second wife of Filmer Jesson, finds it difficult to conform to the methodical ideas of her husband, and the constant interference of his first wife's family, who are continually comparing her unfavorably with Annabel, the first Mrs. Jesson. She discovers by accident that Annabel was an unfaithful wife, and determines to tell what she knows to the Ridgeley family. Filmer's brother, Hilary, knows the truth, but pleads with Nina to let the past be, but he eventually gives in and tells Filmer the truth. Filmer comes to realize the good qualities of Nina and asks her to take her proper place as mistress of his house.

Review Summary

"Tallulah Bankhead plays with a finished ease which encourages the hope that she may shortly be seen in a part better suited to her arresting personality." (*The Bioscope*, March 1, 1928)

"[Tallulah Bankhead's] make-up was wrong, she was not well lit, and some of the angles used from which to photograph her ought to be avoided." (*Variety*, Feb. 26, 1928)

Additional Sources

Reviews: *Kine Weekly* (date unknown)
See Also: *World Film Encyclopedia*

Commentary

In her autobiography (see B001), Tallulah admitted that she had turned down several offers from English film companies, and only accepted this one because of the money. Ideal paid her £500 a week to make this picture, and as indicated by the less than enthusiastic reviews, not much money was left to spend in other areas. Noted *Variety*: "the poverty of technical aid shows." Years later, Tallulah referred to it as "gruesome." Despite the technical inadequacies, the British Board of Review found the story strong enough to give the film an "A" rating, meaning that adolescents could not see it unless accompanied by an adult, but such ratings were common and didn't necessarily indicate objectionable material.

His House in Order premiered in the United States at New York's Palace Theatre on February 24, 1928. It's running time was listed at 71 minutes, and considering that it was copyrighted at 7,400 feet, it is possible (depending on projection speed) that a few minutes worth of film was cut out before its New York showing. (7,400 feet equals approximately 80 minutes.)

F6   TARNISHED LADY *(Paramount)*

Released: April 29, 1931   Running Time: 80 minutes

Credits

Director, George Cukor; Producer, Walter Wanger; Screenplay, Donald Ogden Stewart, adapted from his story, *New York Lady*; Photography, Larry Williams; Editor, Barney Rogan; Recording Engineer, Harold Fingerlin

Cast

Tallulah Bankhead (Nancy Courtney); Clive Brook (Norman Cravath); Phoebe Foster (Germaine Prentiss); Alexander Kirkland (DeWitt Taylor); Osgood Perkins (Ben Sterner); Elizabeth Patterson (Mrs. Courtney); Eric Blore (Jewelry Counter Clerk); Edward Gargan (Man in Bar); Baby Rosemary McHugh (Nancy's Baby).

Synopsis

Nancy Courtney, the daughter of a once-wealthy New York family, has been relying on her friends for money since her father's death. She is in love with DeWitt Taylor, a young writer, but her mother insists that she marry wealthy Norman Cravath. Norman is in love with Nancy, but Germaine Prentiss, a young heiress, is in love with him. Ben Sterner, a kind-hearted man who heads a department store, also encourages her to marry Norman Cravath. She tells DeWitt that although she loves him, she must marry another. They have a last night together, a dinner in a romantic cafe and a stroll on a moonlit beach. Nancy marries Norman the next day, but she is unhappy as Mrs. Norman Cravath. She is still in love with DeWitt who is seduced by Germaine. A few months later, the stock market crash wipes out Cravath's fortune, but Nancy, unaware of the crash, stops by Norman's office and tells him she's leaving, that she's going back to the man she loves. Norman doesn't tell her about his loss, but lets her go. Nancy runs to DeWitt's apartment, only to find Germaine there. She goes to a club and runs into Ben Sterner, who takes her to a series of Harlem nightclubs where she ends up getting drunk. She realizes that she really loves Norman, and although Ben tries to reconcile the couple, Norman says he doesn't want to see Nancy again. Nancy, now on her own, goes in search of work,.but is turned away everywhere. Several months later, still without a job, Ben sees her on the street, but she is not well and faints (being pregnant with Norman's child), and Ben sees that she is taken care of. She implores him to tell no one about the baby. He doesn't, but he does see that she gets a job at his store. Sometime later, Norman and Germaine come into the store and see Nancy. Norman walks out but comes to Nancy's apartment later that night. Nancy says she loves him and wants another chance as his wife. They embrace, and Nancy introduces him to his child.

Review Summary

"Miss Bankhead unquestionably possesses b.o. [box office] possibilities. She has personality, charm, and a voice loaded with s.a. [sex appeal?]. With careful handling and proper treatment, she has a screen future." (*Variety*, May 6, 1931)

"Bankhead acquits herself with considerable distinction, but the vehicle to which she lends her talent, is no masterpiece... Miss Bankhead is at times not unlike Marlene Dietrich, and she has the same deep voice." (*New York Times*, April 30, 1931)

"Tallulah Bankhead, who is a cross between the late Jeanne Eagles [sic] and Nancy Carroll, has plenty of ability but is largely wasted in this story [which is] almost entirely bare of comedy." (*Film Daily*, April 19, 1931)

Additional Sources

Reviews: *Judge* (May 23, 1931); *Life* (May 15, 1931); *Motion Picture Herald* (May 9, 1931); *The New Statesman and Nation* (June 6, 1931); *The New Yorker* (May 9, 1931); *Outlook and Independent* (May 13, 1931); *Rob Wagner's Script* (May 11, 1931); *Time* (May 11, 1931)
See Also: *The Films of the Thirties*, pp 55-56; *George Cukor* (Phillips), pp 31-32.

Commentary

After eight successful and highly publicized years in London, Paramount considered Tallulah Bankhead a sure bet for stardom. They launched an expensive campaign to promote her first Paramount film, describing Tallulah as a "woman-thrill," but to back that up with *Tarnished Lady* was a senseless move. Tallulah was indeed a woman-thrill, a vibrant personality, but *Tarnished Lady* gives her not one chance to sparkle. The film is a shameless melodrama and Nancy Courtney is unhappy during most of its 80 minutes. Even the nightclub scenes, with Nancy whooping it, are rather depressing because she isn't really happy at all; she's merely pretending to be. Tallulah does her best, and even manages to rise above the material occasionally, especially in the touching scene where she tells the young writer she has to marry another man because she depends on his money, but the film as a whole defeated her.

If she had followed *Tarnished Lady* with a successful picture, her film career might have taken a different turn, but as it was, none of her Paramount pictures made money, and she failed to catch on as a movie star. George Cukor had perhaps the best explanation of Bankhead's failure: "On stage she was enormously animated, but never at home on the screen. She was just not naturally photogenic. Her eyes seemed deadly opaque on film and her face never looked radiant, even when she smiled" (see B114). In view of Cukor's opinion, even the "right" vehicle might not have helped.

Tallulah and Clive Brook were reunited twenty years later on radio. He was a guest on NBC's *The Big Show* and Tallulah, as mistress of ceremonies, pulled him aside to chat. "I made a picture with you, Tallulah," Brook remarked. "Remember *Tarnished Lady*? I went back to England right after that." To which Tallulah responded, "Coward!"

F7 MY SIN (*Paramount*)

Released: September 11, 1931   Running Time: 77 minutes

Credits

Director/Adaptation, George Abbott; Scenario, Owen Davis and Adelaide Heilbron, from a story by Fred Jackson; Photography, George Folsey; Editor, Emma Hill; Recording Engineer, Ernest Zatorsky

Cast

Tallulah Bankhead (Carlotta/Anne Trevor); Fredric March (Dick Grady); Harry Davenport (Roger Metcalf); Scott Kolk (Larry Gordon); Anne Sutherland (Mrs. Gordon); Paula Marsdon (Margaret Adams); Lily Cahill (Helen Grace); Jay Fassett (James Bradford); Joe Spurin Calleia (Juan); Eric Blore (Man In Nightclub)

Synopsis

Carlotta, the hostess of a gambling saloon in Panama, has a tainted reputation. After leaving the saloon one night, she is followed to her rooms by her blackmailing husband who attempts to steal her savings. She shoots him and is arrested for his murder. No lawyer in Panama will take her case, so Dick Grady (a former lawyer, now a penniless sot) agrees to take it. He believes Carlotta's story and gets her acquitted. He shows such skill in defending the woman that Roger Metcalf, who watched the trial with great interest, offers him a job with his law firm in the states. Grady goes to tell Carlotta the news and finds her about to commit suicide. He cheers her up, tells her that Carlotta *is* dead, and that she must start over somewhere with a new name. He gives her $1,000 and sends her to New York, where, as Anne Trevor, she becomes a successful interior decorator. She becomes engaged to Larry Gordon, a wealthy young man of social standing, but before they can be married, Dick Grady (who has been harboring a secret love for Carlotta), comes to New York to look her up. She tells him of her upcoming marriage and he decides to leave town. A few days later, Larry's mother invites Anne to a family dinner where she can be introduced properly as Larry's fiancee and meet Larry's uncle from out of town. The uncle turns out to be Roger Metcalf, and he recognizes

Anne as the woman from Panama. He steers the conversation to the Panama trial, making Anne very uncomfortable. She runs away from the table and is comforted by Dick. He promises that he will never tell, but she knows it is useless, that the past will always haunt her. She confronts the family and admits that *she* is the woman from Panama and gives Larry back his ring. A few weeks later, she reads that Larry Gordon is to be married. The same day she is given an interior decorating assignment – the Connecticut home of Larry Gordon. She grits her teeth and goes to the address given, but finds Dick Grady there. *He* has bought the house and he wants Anne to live in it with him as his wife. She accepts.

Review Summary

"Miss Bankhead is of the type who needs careful handling to attract the film public. Just a deep femme voice isn't sufficient." (*Variety*, Sept. 15, 1931)

"Why don't they give Tallulah Bankhead a worthwhile vehicle?" (*The New York Daily News*, Sept. 12, 1931)

"Offers additional evidence to the effect that Miss Bankhead is first class starring material. She has both glamor and ability." (*Film Daily*, Sept. 6, 1931)

Additional Sources

Reviews: *Life* (October 2, 1931); *The London Times* (Oct. 29, 1931); *The New York Times* (Oct. 12, 1931)
See Also: *The New York Times* (Sept. 13, 1977); *Picture Show Art Supplement* (April 9, 1932); *The Films of Fredric March*, pp 76-77.

Commentary

As in her first Paramount film, Tallulah again plays an unhappy woman, but the story is a bit more interesting, and she does have the chance to sizzle (if only briefly) in the gambling saloon in Panama, singing a few lines of a rousing song to an appreciative (mostly male) audience. The sleazy atmosphere has been admirably captured and Tallulah is obviously having a good time. Abbott directs the Panama scenes with surprising flair and the photography is consistently good. Tallulah has been well lighted and appears to good advantage not only in the early scenes, but throughout the film.

Perhaps the most striking scene has Carlotta returning to her shuttered rooms after being acquitted of her husband's murder. She pours herself a glass of some lethal potion, sits before a three-paneled mirror, raises the glass in a pathetic toast and is interrupted before she can drink. The low key lighting, Carlotta's multiple reflection and Tallulah's expert handling of the scene all combine to make this the film's most memorable moment.

Tallulah and Fredric March made a handsome team, and they were reunited eleven years later on stage in *The Skin of Our Teeth*, but political disagreements overshadowed their friendship and they refused to speak to each other. Joe Spurin Calleia, who played Juan, later altered his name to Joseph Calleia and became one of Hollywood's most dependable character actors.

F8　THE CHEAT　(*Paramount*)

Released: December 11, 1931　　　　　Running Time: 65 minutes

Credits

Director, George Abbott; Scenario, Harry Hervey, adapted from original material by Hector Turnbull; Photography, George Folsey; Editor, Emma Hill; Recording Engineer, Ernest Zatorsky

Cast

Tallulah Bankhead (Elsa Carlyle); Irving Pichel (Hardy Livingston); Harvey Stephens (Jeffrey Carlyle); Jay Fassett (Terrell); Ann Andrews (Mrs. Albright); Willard Dashiell (Judge); Arthur Hohl (Defense Attorney); Robert Strange (District Attorney); William Ingersoll (The Croupier); Hanaki Yoshiwara (Japanese Servant); Henry Warwick (Butler)

Synopsis

Hardy Livingston, a wealthy collector of oriental art objects and costumes, has a habit of branding his women with a red hot iron bearing a Chinese inscription meaning "I possess." After Elsa Carlyle, the wife of a young banker, loses $10,000 in a gambling casino ($5,000 of her husband's money, and $5,000 belonging to a charitable organization), he gives her the money. Her husband soon comes into some money of his own through a successful business deal, and when Elsa tries to repay Livingston, insisting the ten thousand dollars was a loan, he refuses to take it and tells her it was gift. She realizes his intent (to "purchase" her as his mistress) and demands that he set things right. He responds by putting the branding iron to her. Elsa shoots him (but not fatally), the husband walks in, takes the blame and is tried for the crime. Livingston, from the witness stand, tries to compromise the young wife by telling an untrue story. To defend her husband, Elsa dramatically uncovers her brand in the crowded courtroom to prove what a beast Livingston is. Carlyle is set free and Livingston is jailed.

Review Summary

"Miss Bankhead more than most actresses has a knack for fitting into these prodigal locals with plausibility. She is at least an actress of elegance and that suffices for this story indeed." (*Variety*, Dec. 15, 1931)

"Giving [the story] a ritzy setting and a very competent cast only serves to emphasize just how meller the plot intrinsically is." (*Film Daily*, Dec. 13,

1931)

"Miss Bankhead, who has been somewhat unfortunate with her previous
screen vehicles, at last appears in one that really merits attention. [She is]
also photographed to better advantage than in her other films." (*New York
Times*, December 12, 1931)

Additional Sources
Reviews: *Judge* (January 9, 1932); *Motion Picture Herald* (December 19,
1931); New York *Daily News* (December 12, 1931); *The New Yorker*
(December 19, 1931); *Rob Wagner's Script* (December 12, 1931); *Time*
(December 21, 1931)
See Also: *Film Weekly* (November 21, 1931)

Commentary
The Cheat had been filmed before (and more successfully) by Paramount in
1915. Cecil B. deMille directed, with Fannie Ward and Sessue Hayakawa
starring. It was remade (again by Paramount) in 1923 as a Pola Negri
vehicle, and a French version, titled *Forfaiture* (with Sessue Hayakawa
reprising his original role as the villain), was released in 1937.

Irving Pichel (1891-1954), a good actor within a limited range and
later a competent director, is often over-looked by film historians. His
most famous film impersonation is probably the guardian of vampire
Gloria Holden in *Dracula's Daughter* (Universal 1936), and his directing
career covered several genres and included such films as *The Pied Piper*
(1942), and *They Won't Believe Me* (1947).

F9   THUNDER BELOW   (*Paramount*)

Released: June 17, 1932   Running Time: 71 minutes

Credits
Director, Richard Wallace; Screenplay, Josephine Lovett and
Sidney Buckman, based on the novel by Thomas Rourke;
Photography, Charles Lang

Cast
Tallulah Bankhead (Susan); Charles Bickford (Walt); Paul Lukas
(Ken); Eugene Pallette (Horner); Ralph Forbes (Davis); Leslie
Fenton (Webb); James Finlayson (Scotty); Edward Van Sloan
(Doctor); Mona Rico (Pajarita); Carlos Salazar (Chato); Enrique
Acosta (Pacheo); Gabry Rivas (Delapena)

Synopsis
Walt and Ken are partners in an oil-hunting expedition in Central America.
Walt is very much in love with his wife, Susan, but she is secretly in love
with Ken. Susan and Ken confess their love for each other and decide to

tell Walt and leave together, but before they can do so, Walt confesses to *them* that he is going blind, and will need their support. And so they put their feelings aside and stand by Walt as his vision fails. Susan loves Ken all the more, and even though she tries to be a good wife to Walt, she weeps silently, not only because of her own unhappiness, but because she realizes.Ken's loyalty to Walt is stronger than his love for her. She demands that Ken choose, and he decides to stay with Walt. A few days later, a young man named Davis passes through, and is attracted to Susan. Susan doesn't love Davis, but uses him as a means to escape her unhappy life. They leave together with plans to book passage on a boat. When Walt discovers them missing, he sends Ken after them. Before Ken arrives at the seaport, Susan tells Davis that she doesn't love him and could never be happy with him. She sends him on the boat alone just as Ken arrives. Susan gives Ken one last chance to decide – "It's either Walt, or us." Ken chooses Susan this time and they make plans to go away together, but before they can leave, Walt arrives, having been led there by one of his workers. Susan stands silently in the back of the room as Walt, thinking that Susan and Davis have gone away, tells Ken that he loves her and was afraid of losing her, that life wouldn't mean anything without her. As Susan weeps silently, Ken tells Walt that Susan didn't run away with Davis, that she is already on her way back to the village. Walt asks Ken to take him home, so they leave. Susan watches them go, then writes a note addressed to Ken, asking him to tell Walt the truth, then she leaps off the balcony onto the rocks below.

Review Summary

"Miss Bankhead [possesses] little for screen appeal. The close-ups are most unkind to her general facial contour, especially around the mouth." (*Variety*, June 21, 1932)

"Can be chalked up as one of the major casualties of the season." (*Film Daily*, June 18, 1932)

"Miss Bankhead's acting is impressive. Her interpretation is convincing and restrained." (*New York Times*, June 20, 1932)

Additional Sources

Reviews: *Motion Picture Herald* (June 25, 1932); *Rob Wagner's Script* (June 18, 1932); *Time* (May 16, 1932)

Commentary

"One Woman – desired, desiring – in a village of lonely men!" And so proclaimed the ads for *Thunder Below*. It sounded promising but, unfortunately, it vies with *Tarnished Lady* as the worst of Tallulah's Paramount films. Its plot is old-fashioned, and causes her to suffer even more than usual. Her suicide at the end is actually a relief! The obligatory song is written into the script for her to sing, but even that is done poorly.

The film crawls along at a snail's pace, and even the light comedy of

Eugene Pallette fails to liven it up. A tragic waste of talent, with the only saving grace (and that only barely) being Charles Lang's photography, especially the evocative shots of Bankhead through mosquito netting.

After a distinguished stage career, Charles Bickford (1889-1967), was in his second year as film actor, and Paul Lukas (1887-1971) later won an Oscar for his fine work in *Watch on the Rhine* (1943).

F10 MAKE ME A STAR *(Paramount)*

Released: July 1, 1932   Running Time: 70 minutes

Credits

Director, William Beaudine; Screenplay, Sam Mintz, Walter DeLeon and Arthur Kobler, adapted from the novel, *Merton of the Movies*, by Harry Leon Wilson, and from the subsequent play by George S. Kaufman and Marc Connelly; Photography, Allen Siegler; Editor, Leroy Stone; Sound Recorder, Earle S. Hayman

Cast

Stuart Erwin (Merton Gill); Joan Blondell ("Flips" Montague); ZaSu Pitts (Mrs. Scudder); Ben Turpin (Ben); Charles Sellon (Mr. Gashwiler); Florence Roberts (Mrs. Gashwiler); Helen Jerome Eddy (Tessie Kearns); Arthur Hoyt (Hardy Powell); Dink Templeton (Buck Benson); Ruth Donnelly (The Countess); Sam Hardy (Jeff Baird); Oscar Apfel (Henshaw); Frank Mills (Chuck Collins); Polly Walters (Doris Randall); Victor Potel, Bobby Vernon, Snub Pollard, Billy Bletcher, Bud Jamison, Nick Thompson (Fellow Actors)

Guest Stars

Tallulah Bankhead; Clive Brook; Maurice Chevalier; Claudette Colbert; Gary Cooper; Phillips Holmes; Fredric March; Jack Oakie; Charlie Ruggles; and Sylvia Sidney.

Synopsis

Merton Gill, a grocery clerk, longs to be a film star, so he goes to Hollywood and gets inside a big studio by telling the casting director that he has a diploma from a correspondence school of acting. He is befriended by "Flips" Montague, a bit player, who gets him a job in a burlesque western as the hero. He plays his role seriously, however, and looks like a buffoon when he sees the preview. He is embarrassed and, thinking himself a failure, starts to leave town, but "Flips" stops him and assures him that he has become a great success as a comic.

Review Summary

"It's the forerunner of the latest Hollywood production cycle dealing with insights on filmland, which gives it another advantage. Picture should do very well considering the investment and times." (*Variety*, July 5, 1932)

"One of the most thoroughly and wholesomely satisfying comedy dramas of the season. Genuine studio background and shots of stars, add much value to the production." (*Film Daily*, July 2, 1932)

Additional Sources

Reviews: *Judge* (August 1932); *Motion Picture Herald* (June 18, 1932); *The Nation* (July 20, 1932); *The New York Times* (July 1, 1932); *Rob Wagner's Script* (July 19, 1932); *Time* (July 11, 1932)

See Also: *The Films of Gary Cooper*, pp 99-100; *The Films of Fredric March*, pp 87-88.

Commentary

Harry Leon Wilson's 1922 novel, *Merton of the Movies*, was a hit on Broadway in 1923, and has been made into a movie three times since: Paramount released a 1924 silent version with Glenn Hunter (who had starred in the stage production) as well as the 1932 remake; Metro-Goldwyn-Mayer purchased the rights in 1947 and made their own version, under the original title, as a vehicle for Red Skelton.

Several of Paramount's most popular stars made cameo appearances in the 1932 version as Stuart Erwin made his way about the studio. Tallulah Bankhead and Gary Cooper, in costume for *The Devil and Deep*, which they were currently shooting, were glimpsed briefly in one scene.

F11 THE DEVIL AND THE DEEP (*Paramount*)

Released: August 19, 1932   Running Time: 72 minutes

Credits

Director, Marion Gering; Screenplay, Ben Levy, from a story by Harry Hervey; Photography, Charles Lang; Sound Recorder, J. A. Goodrich; Costumes, Travis Banton; Art Direction, Bernard Herzbrun; Editor, Otho Lovering

Cast

Tallulah Bankhead (Pauline Sturm); Gary Cooper (Lieutenant Sempter); Charles Laughton (Commander Charles Sturm); Cary Grant (Lieutenant Jaeckel); Paul Porcasi (Hassan); Juliette Compton (Mrs. Planet); Henry Kolker (Hutton); Dorothy Christy (Mrs. Crimp); Arthur Hoyt (Mr. Planet); Gordon Wescott (Lieutenant Toll); Jimmie Dugan (Condover); Kent Taylor (A Friend); Lucien Littlefield (Shopkeeper); Peter Brocco (Wireless Operator); Wilfred Lucas (Court Martial Judge); Dave O'Brien, Harry Guttman, George Magrill (Submarine Crewmen)

Synopsis

Commander Charles Sturm, in charge of a submarine based in a small port on the north coast of Africa, dismisses Lieutenant Jaeckel for negligence of duty. His young and attractive wife, Pauline, however, knows the real reason is jealousy. He had assumed that Paula and the young lieutenant were having an affair, and so do their friends. She confronts him one evening and he accuses her of infidelity and flies into a rage, driving her from the house. Pauline wanders into the village, where the natives are celebrating the Moslem Feast of Beiram. Just as she is almost crushed by the crowd, a young man appears and guides her into a nearby store. To pacify the shopkeeper, the man buys a bottle of cheap perfume. They wander out into the desert and lie on the sand. Pauline spills the perfume on her dress and wipes it off with his handkerchief. The next morning, as he leaves her in town, she tells him that they must never see each other again. Sturm, already suspicious of his wife, becomes even more so when he smells the perfume on her clothing, but his spirits are lifted when Sempter, his new lieutenant, arrives. It turns out to be the same young man who had spent the night with Pauline. During the course of the conversation, Sempter drops his handkerchief, and Sturm recognizes the fragrance. Sturm later confronts Pauline, and although she admits the affair she denies that Sempter loves her. Fearing that her husband will do something drastic, Pauline goes to the submarine to warn Sempter, and when Sturm goes aboard and discovers his wife there, he gives orders for the submarine to submerge. He steers the submarine toward a freighter, and adjusts the periscope so it is not visible when Sempter takes the controls. A collision results, and the disabled submarine sinks to the bottom. Sturm blames the disaster on Sempter and relieves him of duty. He then tampers with the equipment so radioing for help is impossible. He wasn't aware that Pauline witnessed his act, and as Sturm is directing the crews' mounting anger toward Sempter, Pauline pulls a revolver, holds everyone off and tells what her husband has done. The crew revolts and one by one, swim to safety through an escape hatch, but Sturm bolts himself in a cabin, opens a hatchway, and drowns in the rushing water. Pauline and Sempter get out safely.

Review Summary

"A neatly built up theatrical story with a world of dramatic tension which loses much of its grip by the lifeless and superficial playing of the most synthetic of actresses, Tallulah Bankhead, the weak element in a good story for the first time, instead of being the strong factor in a weak [one]." (*Variety*, Aug. 23, 1932)

"They started this one as a vehicle for the specialized talents of Tallulah Bankhead in her usual role of the unhappy love-starved wife... But Charles Laughton as the insanely jealous husband... supplies one of the most unusual characterizations of the year. Miss Bankhead is about the same as in her previous productions." (*Film Daily*, August 4, 1932)

"Not withstanding the unimaginative direction of several of the sequences, the hesitant and often trite dialogue, this melodrama, owing to the excellent work of Mr. Laughton and Tallulah Bankhead, succeeds in being something out of the ordinary and a picture that always holds one's attention." (*New York Times*, August 31, 1932)

Additional Sources

Reviews: *Hollywood Reporter* (July 27, 1932); *Motion Picture Herald* (August 6, 1932); *The New Outlook* (October 1932); *The New Yorker* (August 27, 1932); *Rob Wagner's Script* (August 13, 1932); *Time* (August 29, 1932)
See Also: *The Films of Cary Grant*, pp 38-40; *The Films of Gary Cooper*, pp 101-103.

Commentary

The Devil and the Deep was the fifth and final picture Tallulah made for Paramount. (She was loaned to MGM for her sixth and final picture under her original contract.) The picture is perhaps the best of Tallulah's early talking films, but does not contain one of her better performances. She performs capably, but Pauline Sturm is yet another put-upon, unhappy character. And Charles Laughton's character is so exciting and charged that the entire cast pales beside him. It is fun to watch Sturm abusing his wife with a smile on his face. He is especially venomous in one scene as he is about to strike her. Pauline, defiant yet helpless, screams, "Well, go ahead, why don't you kill me?" Sturm stops and says calmly, "I can wait. I'm in no hurry."

The submarine scenes are particularly exciting. Lang's first rate photography and Bernard Herzbrun's claustrophobic sets create just the right atmosphere, and one scene with Laughton confronting Bankhead and Cooper rings particularly true. "I suppose women find you attractive," Laughton says to Cooper. "That must be a wonderful thing, to look as you do. I've never had that."

This was Laughton's first American film, and when interviewed the following year, he said he made it because "as soon as I read through the story I knew the film was going to be mine, and I didn't bother in the slightest about how my name was going to be billed. I knew the public would find out who I was." He even says he tried to convince Tallulah not to do the film because he didn't want it to be stolen from her (see B285). She should have taken Laughton's advice.

F12　FAITHLESS　(*Metro-Goldwyn-Mayer*)

Released: November 18, 1932　　　　　　　　Running Time: 75 minutes

Credits

Director, Harry Beaumont; Screenplay, Carey Wilson, from an original story by Mildred Cram; Photography, Oliver T. Marsh; Editor, Hugh Wynn; Recording Director, Douglas Shearer; Art Direction, Cedric Gibbons; Gowns, Adrian

Cast

Tallulah Bankhead (Carol Morgan); Robert Montgomery (Bill Wade); Hugh Herbert (Mr. Blainey); Maurice Murphy (Anthony Wade); Louise Closser Hale (Landlady); Anna Appel (Second Landlady); Lawrence Grant (Mr. Ledyard); Henry Kolker (Mr. Carter); Sterling Holloway (Photographer)

Synopsis.

Carol Morgan, a young attractive New York socialite, was left a great deal of money by her father, but she spends it recklessly, and by 1932 her financial guardian advises her to curtail her spending. She pays no attention; she's too busy giving lavish parties and romancing Bill Wade, the young man she loves. She proposes, and he accepts. She wants to spend three months in Monte Carlo on a honeymoon, but he wants to support Carol on his salary – $20,000 a year. She says it isn't enough money and breaks the engagement. A few days later, the bank tells Carol that her extravagant lifestyle has left her penniless. She goes to Bill, tells him she is broke, and begs to be taken back. Bill is broke too, having just lost his job, but he says they can make it together. She doesn't agree and leaves. Bill goes to Chicago to look for work while Carol visits friend after friend, borrowing money and becoming a social panhandler. She ends up in Chicago as a guest of Mr. and Mrs. Blainey. Mrs. Blainey finally orders Carol to leave, and as she is sneaking away in the night, Mr. Blainey stops her and gives her $1,000. She is thankful, but soon realizes that she has been "bought." Mr. Blainey puts her up in an expensive apartment, buys her clothes and jewels and makes love to her. But Carol is desperately unhappy. Bill finds out that she is in Chicago, tracks her down and comes to the apartment. But he leaves when he sees Mr. Blainey there. Carol runs after him, but Mr. Blainey stops her, knocks her down, and says she can never leave him. But she musters up enough courage to walk out and spends days looking unsuccessfully for work. She uses her last dollar to buy a bowl of soup and runs into Bill at the cafe. It is a teary reunion, and they get married that night, although Bill is also unemployed. He finally finds work with a trucking firm, but disgruntled former employees (who warned him not to take the job), run him off the road. He crashes and is badly injured. Unable to pay for a doctor, Carol resorts to prostitution as a means of making money. One night she tries to pick up a man who happens to be Bill's brother. She recognizes him and runs, but is stopped by a policeman who is touched by her story and finds her a job at a local diner. Bill recovers quickly and one afternoon his brother drops by and tells him about seeing Carol on the street. Carol comes in, and, seeing the look on her husband's face, starts packing to leave. Bill tells his brother that if it hadn't been for Carol he would have died. He forgives her for what she did, asks her to stay, and announces that he has found a new job.

Review Summary

"[Miss Bankhead] struggled valiantly with the role, but it was too much for her, even with a new hair comb that makes her look very much like Garbo

from certain angles. Garbo herself couldn't do much with this number."
(*Variety*, Nov. 22, 1932)

"Has the distinction of capable portrayals by Tallulah Bankhead and Robert
Montgomery. Yet, as well as they do here... it is obvious that both would
be better suited to a smart comedy." (*New York Times*, November 19,
1932)

"A pretty bad story again handicaps Tallulah Bankhead." (*Film Daily*,
November 19, 1932)

Additional Sources

Reviews: *Hollywood Reporter* (Oct. 5, 1932); *Motion Picture Herald* (Oct.
15, 1932); *Time* (Oct. 31, 1932)
See Also: *We're in the Money*, pp 51-53.

Commentary

Despite the MGM gloss, the excellent production qualities, and a softening
of Tallulah's look, nicely accomplished by adding some attractive bangs,
Faithless failed to endear the actress to film audiences. The flaw is not in
the film, which is a fine pice of work, but in the casting. Tallulah again had
to suffer, and unlike Helen Twelvetrees and Sylvia Sidney (who could play
ill treated women beautifully, touchingly), she never seemed believable in
such roles. She needed to play strong women, funny women, naughty
women, not poor downtrodden souls!

Carol Morgan had to endure more hard luck than perhaps any of
Tallulah's screen heroines, and it is little wonder that she called it quits
after this film and headed back to the stage. There were a few moments
early in the film where Tallulah could be more herself. When told by her
financial guardian that her expensive lifestyle has meant that the usual
charity contribution to a home for delinquent girls won't be possible, she
laughs and says, "Good. I don't believe in delinquent girls. Silly
weaklings!" But as soon as she loses her money, the suffering begins, and
we never see the funny side of her character again.

F13   STAGE DOOR CANTEEN   (*United Artists*)

Released: June 24, 1943   Running Time: 132 minutes

Credits

Director, Frank Borzage; Producer, Sol Lesser, in association with
the American Theatre Wing; Associate Producer, Barney Briskin;
Screenplay, Delmer Daves; Photography, Harry Wild; Production
Design, Harry Horner; Art Direction, Hans Peters; Talent
Coordinator, Radie Harris; Make-up, Irving Berns; Sound
Technician, Hugh McDowell; Interiors, Victor Gangelin;
Wardrobe, Albert Deano; Assistant Directors, Lew Borzage, Virgil

Hart; Editor, Hal Kern; Music Score, Freddie Rich; Musical
Director, C. Bakaleinikoff; Songs, Al Dubin/Jimmy Monaco;
Richard Rodgers & Lorenz Hart; Joe Moody; Harry Miller/Bob
Reed; Al Hoffman/Mann Curtis/Cy Corbin/Jerry Livingston; Albert
Hay Mallotte; Castro Valencia/Joe Pafumy;

Cast

Cheryl Walker (Eileen); William Terry (Dakota Smith); Marjorie
Riordan (Jean); Lon McCallister (California); Margaret Early (Ella
Sue); Michael Harrison (Texas); Dorothea Kent (Mamie); Fred
Brady (Jersey); Marion Shockley (Lillian); Patrick O'Moore (The
Australian)

Guest Stars

Judith Anderson; Henry Armetta; Kenny Baker; Tallulah Bankhead; Ralph
Bellamy; Edgar Bergen and Charlie McCarthy; Ray Bolger; Helen
Broderick; Ina Claire; Katharine Cornell; Lloyd Corrigan; Jane Cowl; Jane
Darwell; William Demarest; Virginia Field; Gracie Fields; Lynn Fontanne;
Vinton Freedley; Ann Gillis; Lucille Gleason; Vera Gordon; Virginia
Grey; Helen Hayes; Katharine Hepburn; Hugh Herbert; Jean Hersholt; Sam
Jaffe; Allen Jenkins; George Jessel; Roscoe Karns; Tom Kennedy; Otto
Kruger; June Lang; Betty Lawford; Gypsy Rose Lee; Alfred Lunt; Bert
Lytell; Aline MacMahon; Horace MacMahon; Elsa Maxwell; Harpo Marx;
Helen Menken; Yehudi Menubin; Ethel Merman; Peggy Moran; Ralph
Morgan; Alan Mowbray; Paul Muni; Elliot Nugent; Patrick O'Moore;
Merle Oberon; Franklin Pangborn; Helen Parrish; Brock Pemberton;
George Raft; Lanny Ross; Selena Royle; Martha Scott; Marion Shockley;
Cornelia Otis Skinner; Ned Sparks; Bill Stern; Ethel Waters; Johnny
Weismuller; Arleen Whelan; Dame May Whitty; and Ed Wynn

Bands

Count Basie; Xavier Cugat; Benny Goodman; Kay Kyser; Guy Lombardo;
and Freddie Martin.

Synopsis

Eileen, a junior hostess at New York's Stage Door Canteen, meets Private
Dakota Smith. Because Eileen is hoping to meet Broadway producers, she
and Dakota don't hit if off. Her roommates don't approve of her behavior
and the next evening, when he comes to the Canteen she receives him
warmly. They soon fall in love and agree to be married, making a date to
meet at the Canteen at 5 p.m. However, it is the Canteen's rule that
hostesses can not date the servicemen off the premises, and since Eileen has
broken that rule, her pass is taken away. While she is waiting outside, an
Australian soldier brings her word that Dakota sailed that morning
unexpectedly. Katharine Hepburn, Officer of the Day, consoles the girl and
persuades her to continue her morale-boosting work at the Canteen until
the young man can return.

Review Summary

"Film constitutes a terrific institutional ballyhoo for all of show business and what we are doing in this war effort. [The film] is a shining recording of what all forces in stage, screen and radio have been doing for the lonesome servicemen of all the United Nations." (*Variety*, May 12, 1943)

"When Katharine Hepburn and Tallulah Bankhead are cutting their respective capers, Alfred Lunt and Lynn Fontanne are having a domestic-professional tiff, or Gypsy Rose Lee is strip-teasing in reverse, there is no lack of entertainment." (*New York Herald Tribune*, June 25, 1943)

Additional Sources

Reviews: *The Brooklyn Citizen* (June 25, 1943); *The New York Daily Mirror* (June 25, 1943); *The New York Daily News* (June 25, 1943); *The New York Journal American* (June 25, 1943); *New York PM* (June 25, 1943); *The New York Post* (June 25, 1943); *The New York Sun* (June 25, 1943); *The New York Times* (June 25, 1943); *The New Yorker Staats-Zeitung* (June 25, 1943); *The New York World Telegram* (June 25, 1943)

See Also: *The Family Circle* (April 16, 1943); *Movie Maker* (May 1983); *The New York Daily Mirror* (May 23, 1943); *The New York Times* (January 31, July 4, September 3, 1943); *This Week* (April 25, 1923); *Variety* (February 10, 1943)

Commentary

The almost non-existent plot of *Stage Door Canteen* was merely a slight hook on which to hang a galaxy of guest stars, the *real* stars of the *real* Stage Door Canteen (which was located just off Broadway on West 44th Street) where scores of theatre personalities donated their time to help entertain young men serving their country in World War II. In the film the stars were shown washing dishes, serving food, dancing with the soldiers and boosting morale. Others performed songs and memorable moments from memorable plays. Katharine Cornell, for instance, made her film debut here reciting a scene from *Romeo and Juliet*.

The Stage Door Canteen (and the Hollywood Canteen in California, which was the star of its own film) was an important part of the war effort, and the film is a lasting record of the unselfish service by the greats of the theatre. Tallulah has one brief scene in which she shares a private joke with a group of soldiers, her raucous laugh audible before she is seen, and then chats for a moment with a soldier and his date.

Eighty percent of the film's profits went to the canteens operated by the American Theatre Wing in New York City, Washington, D.C., Philadelphia, Cleveland, Hollywood, San Francisco, Boston and Newark, New Jersey. Michael Harrison, who played one of the enlisted men, changed his professional name to Sunset Carson and enjoyed a successful career in western films.

Katharine Hepburn, who had a fairly substantial role in the film, was a "lifelong friend of Tallulah's" according to Brendan Gill, while Anne Edwards, in her biography of Hepburn (see B050), insists that she had little respect for Bankhead. In a 1990 letter to the author, Katharine Hepburn set the record straight. "I know practically nothing about Tallulah. She always assumed that we were much greater friends than we actually were. I thought she was a damned good actress when she cared to be. And a very entertaining personality. But I honestly don't know any more than this."

F14   LIFEBOAT   (20th Century-Fox)

Released: January 11, 1944   Running Time: 96 minutes

Credits

Director, Alfred Hitchcock; Producer, Kenneth Macgowan; Screenplay, Jo Swerling, based on a story by John Steinbeck; Photography, Glen MacWilliams; Editor, Dorothy Spenser; Special Effects, Fred Sersen; Sets, James Basevi, Maurice Ransford; Music, Hugo Friedhofer; Musical Director, Emil Newman; Costumes, Rene Hubert; Sound Engineers, Bernard Fredericks, Roger Heman.

Cast

Tallulah Bankhead (Constance Porter); William Bendix (Gus); Walter Slezak (The German); Mary Anderson (Alice Mackenzie); John Hodiak (Kovac); Henry Hull (Ritterhouse); Heather Angel (Mrs. Higgins); Hume Cronyn (Stanley Garrett); Canada Lee (Joe).

Synopsis.

During World War II, in the mid-Atlantic fog, the smokestack of a torpedoed passenger ship gives a final moan as it sinks below the surface. From a lifeboat, Constance Porter, a well-known journalist and a survivor of the disaster, catches the event on her newsreel camera. One by one, other survivors climb into the boat: Gus, a dance-mad sailor whose leg has been badly injured; Kovak, a left-wing member of the crew; Ritterhouse, a millionaire; Joe, the Black steward; Mrs. Higgins, a young wife who still clings to her lifeless baby; Stanley Garrett, the ship's radio operator; and Alice Mackenzie, a young army nurse. They are soon joined by Willy, a burly man who speaks only German and, as interpreted by Miss Porter, says he is the only surviving crewmember of the U-Boat which had torpedoed their vessel. (Before sinking, the ship had fired at the submarine, and hit it.) As the German watches, the survivors argue as to what to do, who will be in charge, and what direction in which to sail. Gus's leg worsens and nurse Mackenzie decides amputation is the only solution. The German, who says he was a surgeon in civilian life, performs the operation, saving Gus's life. But all of their lives are soon in danger, as days pass and their food and water run out. During a sudden storm as the boat seems sure to capsize, the sullen German suddenly springs to life and starts giving orders in English. He saves the boat, and the weary survivors make him captain. (He had also been captain of the U-Boat.). They instruct him to plot a course for Bermuda, but he secretly uses a compass to guide the boat toward a rendezvous with a German supply ship. While the others suffer from hunger and thirst, Willy is strong and alert. Gus awakes in the night and sees Willy drinking water from a flask which he had concealed from the others. He tries to awaken the other survivors, but Willy pushes him overboard. The next morning, they piece together what has happened, find his water, his compass and discover that he has been eating energy pills. In a rage, they attack him and throw him into the sea, but they are no more organized than before. "When we killed the German, we killed our motor," Connie observes. Their fate seems hopeless when the German supply ship is spotted in the distance, but an Allied ship also appears, fires on the enemy and sinks the German vessel. The tired and hungry group is rescued (but not before another young German is helped aboard and holds them at gunpoint before being overpowered), and the two romances which have flowered on board (Stanley and Alice; Connie and Kovak) appear to have happy endings.

Review Summary

"Tallulah Bankhead... is not photogenically acceptable in the brief, fiercely romantic interludes with Hodiak. The camera treats her unkindly throughout, except in one or two instances." (*Variety*, January 12, 1944)

"Tallulah Bankhead comes into her own on the screen in this picture. As the well groomed commentator on world disasters who finds herself in a microcosm of catastrophe, she is supremely assured and appealing." (*New York Post*, January 13, 1944)

Additional Sources

Reviews: *Commonweal* (Jan. 28, 1944); *Film Daily* (Jan. 12, 1944); *Hollywood Reporter* (Jan. 12, 1944); *Life* (Jan. 31, 1944); *The London Times* (March 16, 1944); *Motion Picture Exhibitor* (Jan. 26, 1944); *The Nation* (Jan. 22, 1944); *The New Republic* (Feb. 14, 1944); *The New York Times* (Jan. 13, 1944); *The New Yorker* (Jan. 15, 1944); *Newsweek* (Jan. 17, 1944); *Rob Wagner's Script* (Jan. 22, 1944); *Time* (Jan. 31, 1944)
See Also: *Agee on Film, Volume 1*, pp 71-72; *Alfred Hitchcock, the First Forty Films*, pp 74-78+; *The Art of Alfred Hitchcock*, pp 145-50; *Film Comment* (January/February 1976); *Films and the Second World War*, pp 200-202; *The Films of Alfred Hitchcock*, pp 118-20; *The Films of World War II*, pp 168-70; *Framework* (Winter, 1977); *Hitchcock* (Trauffaut), pp 155-59; *Literature/Film Quarterly* (Fall, 1976); *Magills Survey of Cinema, Series I*, pp 974-77; *Selected Film Criticism 1941-1950*, pp 119-20.

Commentary

In the years since *Lifeboat* was released, it has developed a reputation as one of Hitchcock's better films, but it was highly controversial in its day. In the middle of World War II, with the United States at war with Germany, reviewers were angered to see a German submarine captain made to appear smarter than Americans. Many were outraged. One critic gave the film "three days to get out of town," and Lee Mortimer, writing for the *New York Daily Mirror*, said the picture, "if captured by the Germans, [could] be shown throughout Europe, without cuts or editing, as propaganda against the American way of life." Hitchcock defended the film adamantly and considered the work a preachment against the Axis. Yes, the German appeared to be the strong one, but his strength was due to thoroughly reprehensible methods, and he was defeated when the others finally acted as a whole. It was Hitchcock's belief that the Axis could only be defeated when the Allied Nations fought together, side by side, with no disagreements.

The film was shot on a specially constructed set with the boat secured in a large studio tank. The actors had to climb in and out of the craft and it became obvious to the cast and crew that Tallulah wore no underwear. A visiting female reporter was shocked by Miss Bankhead's immodesty and asked that something be done. Studio boss Darryl F. Zanuck sent a representative to ask Hitchcock to speak to the actress. He refused, claiming it wasn't his department. "Well, whose department is it?" the man wanted to know. "Make-up," the director answered, "or maybe hairdressing."

Hitchcock was fond of Tallulah but knew better than to cross her. He had first seen Tallulah in 1923 London production of *The Dancers* and had personally selected her to head the cast of *Lifeboat*. "It was the most oblique, incongruous bit of casting I could think of," he later remarked. "Isn't a lifeboat in the middle of the Atlantic the last place one would expect Tallulah? For the sake of realism and suspense, I am partial to people whose faces are not too familiar to the movie audience" (see B066). His instincts were correct; the offbeat casting worked, and for her performance as Constance Porter, Tallulah was named Best Actress of 1944 by the New York Film Critics. She did not receive an Oscar nomination, however, and in her autobiography, she attributes that to the fact that she wasn't under contract to any of the major studios. "I was thought an outlaw."

Hitchcock, who liked to make brief cameo appearances in his films, had a difficult time figuring out how to get into *Lifeboat*. He finally found a solution which resulted in his most ingenious and certainly most famous appearance: the model for a newspaper weight-reduction ad.

The film was nominated for three Academy Awards: Best Director (Hitchcock); Best Original Story (John Steinbeck); and Best Black and White Cinematography (Glen MacWilliams).

F15   A ROYAL SCANDAL   (20th Century-Fox)

Released: March 16, 1945   Running Time: 94 minutes

Credits

Director, Otto Preminger; Producer, Ernst Lubitsch; Screenplay, Edwin Justus Mayer; Adaption, Bruno Frank, from the play by Lajos Biro and Melchior Langyel; Photography, Arthur Miller;

Editor, Dorothy Spenser; Music, Alfred Newman; Musical Direction, Edward Powell; Art Direction, Lyle R. Wheeler, Mark Lee Kirk; Set Direction, Thomas Little, Paul S. Fox; Costumes, Rene Hubert; Special Effects, Fred Sersen

Cast

Tallulah Bankhead (The Czarina); Charles Coburn (Chancellor); Anne Baxter (Anna); William Eythe (Alexei); Vincent Price (Marquis de Fleury, the French Ambassador); Mischa Auer (Captain Sukov); Sig Ruman (General Ronsky); Vladimir Sokoloff (Malakoff); Mikhail Rasumny (Drunken General); Grady Sutton (Boris); Don Douglas (Variatinsky); Egon Brecher (Wassilikow); Eva Gabor (Countess Demidow); John Russell (Guard); Arno Frey (Captain); Harry Carter (Footman)

Synopsis

The Ambassador of France arrives at the palace of Catherine the Great to sign an alliance between his country and Russia. Before he can be presented, a young cavalry officer named Alexei breaks into Catherine's room to warn her of traitors in her army, particularly two generals. Catherine is amused and puts Alexei up at the palace, much to the concern of the Chancellor. Although disappointed to learn that Alexei is in love with someone else, Catherine flirts with him, and elevates him to the rank of major, then colonel and makes him the captain of the palace guards. Alexei's fiancee, Anna, who is Catherine's lady in waiting, warns him that he has become the Czarina's latest plaything, but he defends his empress. Catherine learns who Alexei's fiancée is and has Anna banished from the palace. Meanwhile the generals attempt to win Alexei's confidence, but he continues to defend his empress. However, when he discovers that she has thrown away the 52 edicts he wrote (one to improve the life of the peasants), he realizes the truth and joins the generals in their traitorous plans. The Chancellor also joins in the scheme by saying he always wants to be on the winning side. Alexei dismisses the palace guards and tells Catherine that the army will storm the palace at dawn, kill her and claim the throne. She begs for mercy, but he has none. At dawn it is not the army which arrives but the palace guards, led by the Chancellor. Alexei is arrested and sentenced to die. As Catherine is about to sign the death warrant, the French Ambassador is finally presented and Catherine finds a new plaything. She tears up the warrant and Alexei is set free to marry Anna.

Review Summary

"Miss Bankhead, as Catherine, is excellent. First the storming, irate ruler, then the ardent femme seeking new romantic adventures... she is convincing throughout." (*Variety*, March 21, 1945)

"Tallulah is witty, earthy, charming and just right for this burlesque of the Mother of all the Russians... She could put drama and humor into the reading of the telephone directory." (*The Philadelphia Inquirer*, June 15, 1945)

"Miss Bankhead makes valiant efforts to fan the comic spirit... but inevitably, the script stands before her, upright and impermeable." (*New York Times*, March 12, 1945)

Additional Sources

Reviews: *Commonweal* (April 13, 1945); *Film Daily*, March 26, 1945; *Nation* (April 7, 1945); *New York Herald Tribune* (March 12, 1945); *New Yorker* (April 21, 1945); *Newsweek* (April 16, 1945); *Time* (April 9, 1945)

Commentary

Catherine the Great (1729-1796), who lived to be 67 years old, has been portrayed on screen by several actresses, among them Pola Negri (*Forbidden Paradise*, 1924), Louise Dresser (*The Eagle*, 1925), Marlene Dietrich (*The Scarlet Empress*, 1934), Elizabeth Bergner (*Catherine the Great*, 1934), Binnie Barnes (*Shadow of the Eagle*, 1950), Viveca Lindfors (*Tempest*, 1958), Bette Davis (*John Paul Jones*, 1959), and Jeanne Moreau (*Great Catherine*, 1968). Mae West also impersonated the Czarina in the 1944 Broadway hit *Catherine was Great*. Ernst Lubitsch directed a 1924 version of *A Royal Scandal*, which starred Pola Negri and was titled *Forbidden Paradise*. He was set to direct the 1945 remake with Bankhead, but illness forced him to turn the project over to Otto Preminger.

At forty-two, Bankhead was still glamorous-looking, and she obviously enjoyed playing the nymphomaniac Czarina. Her lines were sharp and funny, and she was supported by an exceptional cast. But a few funny lines isn't enough; the film seems strangely cold and stilted at times. It cries out for the Lubitsch touch. Drama was Preminger's forté (he had just had an enormous hit with *Laura*) and his occasionally heavy direction contrasts badly with the light material. Nevertheless, *A Royal Scandal* looks magnificent. The opulent sets and ornate costumes are pleasing to the eye, and Tallulah, in a role that might have saved her career ten years before, gives bite to her every line. She later claimed that Lubitsch told her she had given the greatest comedy performance he had ever seen on the screen. It's worth noting that when Tallulah made the remark, Lubitsch was no longer alive to contest or confirm the alleged statement.

F16 MAIN STREET TO BROADWAY (*Metro-Goldwyn-Mayer*)

Released: July 22, 1953   Running Time: 102 minutes

Credits

Director, Tay Garnett; Producer, Lester Cowan, in association with the Council of the Living Theatre; Screenplay, Samson Raphaelson, based on a story by Robert E. Sherwood; Photography, James

Wong Howe; Editor, Gene Fowler, Jr.; Production Manager, Norman Cook; Art Direction, Perry Ferguson; Song, *There's Music in You*, Rodgers & Hammerstein; Score and Music Direction, Ann Ronell; Orchestral Arrangement and Conductor, Leon Arnaud; Assistant Director, James Anderson; Make-up, Lee Greenway; Editorial Assistant, Robert Lawrence; Set Decorations, Edward Boyle; Recording Engineer, Buddy Myers; Wardrobe, Margaret Greenway; Hair Stylist, Hollis Banners; Sound, John Kean; Special Effects, Jack Cosgrove; Titles and Optical Effects, Jack Rabin

Cast

Tom Morton (Anthony Monaco); Mary Murphy (Mary Craig); Agnes Moorehead (Mildred Waterbury); Herb Shriner (Frank Johnson); Rosemary De Camp (Mrs. Craig); Clinton Sundberg (Mr. Craig); Gertrude Berg (Neighbor); Jack Gilford (Ticket Seller)

As Themselves

Tallulah Bankhead; Ethel Barrymore; Lionel Barrymore; Florence Bates; Shirley Booth; Robert Bray; Louis Calhern; Leo Durocher; Faye Emerson; Frank Ferguson; Oscar Hammerstein II; Rex Harrison; Helen Hayes; Madge Kennedy; Joshua Logan; Mary Martin; Lilli Palmer; Carl Benton Reid; Richard Rodgers; Arthur Shields; John van Druten; Cornel Wilde.

Synopsis

Anthony Monaco, a young playwright, has come to New York hoping to have a play produced. He meets Mary Craig, a drama student from Indiana, who doesn't like the play he's written. He romances her, but not too successfully, and she announces her intentions to return home to South Terre Haute Junction. His agent, Mildred Waterbury, encourages him to write an upbeat play. While he is still there, Tallulah Bankhead barges in and threatens to fire the agent unless she can find her a play about a nice woman, a good woman. Miss Waterbury introduces Tony to Miss Bankhead and explains that he is going to write a play about wholesome American motherhood. Tallulah is interested, and so the young playwright goes to South Terre Haute Junction to soak up the small-town atmosphere for his play and try again to romance the girl. He succeeds in winning the girl, but his ideas for a play don't seem to work, and he leaves the girl behind and returns to New York. He rewrites the play to make the woman a murderess, and while he is busy working, Mary is being courted by a hardware salesman back in Indiana. Tony sends his new play to his agent but she rejects it, and so does Tallulah. Despondent, he wraps up his play, takes it to the Brooklyn Bridge, and throws it into the East River. The police spot him, consider his actions suspicious and arrest him. His story is picked up by a radio commentator and is broadcast throughout the nation. Mary hears the news and leaves for New York. Also listening in are Lionel Barrymore, his sister, Ethel, and Louis Calhern, who feel sorry for the young man. They decide to help him, bail him out of jail and encourage him to rewrite the play. He doesn't have to because one copy was not destroyed. John van Druten takes the play, convinces Tallulah to star, and it opens on Broadway. It flops, but Tony decides to keep trying, and he and Mary make plans to marry.

Review Summary

"A dreadful boner, and should be withdrawn as soon as possible." (*The Baltimore Sun*, August 22, 1953)

"Tallulah Bankhead appears more frequently...than any of her compatriots and gives a foolish and strident performance." (*Saturday Review*, July 18, 1953)

"Tay Garnett's direction is dull. Several actor's performances are awful. The whole picture has a faintly vulgar air." (*New York Times*, October 14, 1953)

Additional Sources

Reviews: *New York Herald Tribune* (October 14, 1953);*Oregon Journal* (July 28, 1953); *Variety* (Aug. 12, 1953)
See Also: *Christian Science Monitor* (August 12, 1953); *The New York Times* (March 30, 1951, February 10, March 22, August 29, October 20. Nov. 15, Nov. 30, 1952); *The New York Herald Tribune* (Jan. 25, Dec. 2, 1951, March 13, Dec. 5, 1952); *Variety* (Nov. 21, 1951, Feb. 18, 1953)

Commentary

Main Street to Broadway is not a great film, but it is better than the reviews would have it. The primary flaw is an unlikable central figure. Anthony Monaco is unpleasant, disagreeable and often rude. What makes the film entertaining is the steady flow of guest appearances by theatre notables: Shirley Booth signing autographs; Rodgers and Hammerstein composing a song for Mary Martin; Cornel Wilde rehearsing a role; Ethel Barrymore visiting the Empire Theatre before its demolition, etc. Rex Harrison and his wife, Lilli Palmer, even stroll through one scene, arguing about a triple-decker sandwich. The Theatre is the real star of the film, and the flimsy plot soon becomes secondary.

Tallulah has an extended cameo as herself and she all but steals the film from everyone else. She makes her entrance early, bursting into the office of her agent, Mildred Waterbury (Agnes Moorehead, below her usually high standards of character acting), and threatens to fire her. "Every play you send me is about a fiend!" Miss Bankhead complains, then bellows in her inimitable basso voice, "Aren't they writing plays about NICE PEOPLE like me anymore!?" The playwright saves the day by promising to write Tallulah a play about a gentle, pleasant mid-western housewife. Her best scenes follow as, in the playwright's imagination, she acts out a particular scene as Tony writes and re-writes it. She trips lightly into a sunny room, chatting amiably with her husband (Clinton Sundberg, who doubles as Mary Craig's father), then stops suddenly in mid-sentence as the line is changed. And when she tries to put flowers in a vase, she must wait until it is written into the script. These scenes are clever and funny and are the film's highlight. The only drawback is their brevity.

Main Street to Broadway does have its flaws, but it is an often interesting look at theatre life and it's refreshing to see a film which does not follow the predictable young-man-from-nowhere-writes-hit-play-and-is-overnight-success formula.

F17   THE BOY WHO OWNED A MELEPHANT   (*Universal*)

Released: October 6, 1959   Length: 2 reels

Credits
Producer, Gayle-Swimmer-Anthony; Screenplay, Saul Swimmer, Tony Anthony, adapted from a story by Marvin Wald

Commentary
Tallulah narrated this children's film which starred her godson, Brockman Seawell, the son of Eugenia Rawls. The film premiered at the Palace Theatre in New York, and went on to win the 1959 Gold Leaf Award at the Venice International Children's Film Festival. Detailed information about this film is hard to come by since it was apparently neither reviewed nor copyrighted.

F18   DIE! DIE! MY DARLING!   (*Hammer Films/Columbia*)

Released: May 19, 1965   Running Time: 96 minutes (color)

Credits
Director, Silvio Narizzano; Producer, Anthony Hinds; Screenplay, Richard Matheson, based on the novel, *Nightmare,* by Anne Blaisdell; Photography, Arthur Ibbetson, utilizing Eastman Color; Camera Operator, Paul Wilson; Editor, James Needs, John Dunsford; Music, Wilfred Josephs; Music Director, Philip Martel; Sound Editor, Roy Hyde; Sound Recordist, Ken Rawkins; Production Designer, Peter Proud; Make-up, Roy Ashton, Richard Mills; Hair Stylist, Olga Angelinetta; Wardrobe, Mary Gibson

Cast
Tallulah Bankhead (Mrs. Trefoile); Stefanie Powers (Patricia Carroll); Peter Vaughan (Harry): Yootha Joyce (Anna); Donald Sutherland (Joseph); Maurice Kaufman (Alan Glentower); Gwendolyn Watts (Gloria); Robert Dorning (Ornsby); Philip Gilbert (Oscar); Winifred Dennis (Shopkeeper); Diane King (Woman shopper)

Synopsis

Patricia Carroll, a young, attractive American woman, has come to England with her fiance, Alan Glentower, and decides to pay a courtesy visit to Mrs.Trefoile, whose son, now dead, she had been engaged to. Mrs. Trefoile's country home – bleak and unkept, staffed by a sullen housekeeper, Anna, and Harry, her lecherous husband, as well as an imbecile gardener, Joseph – looks unpromising. But the older woman greets Patricia warmly and she decides to spend the night. Mrs. Trefoile is a religious fanatic and demands that Patricia wipe off her lipstick and change out of a red sweater. "Red is the Devil's color!" Patricia endures these eccentricities with good nature, but when she learns that Mrs. Trefoile considers her to be her dead son's wife for eternity, she insults the woman and attempts to leave. Instead, she is locked in her room and held prisoner. Her threats to call the police do no good, and when she attempts to overpower her captor, Mrs. Trefoile holds her at gunpoint and instructs the housekeeper to take her to the attic. Patricia is accidentally stabbed with scissors as she fights with Anna and when she later tries to escape by lowering herself from a window, she is caught by Harry and brought back to the house. Mrs. Trefoile forces her to write a note to Alan explaining that her visit has been extended. Desperate to escape, she flirts with Harry in an attempt to get the car keys, but Mrs. Trefoile interrupts. When Harry threatens to leave and tell the police, the woman shoots him and hides his body in the cellar, telling his wife that he has gone to London for a few days. Patricia makes another attempt to escape and Mrs. Trefoile strikes her violently and forces her into the cellar. Meanwhile Alan is suspicious of Pat's note and comes to Mrs. Trefoile's house looking for her. While Patricia is bound and gagged, Mrs. Trefoile tells Alan that Patricia left a couple days before. On his way out of town, he stops into a pub and recognizes a brooch the waitress is wearing. He had given it to Patricia as a gift. (Harry had stolen it from Patricia and given it to the woman.) Alan races back to Mrs. Trefoile's and finds the woman in the cellar about to sacrifice Patricia in front of Stephen's portrait. He pushes Mrs. Trefoile away, frees Patricia and takes her away in the car. As Alan and Patricia drive away, Anna discovers her husband's body, picks up a knife and kills her employer.

Review Summary

"Expert thesping by Tallulah Bankhead could cause the Columbia release to take off with general audiences the way other horror pix with veteran actresses have done." (*Variety*, April 28, 1965)

"Although [Tallulah Bankhead] towers above the cast and story, her present effort adds little to her record." (*The New York Times*, May 20, 1965)

"Neither the director nor his scenarist has the trick of piling exaggerations into mirthful absurdity. You simply have an elderly Tallulah bumbling foolishly." (*The New York World Telegram*, May 20, 1965)

Additional Sources

Reviews: *BFI/Monthly Film Bulletin* (April 1965); *Film Daily* (April 29, 1965); *Filmfacts* (July 9, 1965); *Films and Filming* (May 1965); *Hollywood Reporter* (April 27, 1965); *Life* (April 9, 1965); *Motion Picture Herald Product Digest* (March 31, 1965); *The New York Daily News* (May 20, 1965); *The New York Herald-Tribune* (May 20, 1965); *The New York Post* (May 20, 1965); *Newsweek* (April 5, 1965); *Saturday Review* (June 12, 1965); *Time* (April 2, 1965)

Commentary

Whatever Happened to Baby Jane (1962), was the beginning of a short-lived but productive sub-genre of motion pictures – the aging actress horror film. Bette Davis, Joan Crawford, Elizabeth Bergner, Barbara Stanwyck, Shelley Winters and even Debbie Reynolds and Lana Turner all had their turn at battling and/or creating evil, and it was only natural that Tallulah would join the ranks; she was the right age, her voice was a deep growl and her throaty laugh could be menacing as well as mirthful. She took on the challenge, and for her role as crone-like Mrs. Trefoile, she wore no flattering make-up (in fact wrinkles were *enhanced*), and her hair was rigidly knotted. If not for her inimitable voice, she would have been unrecognizable.

The film was shot in England during the summer of 1964 at the Associated British Studios, southwest of London, near Elstree. Tallulah was eager to see London again, but her first day there was disastrous. As she was entering the Ritz Hotel (where she had first stayed in 1923), she tripped and fell while posing for photographs. The embarrassing picture appeared in all the London papers and even found its way into the next issue of *Life* Magazine (see B297). She was humiliated, grew depressed and became ill with laryngitis. Studio heads considered replacing her, but she insisted on going through with the picture.

In a 1990 interview with the author, Tallulah's co-star, Stefanie Powers, remembered the first day on the set:

"We were all gathered around the rehearsal table – the producers, the director, Yootha Joyce, Donald Sutherland, Peter Vaughan, all of us – and Tallulah was the last to arrive. She came in wearing slacks and an ankle-length mink coat, with two young men at her side who helped her down the stairs. 'Oh, dahlings, I'm so sorry to hold you up,' she said, 'but I feel *awful*.' On the first day of shooting, everything was done to make her feel at ease. We didn't start shooting until late in the morning, allowing her plenty of time to get there, and we broke for lunch. She had only one scene to do, and then she left. It was the same on the second day. And on the third we went to the studio to see the rushes. She sat with us and watched. There were lots of scenes with the rest of the cast, and then there would be *one* of her, in long shot. That made her angry. Suddenly her laryngitis went away and the next day she was there early, her frailness had disappeared, and she worked."

Powers said one scene required Tallulah to drag her through a doorway. "A stunt man had already been assigned to do the scene for

Tallulah," she said. "He was to dress in Mrs. Trefoile's clothes and do the actual dragging, and it would be intercut with scenes of Tallulah's hands grabbing me under the arms. But Tallulah didn't like the way the stunt man's legs looked in stockings, so she did it herself. She grabbed me under the arms, being sure to feel of my chest first, and with Herculean strength, dragged me through the doorway. And this was the same woman who had needed help down the stairs a few days before!"

The press at the time reported that Tallulah didn't get along with her young co-star, and that Tallulah had made a slap painfully realistic. Powers refutes the story in part:

"During the scene, she did hit me," Powers said, "but there was no malice behind it. The press made a big deal out of it and tried to invent a feud between us, but there wasn't one, really. I enjoyed working with her. But she did think of me as competition, and we were only as friendly as the situation would allow." Powers said that she had tremendous respect for Bankhead. "She was enormously talented. I haven't seen anyone before or since with her ability to cry. I remember one particular scene in which she was seated on a settee, and I was in a chair opposite her. The scene began with her being friendly and telling me how nice it was to see me, and then became more dramatic as she started crying and talking about her dead son. It was her scene, and she did it beautifully. When she started crying, it looked so real. Her eyes became red and swollen, and her nose turned red... I was moved, and when the scene was finished, the director said, 'Miss Bankhead, can you go through that again?' and she said yes. She stood up and composed herself in an instant. It was like some miracle. Her eyes were no longer red and swollen, her nose was no longer red... I was astonished. She sat down and we went through the entire scene again. I asked her about it later and she said she used to practice crying as a child. It was an art with her, not merely a trick."

Die! Die! My Darling! was Tallulah's first and only color film in which she performed (*The Daydreamer* was color, but only her voice was heard.) The film was known as *Fanatic* in England; *Die! Die! My Darling!* was the American title. Tallulah prefered the English title.

The film did rather poorly and Tallulah accepted no other film offers, perhaps because she was aghast to see how bad she looked. At a private screening in New York, the first time she saw the completed film, she is said to have stood up and apologized to the audience "for looking older than God's wet nurse."

F19 THE DAYDREAMER   (*Embassy Pictures/Videocraft Int.*)

Released: July 1, 1966   Running Time: 101 minutes (color)

Credits

Director, Jules Bass; Producer/Screenplay, Arthur Rankin, Jr.,
from the stories of Hans Christian Andersen; Associate Producer,
Larry Roemer; Live-Action Photography, Daniel Cavelli, in

Eastman Color; Animagic Camera, Tad Mochinaga; Music, Maury Laws; Assistant Director, Kizo Nagashima; Staging of Animagic Sequences, Don Duga; Staging of Live-Action Sequences, Ezra Stone; Song, *The Daydreamer*, sung by Robert Goulet; Title Song Orchestration, Don Costa; Sound Technicians, Alan Mirchin, Eric Tomlinson, Peter Page and Richard Gramaglia; Additional Dialogue. Romeo Muller; Recording Supervisor, Richard Cowan;

Cast

Paul O'Keefe (Hans Christian Andersen); Jack Gilford (Papa Andersen); Ray Bolger (Pieman); Margaret Hamilton (Mrs. Kloppleboppler); Robert Hartner (Big Claus); and Larry Mann, Billie Richards, James Daugherty and William Marine.

Voices

Cyril Ritchard (Sandman); Hayley Mills (The Little Mermaid); Burl Ives (Father Neptune); Tallulah Bankhead (Sea Witch); Terry-Thomas (1st Tailor: Brigadier); Victor Borge (2nd Tailor: Zebro); Ed Wynn (Emperor); Patty Duke (Thumbelina); Boris Karloff (Rat); Sessue Hayakawa (Mole)

Synopsis

In the village of Odense, in Denmark, lives ten-year-old Hans Christian Andersen. His father is a poor shoemaker, but he encourages his young son to study hard so he will grow up to be successful. He tells Chris that only in the Garden of Paradise do boys not have to study because everything they eat there contains knowledge. That night Chris decides to go in search of the Garden, writes his father a note and slips out of the house. He takes a little boat out into the river and falls asleep as it drifts downstream. In his dream the boat drifts out to see and breaks apart in a fierce storm. His lifeless body sinks to the bottom where it is found by a little mermaid. Father Neptune tells her that he is dead, but she loves the little boy and, hearing that the Sea Witch has a potion that will restore life to dead humans, pays a visit to the witch. The witch agrees to give the mermaid the potion but only under certain conditions: if the boy returns her love, she must live with him on dry land; if he doesn't, she must live forever as an outcast. She agrees, bring the boy back to life, but he explains that he was on a journey to the Garden of Paradise, and so he swims to shore leaving the little mermaid sobbing. Chris awakes, still in his boat. He steers the boat to shore, climbs out and goes back to sleep sitting under a tree. In another dream, he meets two tailors who are on their way to see the emperor. Unbeknownst to Chris, they have a devious plan to rob the emperor of his gold and silver. Chris accompanies them to the palace where they explain to the gullible emperor that they will make him new clothes out of gold and silver threads. But the clothes will be invisible to fools and will only be seen by wise men. The emperor agrees. The tailors pack up the gold and silver and present the emperor with make-believe clothes. Everyone pretends to see the clothes, but a small child says the emperor is naked. The people realize they have been fooled, and the tailors run away. Chris runs too, falls, and wakes up, still under the tree. He is captured by Big Claus, the game warden, and is told to chop logs. Before he can start, Thumbelina pops out of a flower and tells Chris she too is going to the Garden of Paradise. She tells him to eat a tulip seed which will shrink him down to her size. He does, and they start off together. They come to a snowy land and knock on the door of a rat's house. He invites them in and pretends to be gracious, but intends to make Chris his slave and trade Thumbelina to the Mole in return for grain and a fur coat. The mole agrees to the plan, but a sparrow rescues Thumbelina. She asks Chris to come with her to the land a little people. But he searches for the garden instead. The Sandman appears and tells Chris he has let his own ambitions get in the way of finding happiness. Chris still wants to find the Garden, so the Sandman takes him there. But as soon as Chris eats of the tree of knowledge, the Garden disappears. He is suddenly awakened by Big Claus who has captured another stranger. It turns out to be Papa Andersen who had found Chris's note and was out looking for him. Papa Andersen gives Big Claus his wedding ring as payment, and they are set free. They return to their little house and the Sandman explains that Chris eventually did find his Garden of Paradise -- through his writing.

Review Summary

"*Daydreamer* is skillful, inventive and charming. It should particularly appeal to a pre-teen audience, but with a long list of well-known names voicing the fairy-tale characters. [it] should also get a good play from the older generation." (*Variety*, July 13, 1966)

Additional Sources

Reviews: *Newsday* (Dec. 2, 1966); *New York Morning Telegraph* (Dec. 2, 1966); *New York World Journal Tribune* (December 2, 1966)

Commentary

The Daydreamer, with an estimated budget of $2 million, utilized an animation process called Animagic for the dream sequences (more than half the film) in which three-dimensional figures appear to move on the screen without hands or strings. The process is a form of stop-motion animation (made famous by *King Kong*, 1933) with the position of the figures changed fractionally for each frame of photography.

The film includes three of Hans Christian Andersen's most well known stories – *The Little Mermaid*, *The Emperor's New Clothes*, and *Thumbelina* – and the boy was written into each story presumably to give the picture continuity. The major doll figures had faces which were caricatures of the actors who spoke for them. The Sea Witch (an unmistakable resemblance to Tallulah) is the most striking example. And when the Sea Witch talks, the voice is unmistakably Tallulah's, especially the smoky laugh.

With Jeff Chandler in the 1950 radio dramatization of *Lifeboat*.

5

Radio

Tallulah Bankhead is known primarily for her work in the theatre, but she carved a nice niche for herself in radio as well, beginning with guest appearances in 1933, leading to her own show in 1950 and culminating in her being named 1951's woman of the year by the Radio Editors of America.

Interestingly enough, she admitted in a 1934 interview that she was terrified of radio and would not broadcast before a live audience, preferring to speak from a private, adjoining studio. This section is divided into two parts: *The Big Show,* Tallulah's series for NBC (with each episode listed chronologically); and guest appearances on other programs.

SERIES

R1 **The Big Show** (NBC)

Premiered: November 5, 1950, 6 p.m. (90 minutes)

Produced by James Harvey, Individual programs produced and directed by Dee Englebach. Written by Goodman Ace, Selma Diamond, George Foster, Mort Green, Welbourn Kelley, Joel Murcott and Frank Wilson. Special material by Fred Allen. Musical direction by Meredith Willson. Chorus directed by Max Teer and Ray Charles. Announcers: Bert Cowlan, Ben Grauer, Ed Herlihy and Jimmy Wallington. Mistress of Ceremonies: Tallulah Bankhead.

1 9 5 0

1) (November 5) Guests were Fred Allen, Mindy Carson, Jimmy Durante, José Ferrer, Portland Hoffa, Frankie Laine, Paul Lukas, Ethel Merman, Russell Nype and Danny Thomas.

2) (November 12) Guests were John Agar, David Brian, Fanny

Brice, Frank Lovejoy, Groucho Marx, Ezio Pinza, Jane Powell and Hanley Stafford.

3) (November 19) Guests were Eddie Cantor, Perry Como, Bob Hope and Ray Middleton. (Meredith Willson's *May the Good Lord Bless and Keep You*, which became the program's closing theme, was first performed on this episode.)

4) (November 26) Guests were Fred Allen, Jack Carson, Ed "Archie" Gardner, Portland Hoffa, Lauritz Melchoir and Ed Wynn.

5) (December 3) Guests were Fred Allen, Joan Allen, Douglas Fairbanks, Jr., Portland Hoffa, Phil Silvers and Margaret Truman.

6) (December 10) Guests were Eddy Arnold, Charles Boyer, Joe Bushkin, Imogene Coco and Clifton Webb.

7) (December 17) Guests were Louis Armstrong, Bob Hope, Deborah Kerr, Frankie Laine, Dean Martin & Jerry Lewis, and Dorothy McGuire.

8) (December 24) Guests were Jimmy Durante, Bert Lahr, Robert Merrill, Margaret O'Brien, Edith Piaf and Fran Warren.

9) (December 31) Guests were Vivian Blaine, Sam Levine, Ken Murray and Gloria Swanson.

1951

10) (January 7) Guests were Fred Allen, Phil Baker, Marlene Dietrich, Portland Hoffa, Edward G. Robinson and Danny Thomas.

11) (January 14) Guests were Louis Calhern, Jack Carter, Florence Desmond, Jimmy Durante, Martha Raye and Fran Warren.

12) (January 21) Guests were Fred Allen, Eddie Cantor, Portland Hoffa, Judy Holliday, Gypsy Rose Lee, Vaughn Monroe and Patrice Munsel.

13) (January 28) Guests were Ray Bolger, Gary Cooper, The Delta Rhythm Boys, Danny Kaye, Maxie Rosembloom, Rudy Vallee and Julie Wilson.

14)   (February 4) Guests were Fred Allen, Robert Cummings, Laraine Day, Jimmy Durante, Leo Durocher, Judy Holliday and Jane Pickens.

15)   (February 11) Guests were the Andrews Sisters, Joan Davis, Judy Garland, Gordon MacRae, Dean Martin & Jerry Lewis, and Groucho Marx.

16)   (February 18) Guests were Jack Carson, Dennis King, Beatrice Lillie, Lauritz Melchior, the West Point Choir and Ed Wynn.

17)   (February 25) Guests were Uta Hagen, Jack Haley, Judy Holliday, Paul Kelly, Robert Merrill, Ole Olsen & Chick Johnson, and Monty Woolley.

18)   (March 4) Guests were Fred Allen, Clive Brook, Portland Hoffa, Frankie Laine, Ethel Merman, Margaret Phillips, Hugh Reilly, Herb Shriner and Margaret Truman.

19)   (March 11) Guests were Bob Burns, Jimmy Durante, Billy Eckstein, Celeste Holm, Eddie Jackson, Evelyn Knight, Jack Pearl (Baron Munchausen) & Cliff Hall (Sharlie), and Joe Smith & Charlie Dale.

20)   (March 18) Guests were Fred Allen, Phil Baker, Johnny Burke, Eddie Cantor, Eddie Fisher, Ella Fitzgerald, Portland Hoffa, Jan Peerce and Ethel Waters.

21)   (March 25) Guests were Don Cornell, Jimmy Durante, Rex Harrison, Judy Holliday, Eddie Jackson, Jackie Miles, Carmen Miranda and Lilli Palmer.

22)   (April 1) Guests were Ethel Barrymore, Joan Davis, Judy Holliday, Bob Hope, Van Johnson, Groucho Marx and Ezio Pinza.

23)   (April 8) Guests were Fred Allen, Vivian Blaine, Alonza Bozan, Dr. Ralph Bunche, John Crosby, Ossie Davis, Portland Hoffa, William Marshall, Jane Morgan and Rudy Vallee.

24)   (April 15) Guests were Eddy Arnold, Eddie Cantor, Jack Carson, Olivia de Havilland, Phil Foster, Tommy Henrich and Martha Raye.

25)   (April 22) Guests were Fred Allen, Joan Davis, Portland Hoffa, Judy Holliday, Dennis King, Lisa Kirk, Herb Shriner and Fran Warren.

26)   (April 29) Guests were Milton Berle, Rosemary Clooney, Matt Cvetic, Jimmy Durante, Frank Lovejoy, Gordon MacRae and Ethel Merman.

27)   (May 6) Guests were Fred Allen, Lucienne Boyer, Portland Hoffa, George Jessel, Groucho Marx, Ginger Rogers and Margaret Truman.

28)   (September 30, broadcast on the BBC on September 16.) Guests were Fred Allen, Jack Buchanan, Portland Hoffa, Michael Howard, Vivien Leigh, Beatrice Lillie, the George Michael Choir, Laurence Olivier, George Sanders and Robb Wilton. (This episode launched the second season of *The Big Show*, and was broadcast from the London Palladium.)

29)   (October 7, recorded on September 24.) Guests were Josephine Baker, Gracie Fields, Joan Fontaine, William Gargan, Fernand Gravat, Georges Guitary, François Rosay and George Sanders. (This episode originated from the Empire Theatre, Paris.)

30)   (October 14) Guests were Fred Allen, Shirley Booth, Jimmy Durante, Ethel Merman, Portland Hoffa and George Sanders.

31)   (October 21) Guests were the Andrews Sisters, Marlene Dietrich, Phil Foster, Benny Goodman, Frankie Laine and Margaret Truman.

32)   (October 28) Guests were Jack Carson, Jimmy Durante, Ed "Archie" Gardner, the Ink Spots, James and Pamela Mason, Dorothy Sarnoff and Herb Shriner.

33)   (November 4) Guests were Joan Davis, Herb Jeffries, Evelyn Knight, Groucho Marx, George Sanders and Lurene Tuttle.

34)   (November 11) Guests were Morton Downey, Jerry Lester, Jackie Miles, Ken Murray, Ann Sheridan, Sophie Tucker and June Valli.

35)   (November 18) Guests were Fred Allen, Gertrude Berg, Shirley Booth, Yul Brynner, Cliff Hall (Sharlie) and Jack Pearl (Baron Munchausen), Portland Hoffa and Maxine Sullivan.

36)   (November 25) Guests were Dane Clark, Graham Forbes, Phil Foster, Mary McCarty, George Sanders, Martha Scott and Martha Wright.

37)   (December 2) Guests were Fred Allen, Wally Cox, Dolores Gray, Portland Hoffa, Paul McGrath, Lauritz Melchior, Ginger Rogers and George Sanders.

38)   (December 9) Guests were Eddy Arnold, Jean Carroll, Robert Cummings, Ed "Archie" Gardner, Hildegarde and Ann Sothern.

39)   (December 16) Guests were Jack Carson, Merv Griffin, Rosalind Russell, Phil Silvers, Sarah Vaughan and Henny Youngman.

40)   (December 23) Guests were Milton Berle, Robert Merrill, Ozzie and Harriet Nelson, Alec Templeton and Margaret Truman.

41)   (December 30) Guests were Fred Allen, Gertrude Berg, Joan Davis, Portland Hoffa, Georgia Gibbs, Johnny Johnston and Jackie Miles.

1 9 5 2

42)   (January 6) Guests were Bob Carroll, Joan Davis, Vera Lynn, Jimmy Nelson, Claude Rains and Herb Shriner.

43)   (January 13) Guests were Fred Allen, Tony Bennett, Phil Foster, June Havoc, Portland Hoffa, Betty Hutton, Vera Lynn and Sheppard Strudwick.

44)   (January 20) Guests were Shirley Booth, Phil Foster, Vera Lynn, Jack Pearl (Baron Munchausen) and Cliff Hall (Sharlie), Dick Powell and Earl Wrightson.

45)   (January 27) Guests were James Barton, Tony Bavaar, Victor Borge, Jack Carson, Bob (Elliot) & Ray (Goulding) and Vera Lynn.

46)   (February 3) Guests were Fred Allen, Jerry Colonna, Portland Hoffa, Vera Lynn, Ethel Merman, Jan Murray and Cathleen Nesbitt.

47)   (February 10) Guests were Joan Davis, Phil Foster, Vera Lynn, Jan Miner, Claude Rains and Jean Sablon.

48)   (February 17) Guests were Fred Allen, Hoagy Carmichael, Joan Davis, Portland Hoffa, Vera Lynn and Jane Pickens.

49)   (February 24) Guests were Kay Armen, Gertrude Berg,

Victor Borge, Phil Foster, Ed "Archie" Gardner and Robert Merrill.

50)   (March 2) Guests were Fred Allen, Connee Boswell, Clark Dennis, Rex Harrison, Portland Hoffa, Lilli Palmer and Henny Youngman.

51)   (March 9) Guests were Richard Eastham, Joe Frisco, Peter Lorre, Fibber McGee and Molly (Jim and Marian Jordan), Ethel Merman and Sheppard Strudwick.

52)   (March 16) Guests were Fred Allen, Peter Donald, William Gargan, Portland Hoffa, Helen O'Connell and Frank Sinatra.

53)   (March 23) Guests were Victor Borge, Rosemary Clooney, Marlene Dietrich, Paul Douglas, Jack Pearl (Baron Munchausen) and Cliff Hall (Sharlie) and Earl Wrightson.

54)   (March 30) Guests were Fred Allen, Vivian Blaine, Judy Canova, Phil Foster, Portland Hoffa, Johnny Johnston and Jan Murray.

55)   (April 6) Guests were Toni Arden, Dorothy Claire, Judy Canova, the Continental (Renzo Cesana), Herb Jeffries, Oscar Levant, Jane Russell and Paul Winchell & Jerry Mahoney.

56)   (April 13) Guests were Fred Allen, Portland Hoffa, Peggy Lee, Groucho Marx, Jackie Miles and George Sanders.

57)   (April 20) Guests were Fred Allen, Phil Foster, Gilbert W. Gabriel, Julie Harris, Portland Hoffa, Groucho Marx, Ethel Merman, William Prince, George Sanders, John Van Druten and Earl Wrightson. (This episode marked the end of *The Big Show*, and was the end of radio's glory days. Television had successfully won their audience.)

GUEST APPEARANCES

(NOTE: In addition to the shows listed, Tallulah Bankhead also appeared -- with Georgia Gibbs, the Pied Pipers and Ethel Smith -- in an episode of *Mail Call*, the radio program produced by the Armed-Forces and broadcast abroad, in 1944 [date undetermined]; and starred with Eugenia Rawls in a program titled *Woman at War*. It aired on NBC sometime during January 1944.)

R2   (WEAF) March 13, 1933. (On this local New York City station, an

NBC affiliate, Tallulah spoke briefly on behalf on the stage relief fund..She went on the air, making her radio debut, at 6:55 p.m.)

R3 **The Rudy Vallee Show** (NBC) February 15, 1934. (For her *national* radio debut, Tallulah appeared with Horace Braham and Porter Hall in *The Affairs of Anatol*, a comedy skit by Arthur Schnitzler.)

R4 **Lux Radio Theatre** (NBC) December 2, 1934. (Tallulah starred in a dramatization of *Let Us Be Gay* with Bert Lytell and Edward Woods.)

R5 **The Rudy Vallee Show** (NBC) September 24, 1936. (Tallulah performed *The Waltz* by Dorothy Parker.)

R6 **The Magic Key of RCA** (NBC) January 10, 1937. (Tallulah performed a scene from George Kelly's *Reflected Glory*.)

R7 **The Rudy Vallee Show** (NBC) June 17, 1937. (Tallulah recited *Advice to the Little Peyton Girl* by Dorothy Parker. Appearing with her was Florida Freibus.)

R8 **Radio Playhouse** (CBS) August 30, 1937. (Portraying Viola, Tallulah participated in a dramatization of *Twelfth Night* with Orson Welles, Estelle Winwood, Helen Menken, Conway Tearle and Cedric Hardwicke.)

R9 **The Kate Smith Show** (CBS) September 30, 1937. (Tallulah starred in a twelve-minute version of *Camille*, with Henry Fonda as Armand.)

R10 **For Men Only** (NBC) February 21, 1938. (Tallulah chatted about baseball with two members of the New York Yankees.)

R11 **The Rudy Vallee Show** (NBC) June 23, 1938. (Tallulah appeared opposite her husband, John Emery, in *"L" is for Love*, a comedy by Howard Paris.)

R12 **The Kate Smith Hour** (CBS) March 16, 1939. (Tallulah recited *Sentiment*, a monologue by Dorothy Parker.)

R13 **The Greater New York Fund All-Star Show** (NBC) April 23, 1939. (Tallulah read Dorothy Parker's *The Waltz*.)

R14 **The New York Drama Critics Circle Award Program.** (NBC) April 23, 1939. (Tallulah performed two scenes from her current Broadway hit, *The Little Foxes*.)

R15   **The People's Platform** (CBS) August 20, 1939. (Tallulah talked about baseball with Ford Frick, Lyman Brasson, Bill Corum and Ed Ferguson.)

R16   **Time to Smile** (NBC) March 4, 1941. (Tallulah appeared with Eddie Cantor, Harry VonZell and Dinah Shore.)

R17   **The Campbell Playhouse** (CBS) April 18, 1941. (Tallulah starred in a play titled *The Talley Method.*)

R18   **Time to Smile** (NBC) April 23, 1941. (Tallulah appeared opposite Eddie Cantor.)

R19   **Your Happy Birthday** (NBC) April 23, 1941. (Along with co-host Axton Fisher, Tallulah gave birthday greetings to listeners.)

R20   **Lincoln Highway** (NBC) April 26, 1941. (Tallulah discussed her "already lengthy" career, denounced Hitler and read a love poem.)

R21   **Greater New York Fund Variety Program** (NBC) April 27, 1941. (Introduced by New York City Mayor Fiorello La Guardia, Tallulah and other Broadway stars aided in the city's pledge drive for social agencies.)

R22   **Philip Morris Playhouse** (CBS) October 10, 1941. (Tallulah and members of the Broadway cast performed *The Little Foxes.*)

R23   **Listen, America** (NBC) January 18, 1942. (Tallulah urged Americans to buy war bonds and stamps.)

R24   **The Kate Smith Variety Hour** (CBS) January 23, 1942. (Tallulah appeared in a dramatic sketch. Other guests were Nam Rae and Olyn Landick, the Hackensack Housewife.)

R25   **Philip Morris Playhouse: Johnnie Presents** (NBC) February 3, 1942. (Tallulah starred in a twelve-minute version of *Suspicion.* This was to be the first of a 48-week series of love stories with Tallulah. She appeared in only two others.)

R26   **Time to Smile** (NBC) March 5, 1942. (Tallulah was co-host with Fred Allen.)

R27   **Phillip Morris Playhouse: Johnnie Presents** (NBC) March 17, 1942. (For a dramatic reading, Tallulah was backed by the Ray Bloch orchestra.)

R28   **Command Performance USA** (NBC) March 29, 1942. (George Jessel hosted the program, and guests on this episode included

Tallulah Bankhead, Joan Edwards and Carmen Miranda.)

R29 War Bond Drive (NBC) April 11, 1942. (Tallulah appeared with several stage and screen stars to read pledges from listeners.)

R30 Listen, America (NBC) April 26, 1942. (Tallulah read Carl Bixby's *The Roots of a Tree,* which was written expressly for her.)

R31 Philip Morris Playhouse: Johnnie Presents. (NBC) May 19, 1942. (Backed by Ray Bloch's orchestra, Tallulah read *The Telephone Call* by Dorothy Parker.)

R32 Stage Door Canteen (CBS) September 10, 1942. (Helen Menken, Ethel Barrymore, Cedric Hardwicke, Charles Laughton and Tallulah were among the all-star cast.)

R33 The Infamy of the Axis (WEVD, New York) December 6, 1942. (In this local New York program to promote patriotism, Tallulah and Ella Logan, Paul Muni, Fredric March and Maxine Sullivan represented the theatre.)

R34 Milk Fund for Babies (NBC) January 10, 1943. (Offering her support for this charitable cause, Tallulah appeared with Mayor La Guardia, Mrs. William Randolph Hearst, Lois January, Howard Lindsay and staff members from New York City hospitals.)

R35 That They Might Live (NBC) April 18, 1943. (In the drama, *I Served on Bataan,* Tallulah played the leading role of a war nurse to escaped to Corregidor.)

R36 Radio Reader's Digest (CBS) May 2, 1943. (Tallulah starred as Mrs. Johnnie "Leadville" Brown in *The Unsinkable Mrs. Brown.* Conrad Nagel narrated.)

R37 New York Philharmonic Symphony (CBS) May 30, 1943. (In a tribute to Memorial Day, Tallulah recited *The Blue and the Gray.*)

R38 Stage Door Canteen (CBS) June 10, 1943. (Guests included Tallulah, Fred Allen, Portland Hoffa, Jimmy Durante, Bob Hope and Tom Howard.)

R39 The Radio Hall of Fame (NBC) January 16, 1944. (On this 30 minute program hosted by Paul Whiteman, Tallulah appreared with Frank Lovejoy, Joe Laurie, Jr. and Peter Donald.)

R40 Stage Door Canteen (CBS) January 21, 1944. (Tallulah read Dorothy Parker's *The Little Hours,* and shared the stage with Count Basie, Lena Horne, Elsa Maxwell and George Jessel.)

R41 Words at War (NBC) February 29, 1944. (A re-broadcast of *I Served on Bataan*, originally aired on April 18, 1943)

R42 Million Dollar Band (NBC) May 6, 1944. (Tallulah promised to sing but instead she introduced two songs and joked with Harry James.)

R43 Time to Smile (NBC) May 10, 1944. (In this special episode broadcast from Monmouth, N.J., Tallulah was mistress of ceremonies.)

R44 Stage Door Canteen (CBS) June 10, 1944. (Mike Todd, Harpo Marx, Gypsy Rose Lee, Otto Kruger and Katharine Hepburn were among the guests. Tallulah read Joyce Kilmer's *Trees* and participated in a comedy sketch.)

R45 One Thousand Club of America (NBC) November 6, 1944. (Tallulah urged all Americans to vote for Roosevelt.)

R46 The Rudy Vallee Show (NBC) November 16, 1944. (Tallulah read a poem and starred in a short dramatic play.)

R47 The Frank Sinatra Show (CBS) December 4, 1944. (Again, Tallulah promised to sing, but she traded quips with Sinatra instead.)

R48 This is the Word (CBS) December 16, 1944. (Tallulah urged Americans to buy war bonds.)

R49 The Raleigh Room with Hildegarde (NBC) January 2, 1945. (Tallulah made her singing debut on radio joining Clifton Webb in a rendition of *I'll Be Seeing You*.)

R50 War Bond Show (NBC) January 6, 1945. (Tallulah and Walter Huston starred in *These Are Our Men*.)

R51 The Raleigh Room with Hildegarde (NBC) January 16, 1945. (By popular demand, Tallulah again sang *I'll Be Seeing You*.)

R52 Curtain Time on Broadway (NBC) April 14, 1945. (Appearing with Ethel Barrymore and Elliot Nugent, Tallulah read Nathaniel A. Benson's *Elegy of Remembrance* as a tribute to the late Franklin Delano Roosevelt.)

R53 The Mary Margaret McBride Show (NBC) April 20, 1945. (Tallulah talked about the death of Roosevelt, the status of the war, and the importance of presenting a united effort for President Truman.)

R54 Atlantic Spotlight (NBC) April 28, 1945. (Tallulah urged all Americans to be patriotic.)

R55 The Kate Smith Hour (CBS) April 29, 1945. (Tallulah read *The Waltz* by Dorothy Parker and appeared in a comedy sketch.)

R56 The Jerry Wayne Show (CBS) June 15, 1945. (Tallulah joked with her host then chose the best of currently popular songs.)

R57 The Navy Hour (NBC) August 14, 1945. (Tallulah played the title role in *A Salute to the US Cruiser Helena.*)

R58 The Raleigh Room with Hildegarde (NBC) September 11, 1945. (Tallulah sang *Don't Fence Me In.*)

R59 The Edgar Bergen-Charlie McCarthy Show (NBC) February 24, 1946. (Tallulah fought with Charlie before succumbing to the flattery of Mortimer Snerd, whom she later threatened to reduce to sawdust or firewood.)

R60 The Raleigh Room with Hildegarde (NBC) March 13, 1946. (Tallulah sang *Always*, and Hildegarde's comment was "never again.")

R61 The Chesterfield Supper Club (NBC) March 29, 1946. (With Perry Como hosting, Tallulah and Jack Smith were guests.)

R62 The Fred Allen Show (NBC) May 5, 1946. (Tallulah went "slumming" in Allen's Alley.)

R63 The Penguin Room with Hildegarde (NBC) May 15, 1946. (Tallulah was cited as the most popular guest.)

R64 Radio Reader's Digest (CBS) May 26, 1946. (Tallulah starred in *The Doctor, His Wife and the Clock,* a melodramatic confrontation between a blind physician determined to confess to murder, and his equally determined wife. Raymond Edward Johnson co-starred.)

R65 We, The People (CBS) August 18, 1946. (Tallulah presided over a discussion of summer theatre.)

R66 The Campbell Room (CBS) October 6, 1946. (Tallulah and Hildegarde sang *Anything You Can Do.*)

R67 The Fred Allen Show (NBC) October 27, 1946. (Tallulah and Fred performed, for the first time, a skit titled *The Mr. and Mrs. Breakfast Broadcasting Satire*, which became a radio classic. See D4)

R68   **The Edgar Bergen-Charlie McCarthy Show** (NBC) November 17, 1946. (More joke swapping with Charlie and Mortimer.)

R69   **The Campbell Room** (CBS) November 24, 1946. (Tallulah and Hildegarde chatted about fashions and men. Tallulah also sang, in bits and pieces, *Some of These Days*.)

R70   **The Campbell Room** (CBS) March 30, 1947. (Tallulah read Dorothy Parker's *Here We Are*.)

R71   **Kraft Music Hall** (NBC) April 17, 1947. (Tallulah and Al Jolson debated who was "quicker on the Southern drawl"; she won.)

R72   **Information, Please** (ABC) April 23, 1947. (Answering questions with Tallulah were Franklin P. Adams, Jackie Robinson, Dr. Rufus Clement and John Kiernan.)

R73   **Kraft Music Hall** (NBC) May 1, 1947. (Tallulah and Al Jolson sang *Carolina in the Mornin'* after which Tallulah recited a monologue by Dorothy Parker.)

R74   **Kraft Music Hall** (NBC) June 5, 1947 (Tallulah was on hand as a guest, and sang *When the Blue of the Night* with Bing Crosby.)

R75   **We, The People** (CBS) June 24, 1947. (Tallulah discussed the New York Giants.)

R76   **The Fred Allen Show** (NBC) October 17, 1948. (Tallulah and Fred reprised their *Mr. and Mrs. Breakfast Broadcasting Satire*.)

R77   **Hi, Jinx** (WNBC, New York) December 13, 1948. (On the *Tex and Jinx Show*, Tallulah discussed the recent election and her cover story in *Time* Magazine.)

R78   **A Report to the Nation** (CBS) November 9, 1950. (In this "new experiment in radio news," listeners learned the results of the 1950 elections as told by such celebrities as Everett Dirkson, Tallulah Bankhead, June Allyson, Richard Nixon and Helen Gahagan Douglas.)

R79   **Screen Director's Playhouse.** (NBC) November 16, 1950. (In a dramatization of *Lifeboat*, Tallulah again portrayed Connie Porter. Other cast members included Jeff Chandler, William Wilms, Sheldon Leonard, Barbara Eiler, Bob Glen, Henry Rowland and Ann Diamond. Alfred Hitchcock directed the episode.)

R80   **The Bob Hope Show** (NBC) December 10, 1950. (Tallulah appeared with Gordon MacRae.)

R81 Screen Director's Playhouse (NBC) February 15, 1951. (In an
episode directed by Edmund Goulding, Tallulah starred as Judith
Traherne in *Dark Victory*. David Brian appeared opposite her.)

R82 The Bing Crosby Show (NBC) February 21, 1951. (Tallulah
kidded Bing about the size of his program – half an hour – and
participated with him in a comedy skit built around the song *Just a
Gigalo*. Peggy Lee also appeared.)

R83 Screen Director's Playhouse (NBC) April 19, 1951. (Directed
by Jean Negulesco, Tallulah and Stephen Cochran starred in a
dramatization of *Humoresque*.)

R84 The House of Music (NBC) June 13, 1951. (Wayne Howell
hosted this telescoped audition program with live guests and records.
His guests on this particular program were Fred Allen, Tallulah
Bankhead, Dean Martin and Jerry Lewis, Meredith Willson and
Georgia Gibbs.)

R85 The Jane Pickens Show (NBC) April 7, 1952. (Tallulah
discussed the demands of a radio career.)

R86 Hy Gardner Calling (NBC) September 24, 1952. (Tallulah, via
telephone, talked about the theatre, the talent on Broadway and about
The Big Show.)

R87 The Mary Margaret McBride Show (ABC) September 29,
1952. (Tallulah talked about her name, New England bluebloods,
her career, anxiety, the South, Hollywood gossip, recipes, sponsor
plugs, the theatre and her autobiography.)

R88 Meredith Willson's Music Room (NBC) (Willson discussed the
music he provided for *The Big Show*, especially the song, "May the
Good Lord Bless and Keep You." Tallulah said to her it was "almost
like a hymn.")

R89 The Author Speaks (NBC) October 11, 1952. (Tallulah talked
about her recently published autobiography.)

R90 Theatre Guild of the Air (NBC) November 9, 1952. (Tallulah
was a guest on this particular episode but announced she would star
in the next episode.)

R91 Theatre Guild of the Air (NBC) November 16, 1952.
(Tallulah starred as Margo Channing in a dramatization of *All About
Eve*. Kevin McCarthy and Beatrice Pearson co-starred. See D9.)

R92 Radio City Previews (NBC) November 28, 1952. (Tallulah discussed her recent performnance in *All About Eve*.)

R93 Weekend (NBC) August 1, 1954. (Tallulah was interviewed on the "Women's Page" segment of the program.)

R94 Sunday With Garroway (NBC) September 12, 1954. (Tallulah talked about jazz, home furnishings, politics, baseball and acting.)

R95 Weekend (NBC) September 26, 1954. (Interviewed by Tex McCrary, Tallulah talked about *Dear Charles*.)

R96 A Tribute to Lionel Barrymore (NBC) November 21, 1954. (Tallulah reminisced about the actor and recited a poem; others on the program were Edward Arnold, Gene Fowler, Helen Hayes and Norman Vincent Peale.)

R97 A Call for Foster Parents (NBC) November 28, 1954. (Tallulah, Tex and Jinx McCrary discussed the importance of placing children in foster homes.)

R98 Friday With Garroway (NBC) December 31, 1954. (Tallulah and Dave Garroway wished everyone the happiest of New Year's greetings.)

R99 Biographies in Sound (NBC) March 6, 1955. (In a taped recording, Tallulah talked about the actor as he sees himself.)

R100 This is New York (CBS) November 30, 1955. (With Walter Winchell and Edward R. Murrow, Tallulah talked about New York and said it was her "almost favorite" place.)

R101 Holiday Time (ABC) December 21, 1955. (Tallulah and Estelle Winwood talked about their childhood Christmases.)

R102 Presenting Alfred Hitchcock (NBC) January 25, 1956. (In a pre-recorded interview, Tallulah added her comments to this radio portrait of motion picture director Alfred Hitchcock.)

R103 Biographies in Sound (NBC) May 29, 1956. (Titled "Mr. Allen! Mr. Allen!" this episode reviewed the career of Fred Allen, and Tallulah talked about their many radio shows together.)

R104 This is New York (CBS) July 29, 1957. (Tallulah was interviewed by Jim McKay and Dave Dugan.)

R105 Family Living, '57 (NBC) August 15, 1957. (Tallulah and Ben Gross, radio critic of *The Daily News*, talked about growing up in the South, and participated in a discussion on "How have changes in entertainment influenced your family?")

R106 The Mitch Miller Show (NBC) December 1, 1957. (Peggy Wood, Dennis King and Tallulah enacted the story of *The Little Church Around the Corner*.)

R107 Monitor (NBC) May 27, 1959. (Interviewed from her bed in New York's Flower Fifth Avenue Hospital, the discussion did not center around her health, but on the theatre.)

R108 Monitor's Salute to Jimmy Durante (NBC) February 9, 1963. (A salute to Jimmy Durante on the eve of his 70th birthday. Tributes by Jack Benny, Sammy Davis, Jr., Joey Bishop, Garry Moore, Ethel Merman, Bob Hope, Dinah Shore and Margie Durante. Performances by Tallulah Bankhead, Al Jolson, Clayton & Jackson, Helen Traubel, Garry Moore, Victor Moore, Don Ameche, Bob Hope and Eddie Cantor.)

R109 The Chase & Sanborn 101st Anniversary Show (NBC) November 14, 1965. (Narrnated by Edgar Bergen and Charlie McCarthy, this program featured excerpts from the Fred Allen radio shows, including the famous "Mr. and Mrs. Breakfast Satire" skit that Allen and Tallulah Bankhead did in 1946. It became a classic and was repeated many times.)

R110 NBC's 40th Anniversary Program (NBC) November 13, 1966. (Narrated by Edgar Bergen and Charlie McCarthy, the special contained excerpts from dozens of NBC radio shows of the past, including *The Big Show* with Tallulah Bankhead.)

With Adam West and Burt Ward in an episode of *Batman* (1967).

6

Television

On her radio program, *The Big Show*, television was the butt of many of Tallulah's jokes, but when the program was cancelled in 1952, she gave in and signed with NBC to star in her own series. Titled *All Star Revue*, it was essentially a continuation of the formerly titled *Four Star Revue*, which had debuted in September 1951. Tallulah alternated as mistress of ceremonies with four other celebrities and made one appearance on the program per month. Although she left the series after the first season, Dennis Day took over Tallulah's role as emcee and it continued for a second. Tallulah never again appeared in her own series, but she showed up often as a guest on other shows (she was especially well-liked as "the Celebrity Next Door" on an episode of the *Lucille Ball-Desi Arnaz Show*) and she made several appearances on celebrity talk shows right up until the year of her death. Her television work is divided into two sections: the *All Star Revue* series for NBC (with each episode listed chronologically); and her guest appearances on other programs.

SERIES

T1 All Star Revue (NBC)

First aired: October 11, 1952, 8 p.m. (60 minutes)

Produced and directed by Dee Englebach; Executive production by Sam Fuller; Television direction by Hal Keith; Written by Mort Green and George Foster; Orchestra and chorus directed by Meredith Willson; Choreography by Ron Fletcher; Sets by Richard Day; Tallulah's costumes by Hattie Carnegie. Tallulah, acting as mistress of ceremonies, danced, sang and acted in sketches with her guests. She appeared on one show a month, alternating with three other guest hosts.

1 9 5 2

1)   (October 11) Guests were Ethel Barrymore, Ben Grauer, Meredith Willson and Groucho Marx.

2)   (November 8) Guests were David Niven, Paul Hartman, Vaughn Monroe, Patsy Kelly, Phil Foster and Meredith Willson. (Tallulah and David Niven performed Dorothy Parker's *Here We Are.*)

3)   (December 20) Guests were Louis Armstrong, Jack Carson, Patsy Kelly and Phil Foster.

1 9 5 3

4)   (January 10) Guests were Milton Berle, Dennis King, Phil Foster, Patsy Kelly and Billy Daniels. (In a dramatic sketch, Tallulah portrayed WWI nurse Edith Cavell, winning praise from critics.)

5)   (February 7) Guests were Bert Lahr, Dolores Martin and Patsy Kelly.

6)   (March 14) Guests were Wally Cox, Fred MacMurray, Cab Calloway and Patsy Kelly.

7)   (April 18) Guests were Jimmy Durante, George Jessel, Ben Blue and Connie Russell.

GUEST APPEARANCES

T2   **Answer the Call** (WNBT, New York) March 2, 1953. (Appearing on tape, Tallulah made an appeal with President Eisenhower for the American Red Cross.)

T3   **The Milton Berle Show** (NBC) September 29, 1953. (Tallulah and Frank Sinatra were guests. They both sang, but not together, and Tallulah also dressed as "Uncle Miltie.")

T4   **The Milton Berle Show** (NBC) November 3, 1953. (Tallulah and Wallx Cox appeared in a sketch about rowdy high school students. She also read "dramatically" a Chinese menu.)

T5   **Person to Person** (CBS) November 20, 1953. (Edward M. Murrow visited Tallulah in her townhouse and was introduced to all the pets.)

T6   **The US Steel Hour** (ABC) January 5, 1954. (In her first
dramatic television role, Tallulah starred in the hour-long *Hedda
Gabler* with Luther Adler, Eugenia Rawls, John Baragrey and Alan
Hewitt. The critics were not kind, terming the production "Hedda
Gabby," and Tallulah vowed never to appear in another television
drama. Luckily, she didn't take the vow seriously.)

T7   **The Colgate Comedy Hour** (NBC) February 7, 1954. (Jimmy
Durante hosted this program on which Tallulah and Carol Channing
were guests.)

T8   **Today** (NBC) September 16, 1954. (Tallulah, on audio tape,
discussed the excitement of the opening night of *Dear Charles*, and
reviewed the critics' reaction to the play.)

T9   **The Martha Raye Show** (NBC) September 20, 1955. (Tallulah,
Rocky Graziano and Martha Raye were in a satirical sketch on
television quiz shows. Other guests were Gloria Lockerman and
Dennis King.)

T10 **The Milton Berle Show** (NBC) November 29, 1955. (Guests
were Tallulah, Frank Sinatra, Gale Storm, Vic Damone, Rudy
Vallee, Dick Contino, Fred Clark and Charles Farrell.)

T11 **The Kathy Godfrey Show** (CBS) August 20, 1956. (Tallulah
talked about summer theatre.)

T12 **Campaign Fundraiser** October 20, 1956. (In this 60-minute
program broadcast over a closed circuit network to Democratic
dinners in over 50 cities, Tallulah helped raise funds for the Adlai
Stevenson/Estes Kefauver campaign. Other celebrities participating
included Frank Sinatra, Henry Fonda and Andy Griffith. The
program was written by Alan Jay Lerner and directed by Fred Coe.
Rodgers and Hammerstein contributed special matertial and Mitch
Miller directed the orchestra.)

T13 **Shower of Stars** (CBS) April 11, 1957. (In this television
spectacular hosted by William Lundigan, Tallulah appeared with Jack
Benny, Ed Wynn, Tommy Sands and Julie London.)

T14 **The Steve Allen Show** (NBC) May 12, 1957. (Guests were
Tallulah Bankhead, Pearl Bailey, Billy Graham and Dean Jones.)

T15 **The Arthur Murray Party** (NBC) July 29, 1957. (Tallulah
waltzed with Ted Alexander, and they won. Other contestants were
Raymond Massey and Jose Iturbi.)

T16 **The Tex and Jinx Show** (NBC) August 12, 1957. (Tallulah interviewed Willie Mays.)

T17   Joe Franklin's Memory Lane (WOR, New York) October 2, 1957. (Tallulah talked about music with the other guests, song writers Benny Benjamin and George Weiss.)

T18   The George Gobel Show (NBC) October 8, 1957. (Tallulah and George appeared in a comedy skit. Jeff Donnell was the other guest.)

T19   The Schlitz Playhouse of Stars (CBS) November 8, 1957. (Tallulah starred in *The Hole Card*, the story of a woman who gambled and won. Isobel Elsom, John Bryant, Ottola Nesmith, George O'Hanlon and Jesslyn Fox appeared with her. The program was re-broadcast on July 18, 1958.)

T20   The Polly Bergen Show (NBC) November 30, 1957. (Tallulah sang "Give Me the Simple Life.")

T21   The Lucille Ball-Desi Arnaz Hour (CBS) December 3, 1957. (Tallulah guest starred in an episode titled "The Celebrity Next Door." Richard Deacon appeared as Tallulah's butler.)

T22   The General Electric Theatre (CBS) December 8, 1957. (Tallulah starred as Katharine Belmont in *Eyes of a Stranger*. The program was directed by Ray Milland.)

T23   The Arthur Murray Party (NBC) December 28, 1957. (Tallulah again won by dancing the Waltz with Rod Alexander. Other contestants were Paul Hartman, June Havoc, Hedy Lamarr, Larry Parks, Betty Garrett, Walter Slezak, Sarah Vaughan, Paul Winchell, and Bill and Cora Baird.)

T24   The Jack Paar Show (NBC) October 30, 1958. (Guests were Tallulah Bankhead, Dagmar, Cliff Arquette and Betty Johnson.)

T25   The Jack Paar Show (NBC) November 18, 1958. (Guests were Tallulah Bankhead, Dave Wilcock, Cliff Arquette and May Williams.)

T26   The Milton Berle Show (NBC) January 7, 1959. (Tallulah sang with Berle and acted out a parody of westerns with Jimmie Rodgers.)

T27   The Jack Paar Show (NBC) April 10, 1959. (Guests were Tallulah Bankhead, Phil Ford, Mimi Hines and Coby Dijon.)

T28   The Ed Sullivan Show (CBS) April 19, 1959. (Tallulah performed a subway sketch and recited Dorothy Parker's *The*

Waltz.)

T29   The Big Party (CBS) October 8, 1959. (With Rock Hudson as co-host, Tallulah appeared with Sammy Davis, Jr., Mort Sahl, Lisa Kirk, Esther Williams, Matt Dennis and the Will Mastin Trio.)

T30   The Jack Paar Show (NBC) December 23, 1959. (Guests were Tallulah Bankhead, Joey Bishop, Carl Reiner and Judy Lynn.)

T31   The Jack Paar Show (NBC) February 9, 1961. (Guests were Tallulah Bankhead, Merriman Smith, Betty White and Jack Haskell.)

T32   The Jack Paar Show (NBC) March 29, 1961. (Tallulah appeared on tape in this, the last of the nightly broadcasts of this program.)

T33   The US Steel Hour (CBS) May 5, 1962. (Tallulah starred as Lillian Throgmorton in *A Man for Oona*, written by Michael Dyne. Appearing with her were Nancy Carroll and Murray Matheson.)

T34   The Tonight Show (NBC) October 2, 1962. (Guests were Tallulah Bankhead, Artie Shaw, Shelley Berman and Fran Bennett.)

T35   The Tonight Show (NBC) May 28, 1962. (Guests were Tallulah Bankhead, Malcolm Muggeridge, Bob Hope and Killy Kallen.)

T36   Elliot Norton Interviews (NET Network) June 26, 1962. (Boston drama critic Elliot Norton interviewed Tallulah when she was performing there in *Here Today*.)

T37   The Andy Williams Show (NBC) May 2, 1965. (Guests were Tallulah Bankhead, Sid Caesar and the Beach Boys.)

T38   The Tonight Show (NBC) May 27, 1965. (Guests were Tallulah Bankhead, Henry Morgan and George Jessel.)

T39   What's My Line? (CBS) June 6, 1965. (Tallulah was the "mystery guest.")

T40   The Mike Douglas Show (Group W) October 11-15, 1965. (Tallulah was guest host for a week, appearing on five programs. Among her guests were Lucille Ball, Vivian Vance, Connie Francis, George Gobel, Dr. Joyce Brothers, George Jessel, Bobby Rydell and Jack Jones.)

T41   The Red Skelton Show (CBS) December 14, 1965. (Tallulah danced with Red Skelton.)

T42 **Batman** (ABC) March 15, 1967. (In part one of *The Black Widow Strikes Again*, Tallulah guest starred as the "Black Widow," and at show's end left Batman and Robin tied up in a web.)

T43 **Batman** (ABC) March 16, 1967. (In the conclusion, the Dynamic Duo escape the "Black Widow's" trap and succeed in trapping *her*.)

T44 **The Merv Griffin Show** (Group W) April 21, 1967. (Guests were Tallulah Bankhead, Milt Kamen, Selma Diamond, Bob Considine and Joe Hyams.)

T45 **The Merv Griffin Show** (Group W) May 24, 1967. (Guests were Tallulah Bankhead and Erroll Garner, columnist for *The Boston Globe* and social essayist for *Esquire*.)

T46 **The Smothers Brothers Comedy Hour** (CBS) December 17, 1967. (Tallulah participated in a skit on gun control. The Temptations were also a guest.)

T47 **The Merv Griffin Show** (Group W) January 23, 1968. (Guests were Dirk Bogarde, Jack Carter, Barbara Nichols and Ted Mack)

T48 **The Tonight Show** (NBC) May 14, 1968. (Joe Garagiola hosted, and guests were Tallulah Bankhead, Tony Scotti, Soupy Sales, Lou Thesz, Jack Twyman, Paul McCartney and John Lennon. Tallulah chatted about the origin of her name, baseball and persuaded the pair of Beatles to talk about their music. This was Tallulah's final television appearance.)

T49 **Hollywood: The Selznick Years** (ABC) March 21, 1969. (Included portions of the tests Tallulah made in late 1936 for the role of Scarlett in *Gone With The Wind*.)

7

Discography

D1   **Album of Stars: Great Moments from Great Plays** (Decca, Number DL909–MG2224, MG2225). Released on June 4, 1951, this album contains two scenes from *The Little Foxes* performed by Tallulah Bankhead, Eugenia Rawls, Kent Smith, Paul Byron and Howard Smith.

D2   **Co-Star** (Roulette, Number CS109). Released June 15, 1957, this LP was part of a series in which the listener could "act" with a star by reading a script that was included with each album. In this recording, Tallulah performs scenes from *The Lady of the Camelias, Hedda Gabler, Lady Windermere's Fan, The Importance of Being Earnest, Mr. Chumley and the Giants, Two in a Boat* and *The Truth, Miss Angela.*

D3   **"Don't Tell Him"** (H.M.V., Number B-3687). Tallulah recorded this song (and "What Do I Care?") in England on June 11, 1930.

D4   **The Golden Age of Comedy, Volume I** (Evolution Records, Number 3013). This 1972 release included the famous "Mr. and Mrs. Breakfast Broadcasting Satire" which Tallulah and Fred Allen introduced on radio in 1946. See R67.)

D5   **Greetings From Hollywood** (AEI Mono, Number 2121). This compilation of Christmas songs and greetings was released in 1984. It includes a French carol sung by Edith Piaf, Margaret O'Brien reading "Yes Virginia, There is a Santa Claus," and Tallulah Bankhead's rendition of "Touch Hands."

D6   **"I'll Be Seeing You"** (Columbia, Number 39109). Directed by Mitch Miller and accompanied by Joe Bushkin, Tallulah recorded this title (and "You Go To My Head") on November 27, 1950.

D7   **A Nostalgia Trip to the Stars: 1920-1950**   (Monmouth-Evergreen Records, Number MES/7030).   Includes Tallulah's 1930 recording of "What Do I Care?"

D8   **Nostalgia's Greatest Hits**   (Stanyan Records, Number 10055).   Includes Tallulah's 1930 recording of "Don't Tell Him."

D9   **Tallulah Bankhead as Margo Channing in All About Eve.**   (Moving Finger, Number 002).   This LP is a broadcast quality recording of radio's *Theatre Guild of the Air* program that aired November 16, 1952 (see R91). Tallulah Bankhead starred in the role Bette Davis created in the 1950 film.

8

Awards, Honors, Tributes

A1   Screen Opportunity Contest (September 1917). The contest was
sponsored by *Picture Play* Magazine, and Tallulah was one of twelve
winners. The prize was a role in a movie filmed in New York City.

A2   Best Performance by an Actress (1938/39 Broadway season).
Tallulah was awarded the citation from *Variety* for her performance
in *The Little Foxes*.

A3   Citation (August 17, 1941). The citation was presented to Tallulah
from Major William F. Nee, commissioning her a second lieutenant
in the 22nd Coast Artillery.

A4   Best Actress of the Year (1942 Broadway season). The honor
was from the New York Drama Critics, for Tallulah's performance
in *The Skin of Our Teeth*.

A5   Best Performance by an Actress (1942 Broadway season).
Variety presented her with her second award, this time for her
performance as Sabina in *The Skin of Our Teeth*.

A6   Barter Theatre Award (1942 Broadway season). Presented to
Tallulah by the Barter Theatre, Abingdon, Virginia, for her
performance in *The Skin of Our Teeth*.

A7   Critics Circle Award (1944). Tallulah's performance in the
film *Lifeboat*, was voted the best of any actress by the New York
Film Critics.

A8   Barter Theatre Award (1948). Tallulah was honored for the
second time by the Barter Theare, Abingdon, Virginia, this time for
her performance in *Private Lives*.

A9   Citation (May 13, 1950). From the Night Hawks Social Club, Washington, D.C., for her "democratic stand, opposing discrimination in the theatre arts, and her inimitable acting skill, thus making her a golden inspiration to aspiring, talented persons of all races and religions."

A10   Page One Award (1950). Presented to Tallulah by the New York Newspaper Guild for "putting new life into radio" with *The Big Show*.

A11   Celebrity of the Year (1950). Tallulah was so named by the Celebrity Service, Inc., and the announcement was made by Earl Blackwell, president of the agency, at New York City's Stork Club early in 1951. Tallulah was in good company, with Gen. Dwight D. Eisenhower, John Hersey, Gloria Swanson, Faye Emerson, William (Hopalong Cassidy) Boyd, Margaret Truman, Carol Channing, Phil Rizzuto and Gian-Carlo Menotti receiving similar honors.

A12   Honorary Fellowship Award of Merit (April 9, 1951). Was presented to Tallulah by the George Washington Carver Memorial Institute for her "contribution to the Theatre Arts, Americanism and Human Welfare." The presentation was made in Town Hall, New York City.

A13   Woman of the Year in Radio (1951). Tallulah was so named by the radio editors of America due to her success on NBC's *The Big Show*.

A14   Public Service Award (March 23, 1952). Tallulah received this award from the John Guedel Dinky Foundation for her public service "through radio programs." The producers of *The Big Show* received a similar award.

A15   Nomination (1961). Tallulah was nominated for an Antoinette Perry Award ("Tony") as best actress in a drama for her performance in *Midgie Purvis*. (Other nominees were Joan Plowright, *A Taste of Honey*, Barbara Baxley, *Period of Adjustment*, and Barbara Bel Geddes, *Mary, Mary*. Joan Plowright won.)

Tributes

Tallulah Bankhead has been the subject of many a female impersonator's act, which is certainly a tribute in a sense, but in this section one will find those tributes honoring her memory, talent and achievements.

A16   City Center Showcase (April 27, 1959). An evening of light opera, ballet and drama at New York's City Center was dedicated to

Tallulah Bankhead.

A17   Super Open House in Memory of Miss Tallulah Bankhead
(March 30, 1969). The Players Club, New York City, hosted this
lavish party which consisted of film clips, radio recordings and
television tapes featuring Tallulah. The tribute was produced by
Jean Dalrymple and Gus Schirmer, and included reminiscences by
such guests as Dennis King, Anita Loos, Otto Preminger, Norton
Mockridge and Eugenia Rawls.

A18   Memorial Tribute (April 18, 1971). Eugenia Rawls related
personal anecdotes and recited passages from plays associated with
Tallulah Bankhead in this tribute at the Lincoln Center Library.

A19   Tribute to Tallulah (November 15, 1972). Abercrombie &
Fitch, New York, was the site of this elegant tribute, which served as
a prelude to the publication of Brendan Gill's book, *Tallulah* (see
B003.) The event was co-ordinated by Donald Smith, director of
press and public relations at Abercrombie & Fitch, and guests
attending the opening party included Joan Crawford, Joan Fontaine,
Mabel Mercer, Bobby Short, Helen Hayes, Greta Keller, Bricktop,
Marc Connelly, Glenn Anders, Anne Francine, Mildred Dunnock,
Walter Kerr, Dorothy Stickney, Patricia Collinge, Patsy Kelly,
Emlyn Williams and Tennessee Williams. A display of 300 rare
photographs, film and television footage, recordings and the famed
portrait by Augustus John opened to the public on November 16.

A20   Tallulah (June 14, 1983). This stage musical opened at the TOMI
Terrace Theatre, New York City, and was a remarkable tour de
force for actress Helen Gallagher who was on stage constantly for
almost two hours, singing, dancing, playing dramatic scenes and
carrying on a dramatic monologue. She was portraying Tallulah
Bankhead, of course, and critics complimented her for building a
character "so viable and colorfully drawn that Miss Gallagher
disappears and all we see and hear in Tallulah." The play was little
more than a sketchy chronological outline of Miss Bankhead's life,
from her Alabama childhood to her association with *Private Lives*.
Tony Lang wrote it, David Holgrieve directed and choreographed it,
and (apart from Miss Gallagher), Joel Craig, Robert Dale Martin,
Tom Hafner, Eric Johnson, Richard Larson, Patrick Parker, Rick
Porter and Fran Barnes appeared in it. It left the TOMI Terrace
after a few weeks, but re-appeared for a short run at the West Side
Arts Center, opening there on October 30, 1983, with Russell Nype
replacing Robert Dale Martin as Tallulah's father, Speaker of the
House, William Bankhead.

A21   Tallulah: A Memory (September 20, 1985). In the library of
Boston University, Eugenia Rawls staged this hour-long performance

in honor of Tallulah who was her friend for nearly thirty years. With Tallulah's favorite broach pinned to her red evening dress, Miss Rawls reminisced about the late actress and conjured up the scent of cigarettes and jasmine, and the sound of that bourbon-soaked baritone voice that demanded attention. Miss Rawls reprised her one-woman show in Philadelphia at the On Stage Theatre, where she appeared on September 19, 1986. The program was followed by a champagne reception and a screening of Bankhead's 1945 film, *A Royal Scandal*.

A22 Tallulah Tonight (March 21, 1988). Helen Gallagher and Tony Lang again staged a tribute to the late actress, but instead of dramatizing her life as they did in 1983, this time Tallulah returns from the grave and comments on present day theatre, sings, and flings barbs and bon mots. The one-woman show, nearly 100 minutes long, was likened to a night club act and Miss Gallagher was said to do very little other than what female impersonators do. Written by Lang and Bruce Coyle and directed by Wynn Handman, the "play" had a short run at the American Palace Theatre.

A glamour portrait from the early 1930s.

9

Bibliography

This bibliography (which begins with Tallulah's autobiography and the five Bankhead biographies) does not purport to be a definitive listing of every print reference to Tallulah Bankhead. Such a listing would fill an entire book. What it does, however, is offer an annotated list of books and magazine articles that go into some depth about the life and/or career of Bankhead. It is also impossible to be current as her name continues to appear in articles and books.

B O O K S

By and about Tallulah Bankhead

B001 Bankhead, Tallulah. *Tallulah*. New York: Harper & Brothers, 1952.

Tallulah was paid $30,000 to write her memoirs, and the book became one of the biggest sellers of the year, earning her thousands of dollars in royalties. Ghosted by Tallulah's press agent, Richard Maney, the book is written in a flowery style that is fun and easy to read. It's also exciting to read, although not terribly academic. Tallulah obviously thought very highly of herself and refers to herself more than once as "my favorite actress." She (or Maney, rather) writes about theatre with a keen understanding of the business, and makes no effort to hide her dislike of Lillian Hellman, Billy Rose, Michael Myerberg and Elia Kazan, or her admiration for Katharine Hepburn, Estelle Winwood and Tennessee Williams.

B002 Brian, Denis. *Tallulah, Darling*. New York: Macmillan Publishing Co., Inc., 1972.

1972 was a bumper year for books on Tallulah Bankhead. Four were published. Two were straight biographies, and Brain's is the less academic of the two. It touches most of the bases, but isn't very illuminating. He claims to have interviewed scores of celebrities, but draws mostly on the diaries of Arnold Bennett, actress Marian Seldes's *The Bright Years: A Theatre Life* and Tallulah's own autobiography. Interesting but slight.

B003 Gill, Brendan. *Tallulah.* New York: Holt, Rinehart & Winston, 1972.

A stunning collection of beautifully reproduced photographs is the selling point of this large format coffee table book, which is actually two books in one: a brief biography followed by a photo-biography. Gill, the drama critic of *New Yorker* Magazine, has written honestly about Bankhead, making her appear more human than some others have done, but (as reviews pointed out at the time) it is written in a style resembling an "uptown *Photoplay* Magazine report." Gill also contradicts himself occasionally. After writing about her great talent, he says, "nearly the whole range of classical Greek, Elizabethian, Restoration and 18th Century Drama were closed to her," which indicates a rather *limited* talent. The professional chronology in the back is especially helpful.

B004 Israel, Lee. *Miss Tallulah Bankhead.* New York: G.P. Putnam's Sons, 1972.

A well respected, and well researched biography of the actress. Israel's portrait of Tallulah is by turns warming, outrageous and pathetic, and she writes honestly and with a talent for cutting through the layers of legend and getting to the real woman underneath. There are occasional lapses of fact, but these are minor and represent the lack of material available in 1972

B005 Rawls, Eugenia. *Tallulah: A Memory.* Birmingham, Alabama: The Board of Trustees of the University of Alabama, 1979.

Miss Rawls has been a champion of Tallulah Bankhead for fifty years, since she acted opposite her in *The Little Foxes*. She has assembled letters, telegrams, photographs and touching memories from their long friendship and presents a side of Tallulah Bankhead not many people knew: the *human* side. While *Foxes* was on tour, Miss Rawls kept a daily journal, and many excerpts are included.

B006 Tunney, Kiernan. *Tallulah, Darling of the Gods.* New York: E.P. Dutton & Co., Inc., 1972.

Tunney has written his own personal ccount of Tallulah Bankhead, whom he claims to have known intimately for twenty years. He writes about her affairs, her drinking, her relationships with other women and her theatre ups and downs. And most of it is in her own words. There is a memorable scene with Eric Portman telling Tallulah just what he thought of her: "You're wicked – wicked in the fundamental way – for you've ruined the wonderful, marvelous gifts given you by the Gods. And for that I despise you." Tunney's book caused something of a controversy when Tallulah's attorney said the author was *not* a close friend of the late actress, but rather a man who annoyed her by frequently asking for money.

With substantial mentions of Tallulah Bankhead

B007 Adams, Abby. *An Uncommon Scold*. New York: Simon & Schuster, 1989.

Adams has collected nearly 1,000 quotable quotes from famous women about everything from aging to sex. There are seven quotes from Tallulah Bankhead. Among them, "It's the good girls who keep the diaries; the bad girls never have the time," "Cocaine isn't habit-forming. I should know – I've been using it for years," and her oft-quoted quip, "I'm as pure as the driven slush."

B008 Alpert, Hollis. *The Barrymores*. New York: The Dial Press, 1964.

Hollis reprises the oft-told tale of Tallulah imitating Ethel Barrymore's performance in *Déclassé*, and being slapped for her impertinence. According to Alpert, Miss Barrymore also did not appreciate Tallulah's performance in *The Skin of Our Teeth* (1942), terming it "revolting." She is also quoted as saying that she is more of a baseball fan than Tallulah: "She's a latecomer... and she likes only one team... I like all the teams."

B009 Andrews, Bart. *Lucy & Ricky & Fred & Ethel: The Story of "I Love Lucy."* New York: E.P. Dutton & Co., 1976.

A thorough examination of the popular series which includes information on "The Celebrity Next Door," the 1957 sixty-minute episode in which Tallulah guest-starred. Andrews quotes an un-named assistant director on the show as saying that working with Bankhead during the week of rehearsal was a nightmare. She apparently fought with the director and gave everyone a hard time. "Lucy and Desi were sorry they ever hired her," the assistant director says. He also admits that despite the problems, Tallulah behaved professionally when the program was being taped and gave a splendid performance.

B010 Anger, Kenneth. *Hollywood Babylon II*. New York: New American Library, 1984.

Anger has unearthed more sordid tales from Hollywood for his second volume of star gossip. Tallulah escaped the first volume, but in this one Anger refers to her "ambidextrous AC/DC nature," and says that, to her, "the conquest was all." While on the subject, Anger further states that a "few" of Tallulah's female conquests were Sister Aimee Semple McPherson, Patsy Kelly and Hattie McDaniel.

B011 Arce, Hector. *Gary Cooper. An Intimate Biography*. New York: William Morrow and Company, Inc., 1979.

A well researched biography of Cooper which also contains a few pages worth of information on his *The Devil and the Deep* co-star, Tallulah Bankhead. Arce describes Bankhead's efforts to have an affair with Cooper and also gives a brief history of her disappointing film career at Paramount. "When she made her first picture, the bloom of youth was already gone... Her face didn't move; her eyes didn't come alive. She didn't suggest the uncensored thought. Tallulah wasn't born for the movies."

B012 Arden, Eve. *Three Phases of Eve: An Autobiography*. New York: St. Martin's Press, 1985.

Includes an anecdote dating from the early 40s when Arden was starring on Broadway in *Let's Face It*. A man in the front row was wearing a banner across his chest which, during a dimly lit garden scene, lit up to say "Call for Phillip Morris," Tallulah Bankhead's radio sponsor at the time. Tallulah was seated next to the man, disguised in a long black wig, a diamond tiara, black gown and diamond harlequin glasses.

B013 Aylesworth, Thomas G. and John S. Bowman. *The World's Almanac: Who's Who of Film*. New York: World Almanac, 1987.

Includes an accurate but unexciting synopsis of Bankhead's life with a few film and theatre highlights.

B014 Barrow, Kenneth. *Helen Hayes: First Lady of the American Theatre*. Garden City, NY: Doubleday & Co., 1985.

In this biography of one of the most respected actresses of this or any other century, Tallulah makes an occasional appearance, usually to make a wisecrack, i.e., when Helen Hayes asked Tallulah how she could avoid getting pregnant, Tallulah laughed and said, "Just do what you've always done, dahling." She also advised Miss Hayes not to marry Charles MacArthur due to his reputation as a "skirt chaser." One mention has a degree of poignancy: for Hayes and MacArthur's wedding anniversary, Tallulah had planned a surprise, a portrait of their children. But when their daughter died, the painting was left unfinished.

B015 Barrymore, Ethel. *Memories*. New York: Harper and Brothers, 1955.

Miss Barrymore mentions Tallulah Bankhead only once in her

autobiography, as being a kind and gracious hostess when she had dinner at her London home during the 1920s. Tallulah gets in a few words in a testimonial at the end (others are from Elsie Janis, Katharine Hepburn and Spencer Tracy) in which she remembers seeing Ethel Barrymore thirteen times in *Déclassé*. "She was the most vivid personality I had ever seen on the stage," Tallulah writes, and closes with, "I love you, Ethel."

B016 Behlmer, Rudy, ed. *Memo From David O. Selznick*. Hollywood, Ca: Samuel French Trade, 1989.

A handsome reprinted edition of the original 1972 book which offers an interesting look at the movie-world of David O. Selznick, one of the most prolific memo writers in Hollywood history. During the *Gone With the Wind* period, three of the memos reprinted here concern Tallulah Bankhead. Selznick briefly considered Tallulah for the role as Scarlett (oppposite Ronald Colman's Rhett Butler) but the idea was soon abandoned.

B017 Berg, A. Scott. *Goldwyn: A Biography*. New York: Ballantine Books. 1989.

A well-researched biography of movie mogul Samuel Goldwyn. *The Little Foxes* (1941) was a Goldwyn picture and Bette Davis is quoted as saying that, at first, she did not intend to portray Regina Giddens on film the way Tallulah had portrayed her on stage, but after "being forced" to see the stage production, she decided Tallulah's portrayal was the only way it could be done. William Wyler, the film's director, also wanted Davis to interpret the character differently.

B018 Berle, Milton (with Haskel Frankel). *Milton Berle: An Autobiography*. New York: Delacorte Press, 1974.

Describes Tallulah Bankhead's guest appearance on Berle's television show, which was not a happy experience. During rehearsals she continually drank spirits of amonia in water, and was in a foggy state by show-time. "Nevertheless, she performed, the audience laughed (but not at the jokes she had rehearsed) and they thought she was as outrageous as ever."

B019 Berle, Milton. *BS I Love You. 60 Funny Years with the Famous and the Infamous*. New York: McGraw Hill Book Co., 1988.

An entertaining memoir from one of the most entertaining men in show business. Berle and Bankhead crossed paths many times, and he states emphatically that "there's nobody today like Tallulah." He aptly describes her as a "southern belle and a foul-mouthed free soul with little respect for morals and rules of behavior," and as a "flower child in a Coco Chanel suit, uninhibited, basic and bent on self-destruction." He also relates a few of her personal habits, among them a refusal to close the bathroom door, even when in public, supposedly to ward off claustrophobia.

B020 Blum, Daniel. *A Pictorial History of the American Theatre, 1900-1950*. New York: Greenberg, Publisher, 1950.

This pictorial overview of fifty years of Broadway includes several photographs of Tallulah Bankhead in various plays, among them, *Nice People* (1921), *Reflected Glory* (1936), *The Little Foxes* (1939) and *Private Lives* (1948).

B021 Blum, Daniel. *Great Stars of the American Stage: A Pictorial Record*. New York: Greenberg, 1952.

Similar in size and scope, but less academic than Sheridan Morley's 1986 volume of stage stars, this work was meant for theatre fans as opposed to scholars. It contains lovely illustrations but only slight bios of well known American stage stars (those established prior to 1952). Tallulah is, of course, included.

B022 Blum, Daniel. *A New Pictorial History of the Silent Screen* (revised and enlarged by John Kobal). New York: G.P. Putnam's Sons, 1972.

A magnificently illustrated record of American silent film which includes a still of Tallulah and Tom Moore from the motion picture *Thirty a Week* (Goldwyn, 1918).

B023 Blum, Daniel. *A New Pictorial History of the Talkies* (revised and enlarged by John Kobal). New York: G.P. Putnam's Sons, 1973.

The sound era of American filmmaking is treated identically to that of the silent film in Blum's companion edition. Tallulah Bankhead is well represented in photographs from her Paramount films (1931/32) and from her two film outings in the 1940s -- *Lifeboat* (1944) and *A Royal Scandal* (1945).

B024 Bosworth, Patricia. *Montgomery Clift*. New York: Harcourt Brace Jovanovitch, 1978.

Clift was in the cast of *The Skin of Our Teet*h (1942) and Bosworth describes the tension Bankhead caused backstage. According to Bosworth, Clift kept quiet during Tallulah's many tantrums and is remembered by those involved with the production as a dedicated actor whom Tallulah respected.

B025 Brown, Jared. *The Fabulous Lunts: A Biography of Alfred Lunt and Lynn Fontanne*. New York: Atheneum, 1986.

Brown describes a party at Tallulah's suite at the Elysee to which the Lunts were invited. Tallulah suggested the guests try some marijuana, and most did, but Miss Fontanne declined, explaining that she had a matinee the next day. She chastised Tallulah for her behavior and reminded her that she, too, had a matinee the following afternoon, in a play which the Lunts owned a third each. To prove to Miss Fontanne that partying into the night did not effect her, Tallulah visited the respected actress backstage the next day, bragging about how well she looked after such a wild night. But Tallulah had apparently forgotten to look in the mirror and Miss Fontanne had her do so. Tallulah took one look, screamed out "Oh, my God!" and left.

B026 Brown, John Mason. *Two on the Aisle: Ten Years of the American Theatre in Performance.* New York: W.W. Norton & Co., 1938.

In this collection of essays about plays and performers of the New York stage, Brown presents an intelligent critique of Tallulah's performances in a chapter entitled "Tallulah the Magnificent." Brown praises her as a "performer of uncommon potentialities," but criticizes her lack of discipline. This contrast makes her "wasteful of her gifts," and causes her to be "unsteady in her playing" and "indiscriminate in her use of emphasis."

B027 Buxton, Frank and Bill Owen. *The Big Broadcast.* New York: The Viking Press, 1966.

One of the first books to document the history of radio, this work includes detailed listings of hundreds of radio programs, including NBC's *The Big Show* (1950-52). Buxton offers a sampling of Tallulah's wit and also mentions her as a popular guest on the *Fred Allen Show.*

B028 Callow, Simon. *Charles Laughton: A Difficult Actor.* London: Methuen London Ltd., 1987.

Simon writes that Tallulah Bankhead "loathed" Laughton and did little to hide her feelings while they were filming *The Devil and the Deep* (Paramount, 1932). He does compliment her performance in the film which, although being dismissed by critics (and Tallulah herself) at the time, "now seems an extraordinary and original portrait of an unfulfilled and oppressed woman, bored and unhappy, oddly attached to a paranoically jealous husband."

B029 Carey, Gary. *Cukor & Co., The Films of George Cukor and his Collaborations.* New York: The Museum of Modern Art, 1971.

A film by film look at Cukor's directorial career. Of Tallulah Bankhead, the star of his first feature (*Tarnished Lady*, 1931), Carey writes "the lens did not reveal her delicate beauty. She had a curiously ironic way of playing that was perhaps too *recherche* for the average film audience. She was a curiosity, a *monstre sacre*, too rich for most people's blood."

B030 Carey, Gary. *Anita Loos: A Biography*. New York: Alfred A.
     Knopf, 1988.

This biography of Miss Loos contains several mentions of Tallulah
Bankhead, the most substantial of which details their first meeting in 1918
at the Algonquin Hotel.

B031 Castle, Charles. *Noël*. New York: Doubleday & Co., Inc., 1973.

Includes the story of Tallulah replacing Margaret Bannerman in
Noël Coward's *Fallen Angels* (London, 1924) and learning her lines in
four days. Castle also mentions Tallulah's success in the late 1940s as
Amanda in *Private Lives*.

B032 Clarke, Gerald. *Capote: A Biography*. New York: Simon and
     Schuster, 1988.

A richly detailed biography of one of this century's most well-known
writers. Capote enjoyed a warm friendship with Tallulah Bankhead and, as
Clarke writes, "when it came to the grand flourish... even Truman had to
give way to Tallulah." Clarke goes on to relate an amusing story of
Tallulah showing up for swimming party wearing nothing but a string of
pearls because "I wanted to prove that I was a natural ash blonde."

B033 Cohen, Daniel and Susan. *Encyclopedia of Movie Stars*. New York:
     Gallery Books, 1985.

The title tells all. An ambitious reference volume which includes
hundreds of film performers, but the disappointingly brief biographical
sketches can do little more than scratch the surface. Bankhead is no
exception and gets even less copy than most.

B034 Cole, Lesley. *The Life of Noël Coward*. London: Jonathan Cape,
     Ltd., 1976.

Relates Tallulah's last-minute assignment to star in Coward's *Fallen
Angels* (London, 1924), quickly becoming friends with Coward and his
associates. She apparently confided to a female friend of Coward's that
rumors of her being a lesbian bothered her because she "always thought
about a man when playing with herself." In the 1940s, Tallulah again
crossed paths with Coward when she was playing Amanda Prynne in a
Chicago production of *Private Lives*. He thought she was "extraordinarily
good... a bit course in texture but her personality formidable," that she
"played some of it quite beautifully and all of it effectively." He wasn't as
impressed with Tallulah's leading man, Donald Cook, but he gave Tallulah
permission to bring the play to New York.

B035 Cooper, Gladys. *Gladys Cooper*. London: Hutchinson & Co.,

Publishers, 1931.

Miss Cooper mentions Tallulah occasionally, but not in any depth. She refers to Tallulah as taking over the lead in Michael Arlen's *The Green Hat* (London, 1925), after she left the play before rehearsals started, and makes the questionable remark that Tallulah is not a [theatre] box office draw.

B036 Cotten, Joseph. *Joseph Cotten, An Autobiography: Vanity Will Get You Somewhere*. New York: Avon Books, 1987.

In his memoirs, Cotten includes a couple of anecdotal references to Tallulah Bankhead. While he was appearing in the Broadway play *The Philadelphia Story* (1939), Tallulah cornered him at a bar and gushed with praise then, suddenly, her manner changed and she told him what he could do with himself! Cotten also tells of visiting the set of Hitchcock's 1944 motion picture, *Lifeboat*, and learning of Tallulah's refusal to wear underwear. He also mentions Tallulah's tendency to blink her eyes often, and insists it was not a flirtation device, just a nervous tic.

B037 Coward, Noël. *Noël Coward*. London: Methuen London Ltd., 1986.

A three-part autobiography (comprised of the previously published *Present Indicative* and *Future Indefinite*, and Coward's unfinished *Past Conditional*) in which he compliments Bankhead on her ability (and willingness) to learn her role in *Fallen Angels* (London, 1924) in four days. "She came flying into the theatre with a vitality a little short of fantastic," Coward writes. "She tore off her hat, flipped her furs into a corner and embarked on the first act. On the first night she gave a brilliant and completely assured performance. It was a tour de force of vitality, magnetism and spontaneous combustion."

B038 Cross, Robin. *2,000 Movies: The 1940s*. New York: Arlington House, 1985.

A 256-page pictorial reference book of movies (US and foreign) made during the 1940s. Tallulah is featured in two photographs: *Lifeboat* (1944) and *A Royal Scandal* (1945)

B039 Da, Lottie and Jan Alexander. *Bad Girls of the Silver Screen*. New York: Carroll and Graf Publishers, Inc., 1989.

In this exploration of female wickedness on the screen, there is a still reproduction from *The Cheat* (*Paramount*, 1931) in which Irving Pichel is branding Tallulah with his "I Possess" symbol. The caption criticizes her acting in this particular film, claiming it was "so bad that it cost her the role of Sadie in *Rain*."

B040 Davis, Bette with Whitney Stine. *Mother Goddam*. New York: Hawthorne Books, Inc., 1974.

Davis writes that the similarity of her film performance in *The Little Foxes* (Goldwyn, 1942) to Bankhead's stage performance could not have been helped because Bankhead interpreted the role as it had been written. She also denies the accusation that she was imitating Bankhead in the 1950 film *All About Eve*, and explains that the low, smoky voice she used in the film (which *did* sound like Bankhead's) was due to a throat infection.

B041 Dean, Basil. *Seven Ages; An Autobiography 1888-1927*. London: Hutchinson & Co., 1970.

One of the most most respected names in British theatre, Dean directed Tallulah in *Scotch Mist* and *They Knew What They Wanted* (both 1926), the latter containing one of Tallulah's best performances. Dean makes some very interesting comments about the young, headstrong actress he knew. He compares the squeals of delight from fans at her every performance to a sort of "early Beatlemania," but admits it was a "handicap to critical evaluation of her talent. This she had in plenty, although often wasted through lack of dedication." He is especially complimentary of her performance and professionalism during the run of *They Knew What They Wanted*. "Tallulah set to work enthusiastically, putting herself entirely in my hands and accepting without protest my careful discipline at rehearsals, a process she had never before encountered." It was Dean who hired Tallulah to star in the London production of *Rain*, only to be overruled by the play's author, Somerset Maugham, who fired Tallulah. Dean still defends his choice. "Although comparatively inexperienced for such a big emotional part, she would have been an undoubted box office attraction." Bankhead was replaced with Olga Lindo, an actress, says Dean, "of great competence, but no sex appeal."

B042 Derwent, Clarence. *The Derwent Story: My First Fifty Years in the Theatre in England and America*. New York: Henry Shuman, 1953.

Derwent was a much respected man in the theatre, even becoming president of the Actors' Equity Association. He had a character role in Tallulah's 1947 stage failure, *The Eagle Has Two Heads*, and he reports in his autobiography that Tallulah had no faith in the play from the very beginning "but with her customary fortitude she struggled on..."

B043 Deschner, Donald. *The Films of Cary Grant*. Secaucus, NJ: Citadel Press, 1973.

The entire film output of Cary Grant is explored in the usual Citadel style. His fourth film was *The Devil and the Deep* (Paramount, 1932), starring Tallulah Bankhead. Her performance is not discussed, but she does appear in several still reproductions.

B044 Dickens, Homer. *The Films of Gary Cooper*. Secaucus, NJ: Citadel Press, 1970.

One of the Citadel *Films of...* series. Gary Cooper was the male lead in Bankhead's 1932 film, *The Devil and the Deep*, and although she does not figure prominently in Dickens' discussion of the film, there are several still reproductions in which she appears.

B045 Drew, William M. *Speaking of Silents*. Vestal, NY: The Vestal Press, Ltd., 1989

Drew has interviewed ten leading ladies of the silent screen, among them Lois Wilson (1896-1988) who entered motion pictures via a 1915 beauty contest in Alabama, the state of her birth. In the interview, Miss Wilson states that one of the contest judges was Senator William Bankhead, Tallulah's father. Tallulah, who was only thirteen at the time, also remembered the contest and often referred to Lois Wilson as "my father's godchild."

B046 Drutman, Irving. *Good Company*. Boston: Little, Brown & Company, 1976.

Drutman attempted to write an article about Tallulah in the mid 40s for *Town and Country*, but was unable to complete it. "In part the fault was the reticence of the language allowable in the journalism of the day," Drutman explains, but the easing of journalism's standards makes it printable today. So he revised it, added some additional commentary, and inserted it into his book, titling the piece "Tallulah Means Terrible." Drutman does not concern himself with Tallulah's professional credits but fully develops her personality, and adds some interesting analysis.

B047 Dunning, John. *Tune in Yesterday*. Englewood Cliffs, NJ: Prentice Hall, Inc., 1976,

Includes information on NBC's *The Big Show* (1950-52), radio's "last major gasp in the face of growing TV encroachment." Tallulah Bankhead was the program's mistress of ceremonies.

B048 Eames, John Douglas. *The MGM Story*. New York: Crown Publishers, Inc., 1979.

Tallulah Bankhead made two films for the mighty Metro-Goldwyn-Mayer: *Faithless* (1932) and *Main Street to Broadway* (1953). She merely guested in the latter, but she co-starred with Robert Montgomery in the former. Regarding *Faithless*, Eames states that the film camera "unaccountably dimmed her lustre and crowd magnetism."

B049 Eames, John Douglas. *The Paramount Story*. New York: Crown

Publishers, Inc., 1985.

Contains brief synopses of Tallulah's five Paramount films. In describing her first for the studio (*Tarnished Lady*, 1931), Eames comments on the high hopes Paramount had for the actress, but adds that her "unique personality didn't come through the camera. She was just an efficient actress."

B050 Edwards, Anne. *A Remarkable Woman; A Biography of Katharine Hepburn*. New York: William Morrow & Co., Inc., 1985.

According to Edwards, Katharine Hepburn was not fond of Tallulah Bankhead, whom she considered "rude and foul-mouthed." Interestingly, Edwards also claims that Zoë Akins modelled the heroine of her story *Morning Glory* after Tallulah.

B051 Eisner, Joel. *The Official Batman Batbook*. Chicago: Contemporary Books, Inc., 1986.

A complete guide to every episode of the popular 1960s television series. Tallulah appeared in two episodes as the venomous "Black Widow," a cunning bank robber, and Robert Mintz, the program's chief writer is quoted as saying that he was asked to write those episodes as a vehicle for Tallulah Bankhead, who had expressed an interest in being on the show.

B052 Ellrod, J.G. *Hollywood Greats of the Golden Years: The late Stars of the 1920s Through the 1950s*. Jefferson, NC: McFarland & Co., Inc., 1990.

Includes an awkwardly written entry on Tallulah Bankhead which has several inaccuracies: only her *first* film role can be classified as a "bit," not her first three; her early appearances on Broadway in the late teens and early 20s were not *all* in minor roles (she had the lead in two plays); and she was in London for *eight* years (1923-1931) not ten. The brief sketches of the other eighty Hollywood stars who died before 1987 are similarly written.

B053 Engstead, John. *Star Shots: 50 Years of Pictures and Stories by one of Hollywood's Greatest Photographers*. New York: E.P. Dutton, 1978.

Engstead was assigned to photograph "love stills" of Bankhead and Gary Cooper as publicity for *The Devil and the Deep* (Paramount, 1932), and he says here that Tallulah would show up two hours early to be made up to look especially beautiful for the stills. "Everyone knew that her intention for coming to Hollywood was to lay Gary Cooper." Engstead says that every day Cooper would get to the set too late for the photo session. "I had a sneaking suspicion Coop was trying to tell Tallulah that she wasn't quite the sex goddess she thought she was."

B054 Fairbanks, Douglas Jr. *The Salad Days*. New York: Doubleday & Co., 1988.

In his autobiography, Fairbanks presents a slightly different version of the John Barrymore/Tallulah Bankhead relationship of 1920. According to Tallulah, Barrymore tried unsuccessful to seduce her, but according to Fairbanks, it was the other way around. Fairbanks says it was Barrymore who refused, fearing the trouble such an act might cause, Tallulah being merely a teenager. Fairbanks also mentions Tallulah in connection to a film he was making in 1932 with Lilyan Tashman. Miss Tashman had a reputation for having affairs but, according to Fairbanks, the actress admitted to him at the time that she "was really more interested in her friend Tallulah Bankhead than in anyone else."

B055 Fein, Irving. *Jack Benny: An Intimate Biography*. New York: G.P. Putnam's Sons, 1976.

Describes Tallulah's guest appearance on Benny's show in 1958: she looked old in the rehearsals, unlike the swinging woman the script called for, and she questioned every line and joke. Because of her difficult attitude, Benny was on the verge of replacing her, but when she was made up for the actual taping, she looked wonderful and acted professionally.

B056 Finler, Joel W. *The Movie Directors Story*. New York: Crescent Books, 1985.

An interesting encyclopedic reference guide to American film directors about whom Finley has written detailed and informative essays. Tallulah is mentioned in the entry on George Cukor, the director of her first talking picture, *Tarnished Lady*, 1931. Paramount hoped Cukor could turn the flamboyant actress into a major film star, but something went wrong. Cukor is at a loss to explain what that something was, merely being quoted as saying that her "particular quality of excitement never quite worked on the screen."

B057 Friedman, Drew and Josh Allan Friedman. *Warts and All*. New York: Penguin Books USA Inc., 1990.

In a comic strip fashion, the Friedmans have poked fun at a wide range of celebrities in this sometimes funny, sometimes tasteless collection of rumors and scandals. Rondo Hatton and Tor Johnson seem to be favorite targets, but Tallulah Bankhead also creeps in. As drawn by the Friedman's witty but cruel pen, she is shown in bed with Hattie McDaniel!

B058 Frischauer, Willi. *Behind the Scenes of Otto Preminger*. New York: William Morrow & Co., 1974.

In 1938, Preminger's Jewish parents left Vienna, their homeland, barely escaping the Nazis. They came to the United States but quota laws would not permit them to stay. They were allowed to remain only after Preminger took the matter to Tallulah and asked if her father, then Speaker of the House, could do something to help. He did. Frischauer also describes a day on the set of *A Royal Scandal* (20th Century-Fox, 1945) in which Tallulah starred and Preminger directed. Frank Lloyd Wright came to watch the filming one afternoon (his granddaughter, Anne Baxter, was in the cast) but he grew bored and left. Apparently it was a day when Tallulah had to film a particular scene 27 times.

B059 Goldstein, Malcolm. *George S. Kaufman.* New York: Oxford
      University Press, 1979.

According to Goldstein, Kaufman was offered the role of the department store owner in *Tarnished Lady* (Paramount, 1931), the film which launched Tallulah's unsuccessful American film career. Osgood Perkins took the role and gave a "suave, professional performance."

B060 Greene, Bert. *The Grains Cookbook.* New York: Workman
      Publishing Co., 1988.

Of all the places one would expect to find a reference to Tallulah Bankhead, a cookbook would surely be the least likely. And yet here she is. Greene opens one chapter with an anecdote dating from a performance of *The Little Foxes* in Richmond, Virginia. A young man at the time, Greene went backstage after the show to meet the star, and he describes witnessing a "performance" of a different kind. He even ties it in nicely with the subject of his chapter – grits and hominy.

B061 Griffin, Merv and Peter Barsocchini. *Merv.* New York: Simon &
      Schuster, 1980.

Griffin was a friend of Tallulah Bankhead's and he mentions her several times in his autobiography. He first met her in the early 50s when he was employed by NBC radio and she was the star of their most successful program, *The Big Show.* He remembers one day, before Tallulah arrived for rehearsals, several people on the set were discussing the rumor that Tallulah was a "pot fiend." She walked onto the set and everyone hushed, hoping she hadn't heard them talking, but she walked over and casually remarked, "Has anyone got a reefer?"

B062 Griffith, Richard. *The Talkies: Articles and Illustrations From a
      Great Fan Magazine, 1928-1940.* New York: Dover Publications,
      Inc., 1971.

A nostalgic look at *Photoplay* Magazine. Several of its most representative articles from 1928-40 are reprinted, and many of them mention Tallulah Bankhead, notably Kirtley Baskette's 1937 feature on *Gone With the Wind*.

B063 Haley, Michael. *The Alfred Hitchcock Album*. Englewood Cliffs, NJ: Prentice Hall, Inc., 1981.

Haley's study of Hitchcock and his films includes yet another version of the amusing story of Bankhead's refusal to wear underwear while filming *Lifeboat*.

B064 Halliwell, Leslie. *The Filmgoers Companion*. New York: Charles Scribner's Sons, 1965 (updated regularly)

A helpful listing of hundreds of film players, directors, etc. with thumbnail biographical sketches followed by a listing of notable films. Of Tallulah Bankhead, Halliwell says she titillated London and Broadway during the 20s [actually, she didn't "titillate" Broadway until the 30s and 40s] but that films could never contain her and she later "tended to fritter away her considerable talents by living too dangerously."

B065 Harris, Radie. *Radie's World*. London: W.H. Allen, 1975.

Harris, a Hollywood columnist for decades, has intimately known practically everyone who ever stepped foot in Hollywood. She counted Tallulah Bankhead among her closest friends, and has devoted an entire chapter to the flamboyant actress. With a keen eye for detail, she wonderfully describes an overnight stay with Tallulah at her home in Bedford Village, New York.

B066 Harris, Robert A. and Michael S. Lasky. *The Films of Alfred Hitchcock*. Secaucus, NJ: Citadel Press, 1979.

Part of Citadel's popular *Films of...* series, Harris and Lasky have put together an interesting account of Hitchcock's films (beginning with *The Man Who Knew Too Much*, 1934).Tallulah's most acclaimed film performance was in his 1944 motion picture, *Lifeboat*. It was her first film in twelve years, and Hitchcock is quoted as saying that she was "the most oblique, incongruous bit of casting I could think of."

B067 Haver, Ronald. *David O. Selznick's Hollywood*. New York: Knopf, 1980.

In this intimate look at Selznick and his films, Tallulah Bankhead is mentioned being an early contender for the role of Scarlet O'Hara in *Gone With the Wind*. She was the first "established actress" to be considered, and was tested on December 22, 1936. The test was photographic only, Selznick wanting to be sure the 34-year-old actress could portray the 16-year-old Scarlet. The results were unsatisfactory. Haver also writes that while

Bankhead was appearing on Broadway in *Dark Victory* (1934) Selznick tried to persuade Greta Garbo to let him buy the screenrights as a vehicle for her. She wanted to do *Anna Karenina* instead.

B068 Higham, Charles. *Kate: The Life of Katharine Hepburn*. New York: W.W. Norton & Co., 1975.

According to Higham, one of the most prolific star biographers, Tony Richardson wanted Katharine Hepburn for the role of Flora Goforth in *The Milk Train Doesn't Stop Here Anymore*, the 1964 Broadway play he directed. "I got Tallulah Bankhead instead, unfortunately," Richardson says.

B069 Higham, Charles. *Charles Laughton: An Intimate Biography*. Garden City, N.Y.: Doubleday & Co., Inc., 1976.

Laughton and Bankhead worked together only once (*The Devil and the Deep*, Paramount, 1932) and the experience was apparently not a happy one. Bankhead had publicly called Laughton a "big fat slob" at a New York party some weeks before the filming began.

B070 Higham, Charles. *Bette: The Life of Bette Davis*. New York: MacMillan Publishing Co., 1981.

Most film historians note that Davis's interpretation of Regina Giddens in the film *The Little Foxes* (1941) bore a striking similarity to Tallulah's performance in the 1939 stage production. And, using quotes from Davis to back them up, they further claim that the similarity was intended. Higham's opinion, surprisingly, differs slightly. He writes that "instead of Tallulah's sexuality, her full-blown thwarted voluptuousness, Bette decided to portray a woman whose sexuality had been destroyed by competition with men."

B071 Higham, Charles. *Lucy: The Real Life of Lucille Ball*. New York: St. Martin's Press, 1986.

Lucy and Tallulah weren't the best of friends, and Higham describes the tension that resulted when Bankhead guested on *The Lucy and Desi Comedy Hour* [sic] in 1957. Bette Davis was originally set to portray "The Celebrity Next Door," but a broken back forced her to cancel. Tallulah was called in as a replacement and, according to Higham, during rehearsals "Tallulah was drunk from morning til night, fought with the director, Jerry Thorpe, was unpunctual and insulted Lucy." Lucy and Desi were apparently afraid that she would blow her lines and embarrass the entire company, but to everyone's surprise and relief, she was thoroughly professional on the night of the actual taping. Higham almost defends Bankhead's behavior by explaining that she was suffering from pneumonia at the time.

B072 Higham, Charles. *Brando: The Unauthorized Biography*. New York: New American Library, 1987.

Tallulah and Brando worked together briefly, in the 1947 pre-Broadway production of Jean Cocteau's *The Eagle Has Two Heads*. Higham describes their tense relationship, leading to his dismissal two weeks into rehearsals.

B073 Higham, Charles and Roy Moseley. *Cary Grant: The Lonely Heart*. Orlando, Florida: Harcourt Brace Jovanovich, Publishers, 1989.

Grant worked with Bankhead only once (*The Devil and the Deep*, Paramount, 1932) and, according to Higham, he disliked both her and her drinking. She allegedly made several passes at Grant and, annoyed by his lack of interest, "set off a train of gossip about his lack of virility." It's easy to understand why Grant would dislike Bankhead because, as Higham states, she continually misbehaved while the film was in production, deliberately flubbing her lines, arguing with the director, and laughing at her dialogue.

B074 Hirschhorn, Joel. *Rating the Movie Stars for Home Video, TV, Cable*. New York: Beekman House, 1983.

This book (by the editors of *Consumer Guide*) cannot be taken seriously due to its unscholarly rating system. Stars are rated on a 1 to 4 scale according to the quality of their performances, but to give Eddie Murphy a perfect score of 4 while Katharine Hepburn must settle for a 3.14 will raise many an eyebrow. With a rating of 2.27 (slightly above Catherine Deneuve but below Yvonne DeCarlo), Tallulah's career is briefly but accurately detailed. Too many credits are omitted, but Hirschhorn does truthfully state that she "seemed more adept at generating publicity than movie parts," and that *Die! Die! My Darling!* was a "sad farewell to a vivid and original personality."

B075 Jackson, Carlton. *Hattie: The Life of Hattie McDaniel*. Lanham, Maryland: Madison Books, 1990.

Jackson attacks the rumor that Tallulah and McDaniel were lesbian lovers, insisting there is no evidence to support the claim. He explains that it probably stems from a remark Tallulah once made to the effect that Hattie McDaniel was her best friend.

B076 Kaminsky, Stuart. *Coop: The Life and Legend of Gary Cooper*. New York: St. Martin's Press, 1980.

In this biography of Gary Cooper, Tallulah is mentioned as being his leading lady in the 1931 Paramount film, *The Devil and the Deep*. They first met each other a few months prior to the filming on a blind date arranged by Walter Wanger. Their engagement was announced the following day, but Tallulah insisted the papers had it wrong, that she was engaged to *Jackie* Cooper, not Gary Cooper!

B077 Karney, Robyn, editor. *The Movie Stars Story.* New York: Crescent Books, 1984.

Still another encyclopedic reference volume of film players. To this one various film critics have contributed thoughtful essays on the performers; however Robin Cross fails to achieve any real depth in his brief (albeit informative) entry on Tallulah Bankhead. He mistakenly refers to her father as a "businessman" and includes *A Woman's Law* in the list of Bankhead films. (*A Woman's Law* does not exist, but the error often creeps into Bankhead filmographies.)

B078 Kass, Judith. *The Films of Montgomery Clift.* Secaucus, NJ: Citadel Press, 1979.

In this detailed account of Clift's work in the cinema, Kass also includes a short biography of the actor. Before he entered films, Clift was in the cast of the successful 1942 Broadway play, *The Skin of Our Teeth*, which starred Tallulah Bankhead. Clift is quoted as saying that Tallulah's temper caused "everyone in the show not to show up until curtain time. The play was anti-climatic to her tantrums backstage."

B079 Katz, Ephraim. *The Film Encyclopedia.* New York: The Putnam Publishing Group, 1979.

An indispensable film reference book in which Tallulah isn't allotted much space, but Katz has condensed the highlights of her life rather well. The only error is a reference to a 1928 British film (*A Woman's law*) which he claims she made. She didn't. A complete filmography is included.

B080 Kazan, Elia. *A Life.* New York: Alfred A. Knopf, 1988.

A much touted autobiography of a respected director. Early in his career, Kazan directed Tallulah Bankhead in *The Skin of Our Teeth*, on Broadway in 1942. Their battles have been well documented here, and Kazan, at one point, says, "In my life I have hated only two people, and Tallulah Bankhead was one of them." He certainly presents a good case for his feelings, presenting Bankhead as a demanding, vulgar, trouble-causing woman. He usually refers to her as "the bitch" but does compliment her performance and admits that she "made a director out of me."

B081 Kennedy, Harold J. *No Pickle, No Performance: An Irreverent Theatrical Excursion, from Tallulah to Travolta...*New York: Doubleday & Company, Inc., 1977.

A very funny book of anecdotes culled from Kennedy's many years as a director and "second man" in the theatre. He worked with Bankhead several times in summer stock and his memories of her are both amusing and poignant. He writes about her honestly and seems to have understood her more than most writers, but does admit that "no one has ever captured Tallulah on paper and no one ever will." He repeats some very funny remarks he was privy to, but beneath the wisecracking exterior, Tallulah was very human, and Kennedy remembers taking her home every night after a performance and sitting by her bed until she was asleep. "'Hold my hand,' she would say. And I would take it and hold it firmly until gradually it would begin to slip out of my grasp."

B082 Keylin, Arleen and Suri Fleischer, editors. *Hollywood Album: Lives and Deaths of Hollywood Stars from the Pages of the New York Times*. New York: Arno Press, 1979.

An alphabetical re-printing of obituaries of film stars, from Bud Abbott to Monty Woolley, lifted from the pages of the *New York Times*. Tallulah Bankhead (who died on December 12, 1968) is here, and a filmography is included.

B083 Kobal, John. *People Will Talk*. New York: Alfred A. Knopf, 1985.

Is comprised of 43 interviews, mostly of former Hollywood stars, including Tallulah Bankhead. In Kobal's candid, 21-page interview, he gets her to open up about such things as the feud between she and Bette Davis ("oh, that was just a gag"), the story that she once ordered Adolph Zukor off the set of one of her early paramount films ("absolutely untrue. I never ordered anyone off the set. It would have been discourteous to this older man who was head of this company...") and a possible reason for her failure to become a major motion picture star ("my whole point was my vitality which, if I showed it in pictures, looked as though I had St. Vitis dance. In calming myself down, I lost a certain naturalness, part of my own personality which I had on the stage..."). Throughout the interview, Tallulah talks about a great many things, all at the same time. As she admits at one point, "I'm the queen of non-sequiters."

B084 Kobler, John. *Damned in Paradise: The Life of John Barrymore*. New York: Atheneum, 1977.

Contains another rendition of Barrymore's failed attempt to seduce Tallulah Bankhead in 1919. He is quoted as saying that he spent a "good part of a season trying to impress Tallulah," and characterizes their relationship "loathsomely platonic."

B085 Kotsilibas-Davis, James. *The Barrymores: The Royal Family in Hollywood*. New York: Crown Publishers, Inc., 1981.

Tallulah is said to have been on-hand to watch the opening scene of *Rasputin and the Empress* (Metro-Goldwyn-Mayer, 1932) being filmed. The motion picture was the only film in which all three Barrymores -- Lionel, John and Ethel -- appeared together.

B086 LaGuardia, Robert. *Monty: A Biography of Montgomery Clift.* New York: Arbor House, 1977.

LaGuardia reports that during the run of *The Skin of Our Teeth*, Clift would often visit Tallulah at home, but he makes it clear that their relationship was not sexual. Tallulah thought Clift was a "nice innocuous boy."

B087 Lambert, Gavin. *On Cukor.* New York: G.P. Putnam's Sons, 1972.

A protracted interview with Cukor in which he comments that Tallulah Bankhead (the star of his first film, *Tarnished Lady*, 1931) was a "most exciting brilliant actress" and in real life a "highly entertaining, warmhearted, outrageous and charming creature," but that her quality of excitement never worked on the screen. He says that when they worked together in 1931, she saw herself as another Greta Garbo, with high cheekbones and slightly tubercular hollow cheeks.

B088 Lamparski, Richard. *Whatever Became Of... Eighth Series.* New York: Crown Publishers, Inc., 1982.

Includes a career summary of film comedienne Patsy Kelly, who was once thought to be bad luck because so many of her friends died young (Thelma Todd, Lyda Roberti, Jean Harlow, etc.), but Tallulah Bankhead, who was also a good friend of Patsy's defends her. "She brings nothing but good luck with her," Bankhead is quoted as saying. "I consider myself lucky just to know her." Lamparski says that Bankhead made that remark in 1969, but that is impossible. She died in 1968.

B089 Lanchester, Elsa. *Elsa Lanchester Herself.* New York: St. Martin's Press, 1983.

Long the wife of actor Charles Laughton, Lanchester confesses that she ought not to dislike Tallulah "after what she did for me... generously risking her reputation by sending me to an abortion doctor" in 1920s London, but she did resent Bankhead's rudeness to her husband. She tells of a painful incident (for Laughton) at a New York party where Tallulah pointed to the actor and said, in a loud voice, "look how ugly he is!" And when Laughton died, Tallulah's only comment was, "he had such dirty nails."

B090 Lasky, Jesse L. with Don Weldon. *I Blow My Own Horn.* Garden City, N.Y.: Doubleday & Co., Inc., 1957.

Published the year before his death, Lasky here reveals his triumphs and defeats at Paramount. He recalls one afternoon when his office door slowly opened and a lady's slipper landed in his lap, followed by Tallulah Bankhead. She had just begun filming *My Sin* (1931) and she threw her arms around Lasky and gushed about her leading man (Fredric March.)

B091 Lawton, Richard. *A World of Movies.* New York: Dell Publishing Co., 1976.

374 pages of lovely still reproductions of Hollywood stars and their films, from *The Kiss* (1896) to *Paper Moon* (1973). Includes a stunning, full-page portrait of Tallulah Bankhead. The accompanying paragraph gives a thumbnail personality sketch of the star whose "style, and wisecracks larded with irreligious wit and delivered in her famous husky drawl, blew her reputation out of all proportion."

B092 Leff, Leonard J. *Hitchcock and Selznick.* New York: Weidenfeld and Nicolson, 1987

An academic look at the alliance of these two creative and powerful men. *Lifeboat* (directed by Alfred Hitchcock) was not a Selznick film but it wanders into the discussion nonetheless. Bankhead apparently attempted to do a particular scene her way, but Hitchcock told her gently and politely that only his way would do.   From that point on, she followed his directions. According to Leff, Hitchcock also instructed Ben Hecht to model Alicia Huberman's speech (a character in the 1946 film, *Notorious*, which *was* a Selznick production) after Tallulah Bankhead's -- deadpan, brash and sexy.

B093 Lloyd, Ann and Graham Fuller, editors. *The Illustrated Who's Who of the Cinema.* New York: Portland House. 1983.

An ambitious reference volume complete with photographs (in color and b/w) of hundreds of film personalities. Includes brief summaries of their lives and careers as well as notable film performances. Tallulah Bankhead is allotted little space, but the facts are correct.

B094 Loos, Anita. *Fate Keeps on Happening.* New York: Dodd, Mead & Co., 1984

Published after Miss Loos' death (in 1981), Ray Pierre Cosini has assembled a collection of her writings, including the article "Tallulah," which first appeared in the February 1969 edition of *Playbill*.

B095 McClelland, Doug. *StarSpeak: Hollywood on Everything.* Boston: Faber & Faber, 1987.

Includes a quote from Hume Cronyn regarding Tallulah's lack of modesty while filming Alfred Hitchcock's *Lifeboat* (Fox, 1944). She wore no underwear, and had to lift her skirt whenever climbing into the studio-built boat. "It got boring to the cast and crew," says Cronyn, "but visitors to the set were shocked."

B096 McClelland, Doug. *Hollywood Talks Turkey: The Screen's Greatest Flops*. Boston: Faber & Faber, 1987.

A collection of quotes from actors, directors, etc., regarding their greatest movie disappointments. Includes a quote from Otto Preminger about Tallulah and *A Royal Scandal* (20th Century-Fox, 1945), which wasn't a failure, but wasn't as successful as it could have been.

B097 McDowall, Roddy. *Double Exposure*. New York: Delacorte Press, 1966.

In McDowall's tribute to show business, celebrities write about other celebrities. And who else to write about Estelle Winwood than Tallulah Bankhead. "Throughout my professional life Estelle is the one I've turned to when shattered by the necessity of making a decision," Tallulah writes. "She has never failed me... A world with more Winwoods would be a more desirable sphere on which to fret and fume." [Indeed, Winwood was perhaps Tallulah's closest friend. Their friendship -- sometimes strained, sometimes lesbian (?) -- lasted fifty years, from 1918 until Tallulah's death in 1968.]

B098 McNamarra, Brooks. *The Shuberts of Broadway*. New York: Oxford University Press, 1990.

Tallulah Bankhead appeared in several shows for the Shubert brothers, Lee and J.J., and McNamarra repeats an apocryphal joke in which Tallulah introduces them to a friend of hers: "Dahling," she says, "I want you to meet the Shubert brothers, S.H. and I.T."

B099 MacPherson, Don and Louise Brody. *Leading Ladies*. New York: Crescent Books, 1989.

A large format, handsomely produced celebration in words and pictures of 118 leading ladies of cinema. Under one of Tallulah Bankhead's more flattering portraits, dating from her Paramount period, a brief but well-written profile touches on her life and personality but doesn't get below the surface. The common error of referring to a 1928 British film, *A Woman's law*, creeps in here as well.

B100 Marx, Arthur. *Goldwyn: A Biography of the Man Behind the Myth*. New York: W.W. Norton & Co., 1976.

Playwright and biographer Marx here examines the life of film mogul and producer Goldwyn. *Thirty a Week*, a 1918 Goldwyn film, was one of Tallulah's earliest, and Marx refers to both the film and Bankhead, but he errs in saying it was filmed in Culver City. It was actually filmed in New York City. Tallulah didn't make her first film in California until 1932. Tallulah also figures prominently in the chapter dealing with the 1941 film adaptation of Lillian Hellman's play, *The Little Foxes*. It has often been written that Bette Davis's film impersonation of Regina Giddens was based on Tallulah Bankhead's stage impersonation. Davis has admitted the fact often, but she has also said that it caused friction between she and director William Wyler, who wanted a different interpretation. In this biography of Goldwyn (who produced the film), Marx quotes Wyler as saying that he encouraged Davis to imitate Bankhead's portrayal because Regina Giddens was a woman who was "greedy and high handed, but a woman of great poise, great charm, great wit. And that's the way Tallulah Bankhead had played it on the stage."

B101 Massey, Raymond. *A Hundred Different Lives*. Toronto: McClelland and Stewart Limited, 1979.

Massey knew Tallulah Bankhead in the 1920s, when she was the toast of London, and met her first when she was starring in *Blackmail* (1928.) During that period, he writes, she was "hugely talented but... brash and undisciplined."

B102 Mills, John. *Up in the Clouds, Gentlemen, Please*. New Haven, Conn.: Ticknor & Fields, 1980.

In his his witty autobiography, Mills describes meeting Tallulah Bankhead for the first time: it was 1948, in Westport, Conn., where she was then doing Noël Coward's *Private Lives*. He saw her first at the home of Jack Wilson, Coward's business manager, where "she emerged from the pool house, waved to the guests on the patio, walked to the springboard and executed a perfect swallow dive." It sounds innocuous enough, but Mills then adds that she was completely naked, and that no one seemed to notice or even care!

B103 Morella, Joe, Edward Z. Epstein and John Griggs. *The Films of World War II*. Secaucus, N.J.: Citadel Press, 1973.

Offers synopses, production notes, review summaries and still reproductions of 99 films released in the United States during the Second World War, including *Stage Door Canteen* (1943) and *Lifeboat* (1944), in which Tallulah Bankhead appeared.

B104 Morley, Sheridan. *Gladys Cooper: A Biography*. New York: McGraw Hill Book Company, 1979.

In a letter written in 1941. Miss Cooper says that she has just seen

Tallulah Bankhead in *The Little Foxes*. "It is currently a great success for her though I can't imagine why, unless it's because of the Ethel Barrymore imitations she does, though even they get a bit tiresome after the second act."

B105 Morley, Sheridan. *The Great Stage Stars*. New York: Facts on File, Inc., 1986.

A large book containing brief but amazingly detailed and insightful bios of famous stage stars. The chapter on Tallulah Bankhead has been especially well done. Her dramatic achievements have been strung through a narrative that is both informative and entertaining. Morley writes that Tallulah "revelled in an acid, self-deprecating wit, as though aware that there was always a Boswell within noting distance, and there usually was."

B106 Mosel, Tad and Gertrude Macy. *Leading Lady: The World and Theatre of Katharine Cornell*. Boston: Little, Brown and Company, 1978.

Miss Cornell (1893-1974) is definitely a contender for the title of First Lady of American Theatre, and very early in her career, in 1921, she and Tallulah Bankhead had small parts in Rachel Crothers' *Nice People*. Mosel describes the difficulty Miss Cornell had with some of her comedy lines in the play – she could never get the sure-fire laughs – requiring a lot of coaching from the playwright. He contrasts Miss Cornell with Bankhead "who never needed such special instruction, never had a moment's trouble with the throwaway delivery... because it was at the heart of the art she brought to the theatre and to life." As Mosel explains, Cornell's method was to "ponder and think through, to store up and burnish" and flip lines could never stand up under such studied care.

B107 Moses, Montrose and John Mason Brown. *The American Theatre as Seen by Its Critics, 1752-1934*. New York: W.W. Norton & Co., Inc., 1934.

In this compilation of theatre reviews, Walter Winchell's critique of Tallulah's performance in *Forsaking All Others* is re-printed. It originally appeared in the New York *Daily Mirror* on March 2, 1933, and in it, Winchell says that after seeing Bankhead in the play "you are convinced that she didn't fail Hollywood so much as Hollywood must have failed her. She is a star!"

B108 Neal, Patricia. *As I Am*. New York: Simon & Schuster, Inc., 1988.

After a performance of *Another Part of the Forest* (1948), Tallulah Bankhead came backstage to congratulate Neal, who was impressed by the unpretentiousness of the legendary actress. (She was wearing trousers, considered daring at the time.) Of Neal's performance, Bankhead said "you

were wonderful, darling. If I said you were half as good as I was that
would still be a hell of a compliment."

B109 Nesbitt, Cathleen. *A Little Love and Good Company*. London: Faber
& Faber, Ltd., 1973.

Miss Nesbitt, a well respected English actress, worked with
Bankhead only once, in the 1924 London production of *This Marriage*.
They were co-stars (along with Herbert Marshall), and Nesbitt writes of
the debate between she and Tallulah as to who would inhabit the single star
dressing room. Cathleen insisted Tallulah get it, but Tallulah insisted that
Cathleen get it. Tallulah was the winner, but when she discovered that
Cathleen was still breast-feeding her baby son, and would be doing so
between acts, she gave it up. "I will not have that lovely baby going
upstairs. This room is *yours*."

B110 Paris, Barry. *Louise Brooks*. New York: Alfred A. Knopf, 1989.

An intelligent biography of silent screen star Louise Brooks. Paris
writes that Bankhead and Brooks shared a close and unique friendship in
the 1930s, when Brooks was dancing at the Plaza Hotel. After a show, she
would often stop by Tallulah's suite at the Gotham where [quoting Brooks],
she would "declaim Phaedre in lousy French and read the Bible in her
lovely Alabama accent." Paris quotes one of Brooks's later friends as
saying that the former silent star considered Tallulah Bankhead one of her
most favorite people, and thought she should have run for president.
"Louise thought she [Bankhead] had all the elements that were really
striking in a woman -- she had the intelligence, the generosity, the talent."
Paris also touches on Bankhead's reputation (lesbian affairs, drugs, etc.)
and writes that Brooks and Bankhead were very much alike: "Neither
woman had any real organized set of beliefs of her own, but both were
always open to new and sometimes wild ideas about art, sex and life...
Neither had made very many or very good pictures in America... both had
been undisciplined and ill-advised, yet they could now view their aimlessly
drifting lives with more humor than self pity."

B111 Parish, James Robert and Don E. Stanke. *The Debonairs*. New
Rochelle, NY: Arlington House Publishers, 1975.

An intimate look at several of Hollywood's most debonair actors,
including Robert Montgomery, who starred with Tallulah Bankhead in the
1932 MGM film, *Faithless*. About Bankhead, Parish writes about her bad
luck in Hollywood and mentions the scandalous article from *Motion Picture*
Magazine (see B215.) About *Faithless*, Parish says Montgomery suffered an
appendicitis as the picture was beginning, and although MGM offered to
get her a new leading man, she said she would wait until he was well. "That
was nice of her," Montgomery said later. "Because I was a relatively new
boy."

B112 Peary, Danny. *Guide for the Film Fanatic*. New York: Simon & Schuster, 1986.

Peary has written briefly (but intelligently) about hundreds of films, from the silents through the 1980s. Of *Lifeboat* (1944), the only Bankhead film represented, he is complimentary about the film and the star: "the supercharged Tallulah Bankhead gives bite to her every line."

B113 Peters, Margot. *The House of Barrymore*. New York: Alfred A. Knopf, 1990.

Tallulah Bankhead knew the Barrymores well, especially John and Ethel, and she is often mentioned in Peters's well-researched biography of the famous family. She figures most prominently in the chapter detailing John's activities in 1919, the year he allegedly tried to seduce the still-teenaged Tallulah.

B114 Phillips, Gene. D. *George Cukor*. Boston: Twayne Publishers, 1982.

Tallulah Bankhead was the star of Cukor's first solo directing effort (*Tarnished Lady*, Paramount, 1931), and Phillips writes that she failed to catch on because her personality was too hard and aggressive. Cukor had his own reasons to explain Bankhead's failure: "on stage she was enormously animated, but never at home on the screen. She was just not naturally photogenic. Her eyes seemed deadly opaque on film and her face never looked radiant, even when she smiled. She wanted above all else to be a movie queen, but she didn't have what it takes."

B115 Pratley, Gerald. *The Cinema of Otto Preminger*. New York: A.S. Barnes & Co., 1971.

Pratley intelligently discusses Preminger's career as a film director. Tallulah starred in one of his pictures, the 1945 *A Royal Scandal*, and her performance is briefly discussed.

B116 Preminger, Otto. *Preminger: An Autobiography*. Garden City, NY: Doubleday & Co., Inc., 1977.

Preminger speaks often (and fondly) of Tallulah Bankhead in his memoirs. She played an important part in helping his parents and brother settle in America after Hitler invaded Austria, their homeland, in 1938 (she persuaded her father to pass a law suspending quota limitations of immigrants during the war). Preminger felt indebted to Tallulah because of her kindness, and in 1945, when she was set to star in *A Royal Scandal*, the film he had taken over from an ill Ernst Lubitsch, he insisted that she remain in the cast, despite Lubitsch's efforts to replace her. (Greta Garbo had allegedly expressed an interest in doing the film.) Bankhead was also particularly fond of Preminger, and he writes of an evening shortly before her death. He was seeing her home, and before she entered her townhouse, she turned to him and said, "Otto, we should have gotten together years ago."

B117 Quirk, Lawrence. *The Films of Fredric March*. Secaucus, N.J.: Citadel Press, 1974.

An entry in the Citadel *Films of...* series, Quirk examines the film work of March, including *My Sin* (Paramount, 1921) his first and only film with Tallulah Bankhead. Quirk mentions Paramount's efforts to make a star out of Bankhead and blames this particular film's failure not on its leading lady, but on the inane script.

B118 Quirk, Lawrence. *Fasten Your Seatbelts; The Passionate Life of Bette Davis*. New York: William Morrow & Co., 1990.

Quirk mentions Tallulah Bankhead several times in his biography of Davis, most notably in the chapter dealing with the 1941 film adaptation of *The Little Foxes*. According to Quirk, Davis got the role because Bankhead was not considered box office. John Emery, her husband at the time, said that when told that Davis had been given the part, she threw bric-a-brac, all the while cursing the name of Bette Davis, until her apartment "looked like the London blitz had hit it." Quirk says that Bankhead and Davis met at a party soon after, and everyone expected the two to fight. When Tallulah said cattily, "so you're the woman who gets to play all my parts in the movies. And I play them so much better," people ran for cover. But Davis calmly replied, "I couldn't agree with you more, Miss Bankhead."

B119 Ragan, David. *Who's Who in Hollywood, 1900-1976*. New Rochelle, NY: Arlington House Publishers, 1976.

Ragan has attempted to list every performer who appeared in an American film during the first seventy-six years of this century, along with a brief biographical sketch and a few film highlights. Naturally, more than a few have fallen between the cracks, but Bankhead isn't one of them. Of her, he says she was Broadway's "one of a kind actress who never quite made it in films."

B120 Richardson, Diana Edkins. *Vanity Fair. Photographs of an Age, 1914-1936*. New York: Clarkson N. Potter, Inc., Publishers, 1982.

A magnificent collection of stunning celebrity portraits which appeared originally in the pages of *Vanity Fair* Magazine. Included is Cecil Beaton's 1931 photo of a pensive Tallulah. A portion of the original caption describes the actress newly-signed by Paramount as "the giddiest kind of public idol" whose gowns, gestures, newest plays and house in Mayfair were, for several years, "matters of passionate interest to that curiously eager and plaintive body, the British queue."

B121 Robinson, Alice M., Vera Mowry Roberts and Milly S. Barranger,
   Ed. *Notable Women in the American Theatre*. Westport, Ct:
   Greenwood Press, 1989.

Very helpful reference source with short biographies of hundreds of
important stage actresses, among them Tallulah Bankhead, of whom Erlene
Hendrix (of Old Dominion University) writes, "It is difficult to judge her
now: the legend always obscures the reality with such figures."

B122 Seldes, Marian. *The Bright Lights: A Theatre Life*. New York:
   Houghton, Mifflin, 1978.

Miss Seldes writes of her only encounter with Tallulah Bankhead:
when she played the secretary to Tallulah's Flora Goforth in the disastrous
1964 revival of Tennessee Williams's *The Milk Train Doesn't Stop Here
Anymore*. Her portrait of Bankhead is not a particularly flattering one (she
apparently fought bitterly with director Tony Richardson), yet she does
manage to show the human side, especially when describing a day on the set
when Williams stopped by and gave Tallulah some acting suggestions, then
asked if he were bothering her. "No one's ever bothering me... if they're
helping me," was Tallulah's answer.

B123 Shipman, David. *The Great Movie Stars; The Golden Years*. New
   York: Bonanza Books, 1970.

Shipman has written detailed biographies (and career summaries) of
the most popular film stars from the early silents through the beginning of
World War II. Within the book's nearly 600 pages, one will find, among
others, Billie Burke, Judy Garland, Joel McCrea, Lillian Gish and Tallulah
Bankhead. Shipman achieves little depth in his chapter on Bankhead but
does give a complete synopsis of her professional highlights. He writes that
as talented a stage and screen actress as she was, her reputation as *bonne
vivante* eclipsed both careers. The professional credits are complete
(excepting the 1966 animated film to which she lent her voice) and
Shipman happily makes no reference to *A Woman's Law*, a 1928 British
film that most film historians erroneously attribute to her.

B124 Shipman, David. *Movie Talk: Who Said What About Whom in the
   Movies*. New York: St. Martin's Press, 1988.

About Tallulah, director Irving Rapper is quoted as having said that
she "gave the greatest performance I have ever seen... in the test she made
to play Amanda Wingfield in *The Glass Menagerie*. Karl Freund
photographed the test. He cried. She was that woman. She had promised not
to drink. She could not keep her promise. Jack Warner said, 'Errol Flynn
is enough.' It cost a fortune to do an Errol Flynn picture because he was
always drunk. And thanks to Errol Flynn, Tallulah Bankhead lost the part."

B125 Sillman, Leonard. *Here Lies Leonard Sillman. Straightened Out at Last*. New York: The Citadel Press, 1959.

Sillman was the producer of the *New Faces* series of Broadway musicals that introduced such performers as Eartha Kitt, Henry Fonda Van Johnson and Imogene Coco to an enthusiastic audience. He admits in his memoirs that he and Tallulah Bankhead did not get along, but does relate an interesting tale from the opening night of the first *New Faces* in 1934. Through the drunken haze of opening night celebration, he looked down to see Tallulah kneeling at his feet. "You son of a bitch," she said to Sillman, "I loathe and despise everything you stand for, but I must get down on my knees to you tonight. It's the most devine, heavenly, wonderful musical I've seen in years. Bless you, darling, and thank you for a fabulous evening." She rose to her feet and added, with emphasis, "This doesn't mean, darling, that I *like* you!"

B126 Singer, Kurt. *The Laughton Story*. Philadelphia: The John C. Winston Co., 1954.

Singer describes the relationship between Charles Laughton and Tallulah Bankhead as "workmanlike" while they were making *The Devil and the Deep* (Paramount, 1932) but admits they did not become friends.

B127 Slide, Anthony. *Great Radio Personalities*. New York: Dover Publications, Inc., 1982.

Brief career sketches of radio's greatest stars. Tallulah Bankhead was a popular guest star on various programs and even had her own hit series in the early 1950s. Slide mentions a few of her radio highlights but gives little additional information.

B128 Sobel, Bernard, editor. *The Theatre Handbook and Digest of Plays*. New York: Crown Publishers, 1939.

In a chapter entitled "The Stage as a Career," Tallulah Bankhead wrote that, apart from a good play or typecasting, "I think direction is the most valuable thing in the theatre." She also added that the more talent one has, "the more discipline you need."

B129 Spoto, Donald. *The Dark Side of Genius: The Life of Alfred Hitchcock*. New York: Ballantine Books, 1984.

Spoto explains that Hitchcock saw Tallulah Bankhead for the first time in *The Dancers* (London, 1923), made some mental notes, and remembered her when casting *Lifeboat* two decades later. Relates again Bankhead's lack of modesty (and underwear) while making the 1944 film.

B130 Springer, John and Jack Hamilton. *They Had Faces Then*. Secaucus,

NJ: Citadel Press, 1974.

A celebration of the stars and starlets of the 1930s. Tallulah Bankhead, a failed star of that decade, is described as "the most flamboyant and vibrant of sophisticates." Springer continues, "so why in the world did they [Paramount] tone down the high-powered personality?" The answer to that question will probably never be known.

B131 Steen, Mike. *A Look at Tennessee Williams*. New York: Hawthorne Books, Inc., Publishers, 1969.

Not exactly a biography as much as a collection of interviews with people who knew and/or worked with the famous playwright. Bankhead is not among those interviewed, but she is often mentioned by others. Irving Rapper insists that the test she made for *The Glass Menagerie* (1950) was the best test he ever saw or directed; Geraldine Page says that the Princess in *Sweet Bird of Youth* was modelled on Tallulah Bankhead and Rita Hayworth.

B132 Stenn, David. *Clara Bow; Runnin' Wild*. New York: Doubleday, 1988.

Tallulah Bankhead is quoted as having said the only reason she went to Hollywood was to go to bed with Gary Cooper. Stenn says she chased Cooper into his dressing room and bragged afterwards about their one-night stand.

B133 Stokes, Sewell. *Without Veils: The Intimate Biography of Gladys Cooper*. London: Peter Davies, 1973.

Mentions that Tallulah Bankhead took the lead in *The Green Hat* (London, 1925) after Miss Cooper decided not to do it. She attended the opening night performance, and every eye in the house was on her, waiting for a temperamental reaction. She surprised everyone by remaining calm and reserved.

B134 Swindel, Larry. *The Last Hero: A Biography of Gary Cooper*. Garden City, NY: Doubleday & Co., Inc., 1980.

A lively biography of the late actor which contains an interesting section completely devoted to his association with Tallulah Bankhead, whom he was afraid of at first because of her "man-crushing reputation." They finally met at the home of his friend, Anderson Lawlor, who became a lover of Tallulah's. In fact, according to Swindel, she and Lawlor lived together for a short time in Cooper's house. Swindel goes into some detail in describing Tallulah's disappointing film career before discussing the film she made with Cooper, *The Devil and the Deep* (Paramount, 1932.) The picture was moderately successful, which Swindel attributes to

Cooper's drawing power. He also writes that whereas the camera could bring out something in Cooper "that could never be revealed on the stage, it somehow stifled the incandescence that was Tallulah's in life."

B135 Taylor, John Russell. *Hitch: The Life and Times of Alfred Hitchcock.* New York: Pantheon Books, 1978.

In his discussion of *Lifeboat* (20th Century-Fox, 1944), Taylor describes the relationship between Alfred Hitchcock and his star, Tallulah Bankhead. From all accounts it was a happy one, the two sharing jokes and even browsing through several Beverly Hills art galleries together. Taylor also repeats the oft-told tale of Tallulah's lack of underwear during the filming.

B136 Taylor, Robert. *Fred Allen: His Life and Wit.* Boston • Toronto • London: Little Brown & Co., 1989.

In this biography of one of radio's greatest wits, Tallulah's foray into radio as hostess of NBC's *The Big Show*, is allotted some space, but the information is general.

B137 Thomas, Tony and Aubrey Solomon. *The Films of 20th Century Fox.* Secaucus, NJ: Citadel Press, 1979.

Includes routine plot synopses of Tallulah Bankhead's two films for the studio: *Lifeboat* (1944) and *A Royal Scandal* (1945.)

B138 Thomson, David. *A Biographical Dictionary of the Cinema.* London: Secker and Warburg, 1975.

Includes a brief but intelligently written entry on Tallulah Bankhead and her career. Thomson is especially complimentary of her performance in *Lifeboat* (1944.) It "shows the self-mocking sort of grandiloquence at which she might have excelled had Hollywood not cast her as the sultry maneater." Her films tended to be "banal and dogged," laments Thomson, instead of "nutty and irreverent."

B139 Truffaut, Francois. *Hitchcock Truffaut.* New York: Simon and Schuster, 1967.

In this enlightening interview with Alfred Hitchcock, the director talks about *Lifeboat* and Tallulah Bankhead, but he dwells more on the filming technique than on the performances.

B140 Vermilye, Jerry. *Bette Davis.* New York: Pyramid, 1973.

An entry in the Pyramid Illustrated History of the Movies Series, this look at the career of Bette Davis also includes several mentions of Tallulah

Bankhead, especially in connection with the 1941 film adaptation of *The Little Foxes*. According to Vermilye, Davis said that her insistence that the role of Regina Giddens be interpreted on screen as Tallulah had interpreted it on stage led to a disagreement with director William Wyler who wanted Davis to play it differently. The arguments between Davis and Wyler caused the actress to later say that she felt she had "given one of the worst performances of my life."

B141 Vermilye, Jerry. *The Films of the Thirties*. Secaucus, NJ: Citadel Press, 1982.

The Citadel *Films of...* series does not limit itself to performers. Vermilye discusses 100 films representative of the 1930s, among them *Tarnished Lady* (1931), Tallulah's first film for Paramount.

B142 Wallace, Mike. *Mike Wallace Asks*. New York: Simon & Schuster, 1958.

Includes a two-page excerpt of an interesting conversation with Tallulah Bankhead in which the actress condemns the KKK ("as viscous and horrible as any gestapo"), speaks frankly about the South ("I am proud to be a Southerner. I am not ashamed of the South. I am ashamed of situations [racism] in the South."), and comments on racial tension ("There are wonderfully good and kind people in the South who believe that Negroes should have every opportunity of education and equal facilities, yet they do sincerely believe in segregation. Not believing in integration doesn't necessarily mean that Southerners don't have love, respect and affection for the Negro. I think that Southern Whites, though misguided, have more affection for Negroes than any other people in the United States.")

B143 Wayne, Jane Ellen. *Cooper's Women*. New York: Prentice Hall Press, 1988.

A few mentions of Tallulah Bankhead as one of Cooper's many conquests [or was it the other way around?] but their relationship is not explored.

B144 Williams, Emlyn. *George: An Early Autobiography*. New York: Random House, 1961.

Williams first saw Tallulah Bankhead in England. The year was 1924 and she was performing on stage in *The Creaking Chair*. She made an indelible impression, and he remembers her as "husky-musky and with a face like an exquisite poisoned flower," and says she "was empowered not only to make strong husbands in the stalls moisten their lips behind a program, but to cause girls hanging from the gallery to writhe and intone her first name in a voodoo cantation. She radiated like a lazy catherine wheel." Surely one of the most apt descriptions of the early Bankhead.

B145 Williams, Tennessee. *Memoirs.* Garden City, NY: Doubleday & Co., Inc., 1975.

Tallulah Bankhead is seldom mentioned in this autobiography, which is surprising since she and Williams crossed paths many times, and since he said elsewhere that he had her in mind when writing many of his plays. He does discuss her involvement in the disastrous 1964 revival of *The Milk Train Doesn't Stop Here Anymore*, and says he wishes she could have played the role five years earlier. By 1964, at age 62, she "no longer had the physical stamina to put it over; she was too deep into liquor and pills, and she had great difficulty in projecting clearly past the front of the house."

B146 Zolotow, Maurice. *No People Like Show People.* New York: Random House, Inc., 1951.

A collection of essays about famous people in "the biz," including Ethel Merman, Jimmy Durante, Jack Benny and Tallulah Bankhead, who is the subject of the opening chapter, "The Actor as Absolute." The chapter is basically a condensation of a series of articles Zolotow wrote for the *Saturday Evening Post* in 1947, but the Bankhead personality comes through just as strong. Zolotow calls Tallulah "the most flamboyant stage personality of our time, as powerful in her circle as Catherine the Great was in 18th century Russia." His description of a late-night visit with Tallulah at her country house, fighting off pets of every species while Tallulah talks non-stop about everything from Harry Truman to baseball, is hilarious.

B147 Zolotow, Maurice. *Stagestruck: The Romance of Alfred Lunt and Lynn Fontanne.* New York: Harcourt, Brace & World, 1964.

According to Zolotow, the Lunts had dinner one evening with Tallulah when she was in Chicago starring in *Private Lives*. At the dinner table, besides Tallulah and the Lunts, sat Donald Cook, her co-star, Ivor Novello and Robert Andrews. Tallulah looked around the table, and said in her basso voice, "I've slept with every man at this table, except you, Alfred. And you're next!" Zolotow adds that she never met her objective.

MAGAZINES

Articles by Tallulah Bankhead

B148 Bankhead, Tallulah. "Comment on the Citronella Circuit" *New York Times Magazine.* July 21, 1946, pp 16, 32.

"I work in the summer theatre because I'm usually two jumps ahead of the sheriff," says Tallulah, but she writes about the summer circuit with such enthusiasm, it's difficult to believe she was in it merely for the money. She writes an interesting profile of summer theatre, including bits about its history and funny incidents that have happened at several of the rural theatres. She especially praises summer theatre for providing "dozens of eager and talented youngsters with brief, random assignments, all of which add up to experience."

B149 Bankhead, Tallulah. "Why I Love the Giants." *New York Times Magazine.* June 29, 1947, pp 14, 24-25.

The answer is a simple one: "I like them because I like underdogs, the oppressed, the unbowed but bloody."

B150 Bankhead, Tallulah. "It's not the 'Road,' It's the Detours." *New York Times Magazine.* September 26, 1948, pp 20, 58.

An amusing commentary about her recent tour of *Private Lives.* "I played Joplin, Pueblo, Sacramento, Tulsa and a lot of other towns known to Rand McNally, the census taker and the booking office," she writes, and goes on to defend the "Road," which she claims is not dead, but merely "shamming death in an attempt to escape the assault and battery which it has suffered at the hands of the New York producers." Tallulah has written an interesting account here of life on the road, and she is especially fond of the all night diners in rural America, full of characters "out of Hemingway and Saroyan."

B151 Bankhead, Tallulah. "My Friend, Miss Barrymore." *Colliers.* April 23, 1949, pp 13-14, 92.

Tallulah greatly admired and respected Ethel Barrymore, and here writes a funny and touching tribute to the actress whom she describes as a "great star in the sense that Rachel, Bernhardt, Ellen Terry and Eleanora Duse were great stars."

B152 Bankhead, Tallulah. "Tallulah on Tallulah" *Life.* June 25, 1951, pp 90-97.

Very little text, but a generous supply of photos representing every phase of Tallulah's life. At one point she writes that she has survived fame, fortune and an uncommon thirst "and I have scars to prove it." About her various song recordings, she writes – honestly – that "my vocal range is that of a seal, but what feeling, what passion, what nerve!"

B153 Bankhead, Tallulah. "My Life With Father" *Coronet.* November 1951, pp 56-60.

A pleasant memoir from Tallulah about her famous father, Speaker of the House, William Bankhead. She writes about him with affection, respect and admiration and holds him responsible for her infatuation with the theatre. She says that, to her, her father was "a blend of Aladdin, D'Artagnan, Galahad and Santa Claus."

B154 Bankhead, Tallulah. "The World's Greatest Musician." *Ebony.* December, 1952, pp 102-103, 105-106.

In Tallulah's mind the title belonged to Louis Armstrong, and in this tribute, she writes that he is the "most authentic creative man, endowed with the ability to give meaning to the lives of others not only through his music but from the very fact of his living."

B155 Bankhead, Tallulah. "Not 3-D, but No-T." *New York Times Magazine.* January 31, 1954, p. 14.

Tallulah chastises Hollywood and the movies it produces. "It is going through mechanical convolutions and inflations that will make its pictures wider, deeper, louder, more intricate – and really no better. May I offer the Bankhead plan for a happier, healthier silver screen?" Her solution is for Hollywood to return to silent pictures, and she backs up her stance by naming silent stars who stirred hearts more than the screen idols of 1954. "The screen... should shift its gears... go back where it started. Silent, it will have an appeal, an eloquence and a simplicity sure to be welcomed by all those who seek surcease from the din of our time." [An interesting argument from a woman famous for talking.]

B156 Bankhead, Tallulah. "My Daughter, Barbara." *Cosmopolitan.* April 1954, pp 78-85.

Tallulah was not a natural mother, but she was a foster mother, a fact not often publicized (perhaps she was afraid it would whitewash her image!) In this article, Tallulah writes with motherly warmth about Barbara Nikoli, a Greek girl whom she adopted after the Second World War. She met the badly injured girl for the first time in 1949, when Barbara came to the United States for plastic surgery on her face. Until the girl turned seventeen, Tallulah contributed $180 a month toward her support. The article shows a side of Tallulah seldom seen in public: warm, caring, loving.

B157 Bankhead, Tallulah. "Caught With My Facts Down." *Theatre Arts.* September 1954, pp 22-23, 93.

Tallulah graces the cover of this particular issue, and proves she is a good sport by writing honestly about the factual errors in her autobiography. She encourages would-be memoir writers to "brush up on your spelling, your history, your punctuation and your arithmetic before you write so much as a line." Tallulah reacts to the mistakes as if she had referred to Truman as a Republican, but most of her errors were misspellings.

B158 Bankhead, Tallulah. "What is so Rare as a Willie Mays?" *Look.* September 21, 1954, pp 52, 54.

Tallulah predicts that the New York Giants will win the pennant because of Willie Mays.

B159 Bankhead, Tallulah. "Tallulah: She Sings! She Dances! She even Makes Money!" *Philadelphia Inquirer Magazine.* April 22, 1956, p. 34.

Published as advance publicity for *Ziegfeld Follies*, the revue in which Tallulah headed a cast of 61, the actress writes that after conquering drama on stage and screen, radio and television, she has entered the world of song and dance. "I'm fascinated by danger," she explains, and then cites Rex Harrison's recent success in the musical *My Fair Lady*, his first musical after thirty years of drama. "If Rex can do it, I can do it."

B160 Bankhead, Tallulah. "The Trouble With American Morals." *Esquire.* July 1957, pp 31-34.

Tallulah was hardly qualified to criticize another's lack of morals, and she admits as much here. She never really identifies the "trouble" with America's morals, but she gives her own (rather loose) definition of morals: "gallantry, courage and chivalry." She also comments on certain celebrities who have come under fire because of their moral laxity, including Elvis Presley ("he has a certain lavish, uninhibited rhythm that reminds me of native African dances") and makes the typically Tallulah statement that love is mostly sex. "Why be frightened or ashamed of it? We cannot deny its pleasure. Sex won't be straight-jacketed."

B161 Bankhead, Tallulah. "Your Daughter Really Ought to be an Actress, Darling!" *Good Housekeeping.* March 1958, pp 94, 222-225.

Despite the title, Tallulah spends four pages imploring mothers *not* to turn their daughters loose on the stage. In addition to the hard life an actress must lead, including an average income of $790 a year, she gives several convincing reasons to keep all young women out of the profession. "Like most mothers, you think you're harboring a second Pavlova or a juvenile Helen Hayes. I'll lay you six to one that what you're harboring is a hoyden who's behind in her homework." A strange frame of mind for Tallulah to take, for if her family had acted as she is instructing other familes to do, her life would not have been so glamorous and exciting.

Articles about Tallulah Bankhead

B162 Ace, Goodman. "What's Wrong with Television." *TV Guide*.
December 7, 1957, pp 5-7.

Ace was responsible for the witty dialogue of Tallulah Bankhead's
radio program, *The Big Show*, and he admits here that he is considering
translating the program to television, perhaps with Tallulah again on hand
to swap her unique brand of insults with guest celebrities. "I want to do
that one as simply as possible, though," Ace writes, "no choreography or
any of that stuff you usually find on a TV comedy show. Maybe we'll just
have Tallulah and her guests sit around a living room and talk."

B163 Ace, Goodman. "A Darling is Hushed." *Saturday Review*. January
11, 1969, p. 12.

A nice memory-piece of the late actress, Tallulah Bankhead, from
one of the writers of The Big Show. "It is painfully difficult to imagine
Tallulah at rest," Ace writes. "In the two years I wrote for her in radio...
rehearsal halls echoed to her raucous laughter..."

B164 Ace, Goodman. "Tallu" *Saturday Review*. May 20, 1972, p. 8

Ostensibly written as publicity for Lee Israel's newly published
biography of Tallulah Bankhead, it becomes Ace's personal (and amusing)
memories of the actress. He recalls the first time he met her; she had come
to the NBC studio to complain to the writers about the first script of *The
Big Show*. She questioned every joke, but when the show premiered, she
"got the laughs we promised her. And from then on she was like putty in
our hands. Or was it the other way around?" Ace says that "two years with
[her] went as quickly as a short weekend in the country."

B165 Albert, Katharine. "Charm? No! No! You Must Have Glamour."
Photoplay, September 1931, pp 38-39,100-101.

It is Albert's conclusion that the "ingenue with her friendly, hurt
smile, her bird-like gestures, her coy maidenliness" has been pushed off the
screen by actresses possessing glamour, a word which, according to Albert,
had been newly coined. "They've introduced a new word into ordinary
conversation, started a new fad, begun a new cycle, created a new
standard," writes Albert, and among the actresses responsible for bringing
glamour into the world is Tallulah Bankhead, she says, of the "heavily
lidded, inscrutable eyes."

B166 Allhoff, Fred. "Tallulah the Terrific." *Liberty*. May 9, 1942, pp 54-
56.

A pleasant and diverting interview which covers already familiar ground. Allhoff tries valiantly to capture the essence of Tallulah, but admits that "trying to put the vital Miss Bankhead on paper is something like trying to stuff a tornado into a bottle."

B167 Aubrey, John Churchill. "The Mystery of Tallulah Bankhead."
   Picturegoer Weekly. May 14, 1932, pp 8-9.
   The first of a five-article series examining the career and personal life of Tallulah Bankhead. This first installment serves as an introduction and reports on her doings at Paramount.

B168 Aubrey, John Churchill. "The Darling of the Gods." *Picturegoer Weekly.* May 14, 1932, pp 8-9.

The second installment of Churchill's Bankhead series covers her successes on the London stage, including the frenzy she caused among that city's female theatergoers.

B169 Aubrey, John Churchill. "Love -- and What Then?" *Picturegoer Weekly.* May 21, 1932, pp 8-9.

Continuing with his series, Aubrey, in this installment, dips into Tallulah's love life and chronicles her many affairs and flirtations while in London. Aubrey once asked her why she had come to England. Her answer? "It was sex, just plain sex, with a capital S."

B170 Aubrey, John Churchill. "Untamed -- Yet Loveable." *Picturegoer Weekly.* May 28, 1932, pp 8-9.

Another installment in Aubrey's series which gives another synopsis of her career and throws in several anecdotes from her eight years in London.

B171 Aubrey, John Churchill. "Angel and Fallen Angel in One."
   Picturegoer Weekly, June 4, 1932, pp 12-13.

The final installment of Aubrey's five-part series on Tallulah Bankhead deals exclusively with her life in Hollywood, paying particular attention to her private life, her home and her films.

B172 "Bankhead's Banking." *Newsweek.* December 31, 1951, p. 17.

A report on the Bankhead-Cronin trial. (Tallulah had accused her former secretary, Evyleen Ramsay Cronin, or kiting her weekly paychecks to the amount of $4,284.) Mrs. Cronin claims she raised the amount of the checks to pay for Tallulah's marijuana, cocaine, liquor and sex. Tallulah challenged the secretary's explanation.

B173 "Bankhead's Return." *Newsweek.* September 27, 1954, p. 60.

Evaluates *Dear Charles*, Tallulah's first Broadway play in five years. (She is good, but the play is dated and only sporadically funny.)

B174 "A Bantam from Alabama." *Photoplay*. March 1919, p. 55.

A brief article detailing the blossoming film career of seventeen-year-old Tallulah Bankhead. What is perhaps most interesting is the brief interview with her grandmother, who says "Tallulah has always been perfectly determined to be an actress. She had promised to wait until she was older, but things happened that just took matters right out of our hands."

B175 Baskette, Kirtley. "*Gone With the Wind* Indeed!" *Photoplay*. March 1937, pp 21-23, 101.

An interesting report on the the biggest question in Hollywood at the time: who will play Rhett Butler and Scarlet O'Hara? Possible Rhetts range from Edward Arnold (!) to Fredric March, although Clark Gable is the fans' favorite choice. Actresses being considered for Scarlet include Miriam Hopkins and Bette Davis. Tallulah Bankhead was the first established actress to test for the part, and Baskette says she is "considered the best actress of all the candidates" and that she "could probably recapture a sugar-lipped drawl" but admits that the "years and an aura of sophistication are against her."

B176 Benchley, Nathaniel. "Offstage." *Theatre Arts*. November 1952, pp 8-9.

A preview of Tallulah's soon-to-be published autobiography which concerns itself primarily with the collaboration of Bankhead and Richard Maney, her press agent who ghost wrote the volume of memoirs. Benchley calls this arrangement the "most explosive literary partnership since Addison and Steele," and with Maney supplying most of the prose, the book should make similar books seem "dim and pointless." Benchley characterizes Tallulah as a woman "who makes her presence felt with something of the force of a hailstorm," and who is "as provocative a character as has come down the pike since Attila."

B177 Berger, Meyer. "The Tallulah." *The New York Times Magazine*. Feb. 27, 1944.

Sub-titled "Portrait of an Actress Whose Speech is a Racing Torrent that Engulfs her Visitor," this article presents Tallulah as an opinionated woman who talks non-stop about those opinions. Berger gives a few background details, but quickly brings her to the present: the premiere of Alfred Hitchcock's *Lifeboat*. She defends the film and the director in light of the negative publicity the picture had received. "Hitchie never intended to create the impression that the U-boat captain... was superior to the other characters," she says. "He simply tried to focus, within the confines of a lifeboat, on exactly what had happened in Europe -- German cunning and brute power all but defeating Britain and the small nations, until they united and got the upper hand."

B178 "Best Seller in a Night Club." *Theatre Arts*. April 1953, p. 17.

Tallulah was set to open in a Las Vegas nightclub, and the editors of *Theatre Arts* praise her ability to find success in so many mediums. [her autobiography was currently a bestseller, she had achieved great reclam on radio, had conquered television, and her three-week salary in Vegas was set at $75,000, all this in addition to her theatrical achievements.]

B179 Biery, Ruth. "!!Tallulah!!" *Photoplay*. April 1932, pp 46-47, 125.

A typical fan magazine article of the day, but Biery does include some snappy Bankhead quotes: "If I were well behaved, I'd die of boredom," and "I'm miserable if I'm not in love and, of course, I'm miserable if I am."

B180 "Billy Rose Stages Explosive Sex Tragedy." *Life*. November 24, 1941, pp 53-54.

A brief preview of *Clash By Night*, which was soon to open on Broadway. From the combined talents of producer Billy Rose, playwright Clifford odets and star Tallulah Bankhead, much was expected. "It's star is Tallulah Bankhead who alone among top-flight actresses of the US stage would dare to face a role so brash and grubby."

B181 "Brand New Tallu." *This Week*. November 2, 1952.

Tallulah was considering moving from radio to television, but was apparently unsure of her photogenic quality. She had had new portraits taken for the first time in seven years. One accompanies the article as evidence that Tallulah "is as photogenic as ever, and should have saved her worries for her script."

B182 "The Broadway Plays." *Harpers Bazaar*. November 1958. pp 94-100.

A general description of several plays currently on Broadway and a few more on their way. Tallulah was hopefully "on her way" as the star of *Crazy October* (unfortunately the play closed in California, a long way from Broadway.) She looks rather depressed in the full-page photo on page 96, but the caption describes her as "American Theatre's Grande Dame terrible," whose "personality overwhelms the ideas of mere talent or beauty."

B183 Brown, John Mason. "Grounded Eagle." *Saturday Review of*

Literature. April 12, 1947, pp 40-43.

Complimentary of Bankhead ("There is nothing negative about her [Her] personality is all fire. She smoulders and erupts while others smile and ogle.") but not so complimentary of her stage vehicle, *The Eagle Has Two Heads* ("[Seems] more like a six-months' night in the Arctic Circle than a lively evening in the theatre.")

B184 Brown, John Mason. "Seeing Things." *Saturday Review of Literature*. October 2, 1954, pp 40-41.

A review of *Dear Charles* (then on Broadway) that is more of a personality profile of its star, Tallulah Bankhead. "No performer in our theatre is more colorful than she," says Brown. "None is blessed with a personality more tempestuous or exciting." He then criticizes her for falling into a habit of self parody, and pleads with her to return to the discipline style of acting she showed in *The Little Foxes*.

B185 Burke, Randolph Carroll. "A Talk to Tallulah." *Picturegoer Weekly*. October 31, 1931, pp 16-17.

A brief (but well illustrated) article that criticizes her first Paramount film (*Tarnished Lady*.) "When Tallulah Bankhead went to New York to become a talkie star, I expected great things of her," writes Burke, but he refers to the film as a "foolish affair."

B186 Capote, Truman. "Three Neighbors." *Esquire*. December 1987, pp 223-24.

Capote writes about three famous women who were his neighbors at one time or another: Katharine Hepburn, Dorothy Parker and Tallulah Bankhead. He says the latter was a pest and would call him up at three or four in the morning to discuss her sexual activities. He repeats a typical conversation revealing a woman both witty and insecure.

B187 Carroll, Joseph. "Miss Bankhead Brought to Book." *Theatre Arts*. November 1952, pp 50-51.

An appreciative review of Tallulah Bankhead's just-published autobiography.

B188 Carvel, Madge. "Hollywood Speaks Its Mind about Tallulah Bankhead." *Movie Classic*. May 1932, pp 26, 60.

A collection of comments from Hollywood stars about Tallulah. Among those interviewed were Marie Dressler ("Is she as original and interesting as I hear she is? Tell me at once all the witty and daring things she says. I assure you I am not too young to hear."); Carole Lombard

("Her clothes are so unHollywoodish..."); and Fredric March ("Tallulah is one swell scout to work with. She's never temperamental, except with important people.")

B189 "Censorship for Interviews. Hollywood's Latest Wild Idea." *Cinema Digest.* January 9, 1933, pp 9-12.

Reports on the effort to establish censor boards in the studios to pass on all interviews before writers submit them to their publishers. These censors would delete all items they considered in bad taste or detrimental to the studios. Tallulah Bankhead was responsible for the sudden cry for censorship, after speaking frankly about her need for a man in a fan magazine interview (see B215).

B190 Cheasley, Clifford W. "There's a Wedding Ahead for Tallulah Bankhead." *Movie Classic.* October 1932. pp 51,68,74.

Cheasley, a noted numerologist of the day, predicts that Tallulah would be married between the age of 37 and 46. [He was wrong; she married at 35.]

B191 Clark, Jacqueline. "Female Falstaff." *American Mercury.* December 1952, pp 110-111.

A pleasant review of Tallulah's recently published autobiography. Clark compliments Richard Maney for a superb job of ghost writing ("This gentleman deserves a publisher's medal for heroic action on what must have been a battlefield of conversational confusion") and says the best part of Tallulah's book is the chapter detailing her London success of the 20s, in which she emerges as something akin to one of Fitzgerald's "beautiful and damned" heroines.

B192 "The Clever Use of Fascinating Materials." *Town and Country.* November 1, 1922.

Tallulah Bankhead models fashionable evening clothes in photographs by Ira L. Hill.

B193 Cohen, John S., Jr. "Alabama and London." *Photoplay.* August 31, 1931, pp 46-47, 110.

An entertaining profile of Tallulah Bankhead, described as the "modern of moderns," and as a woman who possesses "the mind of a man, in fact, of an adventurous, reckless, pleasure-loving man with a ruddy Elizabethan vocabulary."

B194 Crouse, Russell. "Close-Up: Richard Maney." *Life.* May 14, 1945, pp 55-56, 58, 60, 62.

Maney was Tallulah Bankhead's press agent, friend and drinking companion, and she is mentioned often in this interesting profile, especially in relation to *Foolish Notion*, Tallulah's latest Broadway play. When signing the contract she insisted on two things: footlights and Maney.

B195 Cruikshank, Herbert, "Why London's in a Fog." *Motion Picture.* June 1931, pp 33, 90.

Described as a "threat to Garbo, a menace to Marlene," Tallulah Bankhead is praised here for her success in London, and Cruikshank predicts similar success as an American film star. He says she "screen divinely, with a sort of somber, fascinating beauty that reaches way inside to disturb your heart and soul."

B196 DeBlois, Frank. "Don't Say I Called You 'Darling'!" *TV Guide.* December 7, 1957, pp 8-10.

DeBlois interviews Tallulah about her recent television activity (*The GE Theatre, Schiltz Playhouse*) and especially her guest appearance on the *Lucille Ball-Desi Arnaz Comedy Hour*. She denies the rumor that "fur flew" but does admit that Desi Arnaz has a temper. "But that's because he's fat. It worries him." Arnaz was also interviewed and his story supports the rumor.

B197 Denton, Frances. "Here Comes Tallulah." *Photoplay.* May 6, 1931, pp 46, 104.

An innocuous personality profile of Bankhead published as *Tarnished Lady*, her first Paramount film, was being readied for release. "This Tallulah's going to be big – a big hit, or a big flop," writes Denton. "There's nothing halfway about the Bankhead lass." [A year later the verdict was in; she was a flop.]

B198 "Dunk it, Dahling." *Newsweek.* March 19, 1951, p. 28.

Tallulah had been to Washington to plead for more money for medical research, and although visitors were not allowed in the private House dining room, she swept past the guard anyway and ordered coffee and cake.

B199 "Et Tu, Tallulah?" *Life.* May 12, 1952, p. 101.

A brief article (illustrated with two pictures) in which Tallulah Bankhead waxes enthusiastic over singer Johnnie Ray. "He's divine! I want to adopt him!" she says. She saw him at a party given in honor of Ethel Merman, at The Pen and Pencil, a New York City restaurant. She stayed until 4:30 a.m., "weeping buckets" while he sang.

B200 Eustis, Morgan. "Footlight Parade." *Theatre Arts Monthly*. October
1939, pp 718-19.

Several Broadway luminaries are featured in this issue, among them
Arthur Byron, Gertrude Lawrence, Robert Morley and Tallulah Bankhead,
who was currently enjoying her greatest success as Regina Giddens in *The
Little Foxes*. Eustis gives a brief history of Tallulah's theatrical successes
and failures and concludes by saying that "if the future holds even half as
much fulfillment as the past did promise, her 'special brand of magic'
should be an important and vital factor in the history of contemporary
histrionics."

B201 "Express." *Newsweek*. February 20, 1956, p. 54.

Tallulah was preparing to board the express train from Miami to
New York where she was scheduled to open as Blanche DuBois in *A
Streetcar Named Desire*. She complains that the role "is harder than
eighteen King Lears, with a Hamlet thrown in," and insists that she was
"brainwashed... into doing this."

B202 "Fashion as Interpreted By the Actress." *Theatre Magazine*.
December 1922.

The actress, in this case, is Tallulah Bankhead, and the fashions she
models in three striking photographs are from her current play, *The
Exciters*.

B203 "Flashback." *Vanity Fair*. April 1990, p. 128.

A regular feature in *Vanity Fair* is to reprint a photo from an older
issue, in this case, the famous Cecil Beaton portrait of a pensive Tallulah
Bankhead which first appeared in the April 1931 issue.

B204 Fletcher, Adele Whitely. "Banking on Bankhead." *Photoplay*. April
1944, pp 51, 96-98.

A quiet chat with Tallulah Bankhead (who had just returned to the
screen as the star of *Lifeboat*) which is a rarity. Instead of ranting about
five different things at once, she calmly shares her homespun views of life
and talks about her home in rural New York. "In growing older -- and I
don't mean I'm Mrs. Methuselah -- I felt the same need to walk on my own
land that all the farmers I spring from always have known." She also says
that women shouldn't be ashamed of their age and admits that she is forty
[she was actually forty-two!] Fletcher says that when Tallulah gets the
notion to do something, she does it. For instance, just before Christmas one
year [probably 1940) she decided to send a message to Winston Churchill.
The cable read: "Stop running out and watching air raids. Very important
you take care of yourself. The whole wide world needs you. Safe

Christmas and Victorious New Year to you and your great people." A few days later, a cable arrived from England. "Thank you. Winston Churchill."

B205 Frazier, George. "Tallulah Bankhead; Broadway's Brightest Star." *Life*. February 15, 1943, pp 46, 49-51.

Frazier writes and writes about Tallulah Bankhead, but he rarely gets below the surface. He does make several amusing comments, however: when visitors arrive at New York's Elysee Hotel to see Miss Bankhead, "they are subjected to a grilling that barely stops short of demanding proof of a negative blood test, membership in the American Kennel Club and the ability to play a bassoon." He also writes in a style similar to Maurice Zolotow's when describing her conversational habits: "It is quite a performance, and into it she interpolates the wringing of her hands, glances heavenward, sudden halts, a twitching of the eye and a sibilant sucking in of her breath." He also relates an anecdote involving Heywood Broun which Tallulah later denied (see B230).

B206 Garland, Robert. "The Drama." *Pictorial Review*. October 10, 1948, p. 16.

Bankhead was currently starring in a Broadway revival of Noël Coward's *Private Lives*, but Garland is critical of both play and star. He charges that Bankhead is "in need of discipline, productional, directional, and all," and further states that the subject of his "more in anger than in sorrow essay, is that too fine a lady is allowed to get away unchallenged with the corny convolutions to be seen and heard in the undisciplined revival of *Private Lives* which never should have been dug up and acted by anybody!"

B207 Gelman, Morris. "A Theatre Portrait: Tallulah Bankhead." *The Theatre*. August 1960, p. 15, 46-47.

An entertaining profile of the actress, too brief, but Gelman has done an admirable job of synopsizing her life and career. He aptly describes her as "probably the most colorful, propulsive female entertainer since Madame du Barry" who "has been the subject of more anecdotes, madcap vignettes and preposterous legends than a combination of Paul Bunyon and Zsa Zsa Gabor."

B208 Gill, Brendan. "Profiles: Making a Noise in the World." *New Yorker*. October 7, 1972, pp 45-46, 48, 50, 52, 55-56, 58, 60, 62, 64, 65-66, 71-72, 74, 76-78, 83-84, 86-90, 95-99.

A well-researched and breezily written profile of Tallulah Bankhead, which was re-printed virtually word-for-word as the text in Gill's book, *Tallulah*, published the same year (see B003).

B209 Gill, Brendan. "Profiles: Making a Noise in the World." *New Yorker*. October 14, 1972.

Part two of Gill's profile of actress Tallulah Bankhead.

B210 Gill, Brendan. "Tallulah" *Harper's Bazaar*. November 1972, pp 102-103.

An interesting but ultimately depressing profile of the actress that might well have served as an introduction to Gill's book. It is sad because Bankhead was such a talented and exciting woman in her youth, but "when she died in 1968... she was more famous than ever, but she was old and frail and there were few to love her."

B211 Graham, Lee. "Man About Town." *Hollywood Studio Magazine*. May 1977, pp 34-35.

Graham reports on the recent tribute to the late actress Tallulah Bankhead at USC. Among those present to tell Tallulah stories were 94-year-old Estelle Winwood, and Patsy Kelly, who said, "I'm sure she's in Heaven. They wouldn't dare refuse her admittance." Graham relates a few of his own experiences with the "leading lady of non-conformity" and throws in a few biographical details as well.

B212 Graham, Lee. "Man About Town." *Hollywood: Then and Now*. November 1990, p. 32.

Nothing more than a string of anecdotes involving Tallulah Bankhead and such celebrities as Estelle Winwood, Patsy Kelly and columnist Mike Connolly.

B213 Grayson, Charles. "The Star Who Has Hollywood Guessing." *Motion Picture*. April 1932, pp 58-59, 82, 85.

A simple, unpretentious personality profile of Tallulah Bankhead which dwells more on her likes and dislikes than on her professional credits.

B214 Green, E. Mawbry. "Echoes From Broadway." *Theatre World*. November 1936, p. 231.

Green reviews several plays newly opened on Broadway, among them Love from a Stranger, Night Must Fall, St. Helena and Reflected Glory, with Tallulah Bankhead, which was deemed "the first new hit of the season."

B215 Hall, Gladys. "Has Hollywood Cold-Shouldered Tallulah? Here's Her Own Opinion." *Motion Picture*. September 1932, pp 47, 86, 89.

Hall says that Hollywood's most elite hostesses (Marion Davies, Constance Bennett, Bebe Daniels, etc.) prefer not to be home to Tallulah because of her behavior, primarily her language. "She reveals all. She disguises nothing. She gives to all functions of living and loving, of body and soul, their round Rabelaisian, biological *names*... She is like a gilded bomb invited to rest among lilies of the field." Tallulah denies feeling the chill of a cold-shoulder, but does voice her opinion very clearly about love. "I'm serious about love. I haven't had an *affaire* in six months... too long! I am not promiscuous... Promiscuity implies that attraction is not necessary. I may lay eyes on a man and have an *affaire* with him the next hour. But it is serious." Tallulah concluded her thoughts on love by announcing, "I WANT A MAN!" Her risque comments shocked the industry, and the studios demanded that all future star interviews be censored.(The Tallulah who speaks in this article doesn't seem terribly naughty, just human, honest and lonely.)

B216 Haven, Scott. "A Light Goes Out." *Photoplay*. March 1969, pp 16-17, 32.

The light was Tallulah Bankhead, who had died four months earlier. Haven briefly synopsizes her life and career, making a few errors, but some interesting observations as well: "Throughout her film career Tallulah had a rare knack for being in the right place at the right time. And yet this was not enough to guarantee success." In the late teens, when Tallulah was making her few American silent films, the motion picture was developing into an art form and new personalities demanded immediate attention, yet she made virtually no impression. And in the early 30s, with Hollywood desperately in need of stage-trained actors, Tallulah failed where lesser talents succeeded.

B217 Hayes, Richard. "A Toast to Tallulah." *Commonweal*. October 1954.

In a letter to the editor, Hayes has written a rather pretentious personality profile of Tallulah Bankhead and describes her as a "personality in the widest sense of that abused and narrow term; she has, that is, made a commodity of her personal relations with the world, and it is a sign of her unquenchable authority that she so successfully imposes the facts of that relation upon us."

B218 Hayes, Richard. "Miss Bankhead vs. Henry James." *Commonweal*. March 22, 1957, pp 638-39.

High brow commentary of Bankhead's recent Broadway failure in Henry James's *Eugenia*. Hayes writes that the play failed to re-awaken the "sleeping artist" in Tallulah.

B219 "Here are Big Moments for Stars in Summer Plays." *Life*. August 5, 1940, p. 31.

Gertrude Lawrence, Miriam Hopkins, Richard Haydn, Lili Damita, Irene Castle and Tallulah Bankhead were among the Broadway stars taking their plays to the summer theatres, and this article reports on their successes.

B220 Hewes, Henry. "Broadway Postscript." *Saturday Review of Literature*. March 3, 1956, p. 22.

Hewes praises Tallulah Bankhead for a "surprisingly disciplined piece of acting" in *A Streetcar Named Desire*.

B221 "A Hit and a Miss." *Newsweek*. October 20, 1952, pp 114, 116.

Reviews both Tallulah's debut on television on *All Star Revue* ("a miss") and her autobiography ("a hit").

B222 Hoffman, Theodore. "We Like Tallulah." *New Republic*. November 17, 1952, p. 30.

A favorable review of Tallulah Bankhead's autobiography. Hoffman is surprised by the actress's "intellectual vitality," but does admit the book occasionally falls victim to the "Broadway affectations and circumlocutions of the school of Billy Rose."

B223 "Holt's New Photo-Biography Shows Another Tallulah." *Publishers Weekly*. August 14, 1972, p. 35.

An interesting account of how Brendan Gill happened to write his pictorial tribute to actress Tallulah Bankhead (see B003). According to the book's editor, Steven Aronson, the idea came about because of several pieces of Bankhead memorabilia shown to him by Eugenia Rawls, a friend of Tallulah's. "I knew about the drinking and the lesbianism," says Aronson, "but the memorabilia proved to me that there was another, more human story to tell." He contacted Gill and gave him the assignment. He says Gill's finished product "is a tastefully indiscreet" biography. "He deals honestly but not sordidly with her drinking and sexual excesses."

B224 Hughes, Kathleen. "Leading – and Vibrant – Leading Ladies." *New York Times Magazine*. January 4, 1942, pp 10-11, 21.

Hughes spotlights five women of the New York Stage: Ethel Barrymore, Helen Hayes, Lynn Fontanne, Katharine Cornell and Tallulah Bankhead. The latter, currently appearing in *Clash by Night*, is described as a "blond stick of dynamite with a mind that works like a racing motor."

B225 Koll, Don. "Tallulah." *Film Fan Monthly*. January 1969, pp 23-23.

A brief but interesting account of Bankhead's career, peppered with comments from her about her film and television appearances.

B226 Krutch, Joseph Wood. "Drama" *Nation*. April 5, 1947, p 403.

Krutch reviews *The Eagle has Two Heads*, but apart from Tallulah's dramatic death scene (falling head first down several stairs), he finds the play drab and unbelievable.

B227 Lardner, John. "Tallulah Goes to the Ballgame." *Woman's Home Companion*. September 1951, pp 26-27, 80, 81.

Lardner accompanied Tallulah to a New York Giants game, and he reports that, as a baseball fan, she combines the intelligence of Ethel Barrymore with a wild, free vocal spirit.

B228 Lardner, John. "The Air: A Crumbling Illusion." *New Yorker*. November 21, 1959, pp 122-28.

A review of *The Big Party*, a new television show. Tallulah Bankhead was on hand for the opening episode and, according to Lardner, she gave the show most of its humor.

B229 "Letters and Art." *Literary Digest*. February 23, 1935, p. 20.

An editorial that praises Tallulah's performance in *Rain* and discusses her eleven year interest in the role. It is the opinion of the uncredited author that Somerset Maugham made a mistake when he dismissed Tallulah from the London cast in 1924 and "it is strongly wished that he could come to New York and see her in a finished performance in the role for which he rejected her."

B230 "Letters to the Editor." *Life*. March 8, 1943.

Tallulah Bankhead responds to George Frazier's profile of her published in the February 15th edition of the magazine (see B205.) She calls the article "befuddled" and "maudlin," and regarding the remark she allegedly made to Heywood Broun ["I've never made love to gargantuan, ill-kept, porcine, sweating old Heywood Broun, and I'm going to tonight"], she advises Mr. Frazier to "give up fiction."

B231 "Life's Cover." *Life*. March 6, 1939, p. 9.

A stunning portrait of Tallulah wearing the pompadour and décolletté gown from *The Little Foxes* graces the cover of this particular issue, and the brief article comments on the play (her first US hit), and her role (her first as a mother). She is complimented for not using her family name to achieve success but relying instead on her own talent.

B232 Linen, James A. "A Letter from the Publisher." *Time*. December 6, 1948, p. 14.

Times's publisher, James Linen, reveals what it was really like for the reporters who interviewed Tallulah Bankhead for *Time*'s November 22 cover story. (See B246). "Tallulah danced the Charleston for them, played piano, told jokes, did imitations, tossed off some mint juleps, fed them shrimp and mushrooms and showed them the house." Linen also admits that separating facts from legends proved "in many instances to be virtually impossible."

B233 "Lioness in the Living Room." *Time*. January 18, 1954, p. 70.

A review of Tallulah's television performance of *Hedda Gabler*. ("Tallulah turned Ibsen's devious, subtly evil heroine into a flamboyant, shouting hussy.")

B234 *"The Little Foxes*. Tallulah Bankhead has her First US Hit." *Life*. March 6, 1939, pp 70-73.

A brief history of Tallulah's theatrical experiences, particularly praising her performance as the "pathetic waitress" in *They Knew What They Wanted* (London, 1926), and complimenting her success in *The Little Foxes*. "The strange electric woman with the languid eyes, the panther's step and the siren's husky voice" has finally found a role "big and fierce enough for her talent."

B235 "Living Legends." *Today's Health*. May 1959, p. 58.

A regular feature in this magazine was a series of little known human interest stories about the world's best known people. The name of the person was withheld, and the reader was supposed to guess who it was. The "mystery celebrity" in this particular issue is Tallulah Bankhead, and the story told is about her sending in her photograph to the movie magazine in 1917.

B236 "The Long and Short of the New Mode in Street and Evening Wraps is Here Expressed." *Vogue*. November 15, 1922, pp 68-69.

Tallulah models several popular outfits for a two-page spread of fashion photos.

B237 Loos, Anita. "Tallulah." *Playbill*. February 1969, pp 7-12.

Miss Loos (who met Tallulah Bankhead in 1918) describes the humorous exploits of the young Tallulah, from matching wits with Alexander Woollcott at New York's Algonquin Hotel to swimming nude in a Hollywood pool and disrupting the construction of a house next door.

"She lived at high speed," Miss Loos writes, "behaving as a great many of us would have done, had we ever dared."

B238 Loos, Anita. "Unforgettable Tallulah." *Readers Digest.* July 1969, pp 130-34.

Very similar to Miss Loos's article in the February 1969 issue of *Playbill* in that she again recounts some amusing incidents from Tallulah's life, primarily from her early life as a professional.

B239 McKegg, William H. "A Lady for Legends." *Picture Play.* May 1932, pp 24-25, 64-65.

An over-written but nonetheless interesting profile of Tallulah Bankhead. Her talents aren't praised as much as her personality. In certain quotes, she comes across as being somewhat conceited. For example, when reached by telephone, she said, "You really *must* meet me! You'll *rave* over me! Everybody is *crazy* about me! I'm perfectly *divine!*"

B240 "Milestones" *Time.* December 20, 1968, p. 60

Reports that Tallulah Bankhead has died, and characterizes her as a woman "lavish beyond redemption, garrulous beyond recall..."
B241 "Mariegold in Society." *Sketch.* October 2, 1929.

Reports on Tallulah's first experience eating bread-and-butter pudding "which she liked so much she threw discretion to the winds and ate pudding and cream regardless of her hard-won slimness."

B242 "Miss Bankhead Shines in Hysterical 'Dark Victory.'" *Newsweek.* November 17, 1934, p. 26.

Reviews Tallulah's latest Broadway offering, but Tallulah is found far superior to her vehicle.

B243 Morrison, Hobe. "Tallulah." *Critics Choice.* January 15, 1969, p. 6

A brief but interesting profile of Tallulah Bankhead, published a month after her death, which presents her as "American Theatre's Grand Dame terrible," and a "quixotic public cut-up addicted to extravagant escapades and excesses."

B244 Mosley, Leonard O. "I'm Leaving, But I'll Be Back." *Motion Picture.* February 1933, pp 34, 79, 81, 85.

As Tallulah Bankhead was preparing to mark her return to Broadway, she looks back honestly and intelligently at her failed film career, admitting that her lack of success was due, in equal amounts, to her lack of experience in the medium and to the poor story quality of her films. She does intimate that she hasn't given up on films, and will probably return the following year "to begin afresh." [She didn't make another film until 1944, when Alfred Hitchcock persuaded her to star in *Lifeboat.*]

B245 "Mrs. John Emery – Formerly Tallulah Bankhead." *Sketch.* September 8, 1937.

Reports on Tallulah's marriage to John Emery.

B246 "One Woman Show." *Time.* November 22, 1948, pp 76-80.

A well-written and insightful article, full of pithy observations and interesting bits of information. The anonymous author writes that Tallulah Bankhead can be "perfectly at ease in a San Francisco waterfront dive, in the Royal Enclosure at Ascot, or playing poker with stagehands," and that the "one tested formula for getting along with Tallulah [is to] give into her." The article is honest ("she lacks the discipline and stability to keep her gifts under control") yet complimentary ("for all her garish conduct, Tallulah is capable of great charm, dignity and conduct.") For a behind-the-scenes report of the actual interview, see B232.

B247 "The Order of the P.A." *Cue.* October 2, 1937, p. 48.

Reports on Tallulah's marriage to John Emery.

B248 O'Shaughnessy, Patrice. "Who Said That?" *Parade.* September 25, 1983.

The idea of this article is to list a "quotable quote," and then give a short profile of the person who uttered the witty words. The quote listed here is "I'm as pure as the driven slush." Attributing the remark to Bankhead is right, but in most other areas the article is wrong. To correct a few of the many factual errors: she did not go to London in 1922 (it was 1923): she did not star on Broadway in the late 30s in *Dark Victory*, nor did it bring her fame (it opened in 1934 and was a flop); and her most memorable portrayal was not Sadie Thompson in *Rain* (most critics agree that it was Regina Giddens in *The Little Foxes.*)

B249 Pedell, Katherine. "It's Tallulah, Dahlings." *TV Guide.* February 12, 1954, pp 17-19.

An innocuous chat with Tallulah in her rural New York home "which she shares with three dogs, a cat, a myna bird, a chauffeur, a cook, her secretary... any number of neuroses, and on weekends, any variety of high – and low – brows." At the time, Tallulah was talking off and on to Bill Todman who had "an audience participation show in the works, tailor-made for Tallulah." Bankhead, however, wasn't so keen on the idea, having been told that "panel shows are on their way out."

B250 "People." *Time.* March 12, 1956, p. 45.

Reprints a portion of the letter Tennessee Williams wrote to the New York *Times* regarding the performance of "uptrodden Tallulah Bankhead as downtrodden Blanche DuBois" in his *A Streetcar Named Desire.* Williams says that when the play was trying out in Florida, Tallulah's reading of Blanche "was the worst I've ever seen." He denies having said that she ruined his play, and sets the record straight by admitting that when it debuted at New York's City Center, Tallulah "magnificently steered *Streetcar* back on track."

B251 "Pin-Up of the Past." *Films and Filming.* July 1973, p. 68.

A flattering full-page glamour shot of Tallulah Bankhead dating from her short-lived career at Paramount in the early 30s. The caption mentions her film highlights but mistakenly refers to her role in *Fanatic* (1966) as a "guest spot."

B252 Rawls, Eugenia. "Another Tallulah." *Equity.* January 1969, pp 12-23.

A loving, warm, sentimental article written in praise of Tallulah Bankhead by her friend and co-star of *The Little Foxes*. Miss Rawls does not write about Tallulah Bankhead the vibrant, living legend, the glamorous superstar, but the Tallulah Bankhead whom she describes as "the quiet, prodigious reader, the introspective person, the tender, very good friend." She writes about the actress's dedication to her craft, as illustrated by her insistence that the show go on, even when a raging blizzard in Minnesota kept all but thirteen people away from a performance of *The Little Foxes*. A touching tribute.

B253 Ray, Marie Beynon. "The Ends of Fashion." *Colliers.* September 1931, pp 17, 69.

Tallulah Bankhead reveals her fashion likes and dislikes, and doesn't once mention her career. She does say at one point, however, that "in spite of all this ballyhoo about Tallulah the Mysterious, Tallulah the Exotic, I'm just a good healthy girl with a husky voice and the strength of a horse."

B254 "The Readers Always Write." *Cats Magazine.* February 1954, p. 4

An amusing letter to the editors written by Tallulah Bankhead in praise of a long-haired cat named Cleo. She "is the most queenly cat I have ever seen," writes Tallulah, "and what impresses me is the regality with which she carries off the role of Cleopatra."

B255 *Red Book.* September 1921.

A lovely portrait of Tallulah Bankhead by Edward Thayer Monroe graces the cover of this particular issue, and although there is no accompanying story or even a caption, the beauty alone of this little-known photograph warrants its being included here.

B256 "Reflecting Glory." *Literary Digest.* May 29, 1937, p. 22

An account of the reception given Tallulah while she toured the south in *Reflected Glory.* She played to packed houses in Birmingham and Montgomery (in her home state of Alabama) and it is reported that at one performance "the audience clapped, stomped, hollered and carried on so, she had to give five curtain calls."

B257 Rogow, Lee. "She Tells All?" *Saturday Review.* September 27, 1952, pp 11-12.

Another flattering review of Tallulah's autobiography. "It is Tallulah who speaks from these pages, Tallulah flamboyant, intense, comic, sentimental..."

B258 Romero, Ramon. "Great Roles Reborn." *Theatre Arts.* November 1952, pp 25, 92-94.

An interview with actress Bette Davis in which she discusses the changes in role interpretation from stage to film. By 1947, Davis had already recreated more famous Broadway characterizations for the screen than any other actress, and two of her more famous roles were originally performed on the stage by Tallulah Bankhead -- Judith Traherne (*Dark Victory*) and Regina Giddens (*The Little Foxes*). Bankhead's critically acclaimed performance as Regina Giddens was her greatest triumph, and Davis is quick to compliment the actress. "Miss Bankhead's characterization of Regina Giddens in unequalled. It made no concessions to sympathy, Legions of Decency or accounting departments. It was a flesh-and-blood realization of what Miss Hellman had written."

B259 "A Royal Scandal." *Theatre Arts.* April 1945, p. 227

Under a flattering portrait of Tallulah Bankhead from the motion picture, *A Royal Scandal*, the caption explains that as the film opens, so does a new Bankhead play, *Foolish Notion*, by Philip Barry.

B260 *Saturday Review.* January 4, 1969.

An untitled article which briefly describes the memorial service for Tallulah Bankhead at St. Bartholomew's Church in Manhattan. A few quotes from eulogies are included.

B261 Schulberg, Budd. "What Price Glory?" *The New Republic*. January 6 & 13, 1973, pp 27-31.

Schulberg not only reviews Brendan Gill's newly published book, *Tallulah* ("neither detailed nor incisive biography, but rather a blown-up *New Yorker* profile"), but writes his own enlightening profile of Tallulah Bankhead. He manages to peel away the layers of self-indulgence, narcissism and personality-peddling to reveal a woman who had guts and talent, but who was also a "willful, spoiled, self-centered trouble-maker whose better instincts and professional intelligence were increasingly sacrificed to her weakness for allowing extrovert personality to take over from inner performance."

B262 Shane, Ted. "Tallulah to You." *Colliers*. April 16, 1947, pp 22-23, 72.

A delightful article. Shane visits Tallulah Bankhead at her country home near New York City, and he reports what happened. She talked non-stop, naturally, and he quotes her verbatim in sentences and paragraphs that are often non-sequiter and always without punctuation. "In a cross between a British and a Southern accent, in a whiskey tenor, in italics, she smiled, sang and danced, poured liquor, spouted epigram, good sense and anecdote," says Shane and admits that for days after his visit, his "head rang with phrases and bits of Tallulah."

B263 "The Shape of Things." *Nation*. March 26, 1949, p. 347

A brief editorial complimenting Tallulah for initiating a $1 million lawsuit against those responsible for the Prell Shampoo jingle using the name "Tallulah." "There is no adequate adjective for the gall of a company or an agency that would exploit in such a way a name which could only refer to one person."

B264 "Slight Exaggeration." *Newsweek*. February 24, 1958, p. 53.

A brief news item explaining that an anonymous phone call received by the New York City police imploring them to hurry to Tallulah Bankhead's apartment because she was dying, was a "wasted worry." The actress was suffering from a kidney ailment and had already been taken to the hospital.

B265 Smallwood, C.L. "That Gal from Alabam." *The New Movie Magazine*. December 1932, pp 28-29, 70, 72.

This issue promised readers the "most revealing story you have read of Tallulah Bankhead," but the article falls far short of its goal. It is merely an innocuous list of several anecdotes from Tallulah's childhood, and a hurried history of her theatre and film roles to date. Smallwood's style is readable, and the article is pleasant, but it does contain some errors, among them naming Tallulah's step-mother as the one who sent Tallulah's picture to *Picture Play* Magazine. (It was Tallulah who sent the picture; her step-mother strongly disapproved of the teenager going to New York as one of the contest winners.)

B266 "Sobering Thoughts?" *Theatre Arts*. June 1956, pp 10-11.

Tallulah Bankhead is pictured rehearsing a number with Julie Newmeyer from *Ziegfeld Follies*. The show was opening out of town in preparation for Broadway [it never made it.] The editors also comment on Tallulah's recent Broadway revival of *A Streetcar Named Desire*.

B267 "Sound of a Bell." *New Yorker*. April 2, 1949, pp 25-26.

Reports on Tallulah's lawsuit against those responsible for the Prell Shampoo jingle that uses the name "Tallulah." in its lyrics. "I have never allowed my name to be attached to soap or spinach," says an angry Tallulah. "Suddenly, I find it attached to this damn shampoo."

B268 Spelvin, George. "A Basket of Pomegranates for Tallulah." *Theatre Arts*. November 1952, pp 25, 92-94.

Tallulah's autobiography had just been published, and Spelvin compliments her, not as a writer, but as a critic. "The autobiography indicates she knows more about the theatre than anybody else," says Spelvin, "and has strong, loud opinions. And when she has an opinion, she sticks with it, instead of taking it all back and reversing herself in the last paragraph." These qualities earned her the award as Critic of the Month.

B269 Stoneman, E. Donnell. "Eugenia Rawls Remembers Tallulah Bankhead." *Interview*. June 1973.

Not so much an article, or interview, as it is a long quote from Miss Rawls, and in this quote, she talks about Tallulah Bankhead's insecurities, eccentric habits and capacity for fun. "I think she was one of the great souls," says Rawls. "A joyful spirit, a joyful, generous spirit."

B270 Sutton, Horace. "Tallulah the Tourist" *Saturday Review of Literature*. November 24, 1951, pp 36-37.

A rather tedious account of Tallulah's recent travels to London and Paris (to kick off the second season of *The Big Show*.) Tallulah talks non-stop, naturally, about the English, her house and her pets. Nothing startlingly new; all has been said before, and Sutton adds very little of his own impressions of interviewing the actress which would have given the article some needed depth.

B271 "The Talk of the Town." *New Yorker*. November 13, 1954, pp 31-32.

Tallulah Bankhead was always the talk of the town, but in this article, it is she who does the talking. A reporter had recently paid her a visit, and her non-stop monologue is printed verbatim. She talks about her likes (meat burned to a crisp; vichyssoise for breakfast, sent from the Stork Club every morning in a milk bottle) and her dislikes (charity play performances.) She talks about her beautiful legs, feet and shoulders, claims to be penniless and admits to having weighed as much as 140 pounds "but I weigh 110 at the moment."

B272 "Talking about Tallulah." *Readers Digest*. April 1951, pp 53-54.

A selection of Tallulah Bankhead anecdotes, culled from various sources, including the Whistler's Mother crack by Dorothy Parker, and Grouch Marx's bon mot during a rehearsal of *The Big Show* when Tallulah's lines were being cut one by one because of a time requirement, and Tallulah was screaming every time another line was blue pencilled. Marx, standing nearby, was heard to remark, "Quite a production eh – this timing of the shrew?"

B273 "Tallu Hullabaloo." *Newsweek*. December 24, 1951, pp 22-23.

Reports on the Bankhead-Cronin trial, paying particular attention to Mrs. Cronin's testimony and Tallulah's reaction from her seat (whispering, making facial gestures.)

B274 "Tallulah." *Picturegoer*. January 6, 1945.

A pleasant but too-brief article covering 25 years of Bankhead's career, concentrating on her (half-hearted) suicide attempt in 1925 and her 1940s film work.

B275 "Tallulah" *Newsweek*. December 23, 1968, p. 80

A brief but informative profile of the recently deceased Tallulah Bankhead. "Latterly she had become more of a character than a character actress. But what a character! And when she performed, what an actress!"

B276 "Tallulah's Almanac." *Show Business Illustrated*. January 2, 1962, pp 25-27, 120-24.

A look at the wit and wisdom of Tallulah Bankhead -- in the guise of an almanac. For every letter of the alphabet, she has written a commentary about someone or something whose name begins with that letter, i.e., "A is for analysis: I'm not a girl who believes she should pay to talk about herself... C is for crowds, columnists and critics: I love people but crowds frighten me..." She also writes about good manners, Elvis Presley, Dr. Joyce Brothers, public appearances, on-stage drinking, and death.

B277 "Tallulah's 5 Lives." *Look*. February 24, 1953, pp 83-86.

The "5 lives" are the five different fields in which Tallulah Bankhead has had success -- theatre, motion pictures, radio, television, and as autobiographer. There are pictures representing each entertainment medium, and an excerpt from her book.

B278 "Tallulah's Tantrums." *Life*. December 27, 1948, pp 64-65.

A report in words and pictures of Tallulah's latest Broadway play, a revival of Noel Coward's *Private Lives*, in which the "galvanic Bankhead, shedding her dignity as a grand lady of the theatre, combines highly polished acting with outrageous clowning." Much of that clowning was a fight with Donald Cook on a sofa prop. The sophisticated roughhousing was said to have the same appeal for adults as a Punch and Judy Show has for children.

B279 "Tallulah's Three Loves." *Life*. October 4, 1954, pp 105-06.

Tallulah Bankhead was currently starring on Broadway in *Dear Charles*, and her character had to choose between three men, hence the title of the article. A brief synopsis of the story is punctuated by several photos of scenes from the play.

B280 "Tallulah Bankhead." *Billboard*. September 10, 1921.
A pleasant interview with the actress who was preparing to open in *Everyday*. She evades the question asked (why did she become a member of Actors Equity), but she does discuss, in long, run-on sentences, how she happened to go on the stage.

B281 "Tallulah Bankhead." *Silver Screen*. June 1931.

Under a full-page, full-length glamour portrait of Tallulah, the caption introduces readers to Paramount's newest star, the "greatest find since Dietrich." It is said that she rouges her toenails and calls men ginks. "She is very different."

B282 "Tallulah Bankhead." *Cinema Digest*. October 3, 1932, p. 11

Reports on Tallulah's seeming inability to catch on with film audiences, and the likelihood that Paramount will not renew her contract when it expires on November 7. "Screen audiences have not responded to her charms as they were expected to. Add to this a string of poor stories and the inability of the best makeup and camera workers to get consistently beautiful shots of her and you have sufficient cause for the downfall of any aspirant to screen fame, no matter what their previous record."

B283 "Tallulah Bankhead." *Cinema Digest*. October 31, 1932, p. 15

An editorial criticizing Paramount for the poor story quality of Tallulah's films. "Instead of giving the gay and unconventional Miss Bankhead an occasional gay and unconventional character to impersonate, they have banged away on the drab and dreary." Paramount had decided not to take up her option, so it is hoped that the quality of her films will improve since she is now a free agent.

B284 "Tallulah Bankhead." *Cinema Digest*. December 12, 1932, p. 10.

An unusual article in that it criticizes Bankhead for being so hostile toward Hollywood in light of her having failed to become a star. "Is is not those who fail who complain the loudest? Miss Bankhead might shoulder some of the blame for her meager accomplishments, for either she did not make use of her talents, or there are well-defined limits to those talents which she possesses."

B285 "Tallulah Bankhead." *Cinema Digest*. February 20, 1933, pp 9-10.

Reprints a review of Tallulah's current Broadway play, *Forsaking All Others*, followed by an insightful interview. Bankhead talks frankly about her failure in Hollywood, and when asked why she was given "such sad roles," she explains "because they didn't know just what to do with me. They were trying to figure me out. They had never seen me act. Maybe they had heard I had done *They Knew What They Wanted* or *Camille*."

B286 "Tallulah Bankhead." *Current Biography*. 1941.

A richly detailed biography of the stage star, currently riding high on the success of *The Little Foxes*. Her professional credits are complete (except for a couple of her London plays) and her off-stage activities and hobbies are also well-represented. Her constant activity leads the anonymous author to say that she is "a complete rebuttal of the idea that Southern females are languorous."

B287 "Tallulah Bankhead." *Current Biography*. 1953.

A more fully developed biography that supersedes the 1941 entry and also adds another twelve years worth of credits and activities.

B288 "Tallulah Bankhead." *Film Dope*. March 1973, pp 34-35.

A brief biographical sketch with an incomplete filmography. It is the anonymous author's opinion that none of Bankhead's "infrequent film performances came anywhere near to communicating her magical stage qualities (though I would dearly love to see her 1931 films.)" [I fear the author would be disappointed by Tallulah's 1931 films, and also those from 1932.]

B289 "Tallulah Bankhead Comes to Stamford." *Cue*. June 17, 1944, p. 14.

Announces that Tallulah Bankhead will open in Noël Coward's *Private Lives* at the Strand Theatre in Stamford, Connecticut.

B290 "Tallulah Bankhead in *Rain*." *Theatre Arts*. March 1935, p. 233.

A striking portrait of Tallulah in costume for *Rain*. The caption heralds the return to Broadway of Somerset Maugham's story with Tallulah as Sadie Thompson.

B291 "Tallulah Bankhead: the Pollyanna Kid." *Cue*. March 10, 1945, p. 12.

A report on the success of *Foolish Notion*, Tallulah's latest play, currently trying out in Washington and playing to a packed house. She refers to herself as Pollyanna because she "adores" everything -- making *Lifeboat*, making A Royal Scandal, her directors and her new play.

B292 "Tallulah Bankhead's House." *Vogue*. July 1, 1943, pp 56-57.

A brief description of Tallulah's country home in Bedford Village, New York, with several photos of the rooms and pieces of furniture.

B293 "Tallulah in D.C." *Newsweek*. April 27, 1959.

A news item reporting Tallulah Bankhead's arrival in Washington to support a Congressional bill that would benefit unemployed thespians. "I had to get up at five a.m. to get here," she told the committee. "So for that reason alone I think the bill should be passed."

B294 "Tallulah Looted." *Newsweek*. January 15, 1951, p. 24.

Reveals Tallulah's accusation that her former secretary has cheated her out of $4,284 by raising the amount of her weekly paychecks.

B295 "Tallulah Shows the Way." *Colliers*. January 13, 1951, p. 74.

An interesting editorial (illustrated with a drawing by Sam Berman) praising *The Big Show*, Tallulah Bankhead, and NBC for prolonging the life of radio. Hiring Tallulah to host the popular series was, in the author's opinion, "quite likely the most progressive step that radio has taken since the loud speaker replaced headphones."

B296 "Tallulah Sings." *Newsweek*. December 18, 1950, p. 86.

Reports that Tallulah has completed her first commercial American singing recording, but does admit that the finished product is made up of "bits and pieces of many 'takes' recorded on tape and then patched together to get the best overall result."

B297 "Tallulah Takes a Tumble." *Life*. September 4, 1964, p. 38.

An entire page of photos, showing Tallulah in different stages of her famous fall on the steps of The Ritz Hotel in London, where she had gone to film *Die! Die! My Darling!*

B298 "Tallulah Talks about Life and *Lifeboat*." *Cue*. January 15, 1944, p. 7.

Tallulah talks very little about either in this brief article. It is the reporter who does all the talking, describing Tallulah's hair, the sound of her voice and her country house. When Tallulah does get to speak, she says that *Lifeboat* is a good film, "adult but not highbrow," and that Alfred Hitchcock, the director, is a "great man."

B299 "Tallulah Tees Off." *Cue*. September 11, 1954, p. 15.

A preview of *Dear Charles*, soon to open at New York's Morosco Theatre, and a brief history of the play.

B300 "Tallulah the Actress vs Tallulah the Tube." *Life*. March 28, 1949, pp 36-37.

In 1949, Tallulah initiated legal proceedings against the Proctor & Gamble Company, Columbia Broadcasting System, National Broadcasting Company and Benton and Bowles Advertising. She was distressed over a Prell Shampoo advertisement which used the name "Tallulah." She insisted the name belonged to her alone, and no one had a right to use it in any way. This article reports on the case, and offers proof that the name "Tallulah" does not necessarily belong exclusively to Miss Bankhead by picturing other Tallulahs: a hound dog, a housemaid, a fire engine, and a gorge in Georgia.

B301 "Tallulah the Great." *New York Times Magazine*. March 18, 1945, p. 28.

A one-paragraph preview of Tallulah's latest movie, *A Royal Scandal*, soon to open in New York. Several photographs from the film included.

B302 "Tattling on Tallulah ...by Tallulah Bankhead." *Cue*. September 27,

1952, pp 12-13.

Strings together a series of quotes from the actress's newly published autobiography. Lifted from the book are her views on men, her fights with Billy Rose and her fondness of Katharine Hepburn.

B303 "The Theatre." *Time*. February 25, 1935.

A brief commentary on Tallulah Bankhead's eleven year desire to play Sadie Thompson in *Rain*. She had gotten her wish, and although critics complimented her performance, the memory of Jeanne Eagels remained undimmed.

B304 "The Theatre." *New Yorker*. January 22, 1938.

Tallulah is mentioned as being a friend of Clifford Odets, and perhaps, at one time, a little more than a friend.

B305 "The Theatre." *New Yorker*. April 30, 1938, p. 28.

Includes a brief commentary on Tallulah's role in Broadway's revival of *The Circle*.

B306 "Theatre." *Newsweek*. December 23, 1968.

Published two weeks after her death, this article summarizes the life and career of Tallulah Bankhead, paying particular attention to her outrageous behavior. "In her long, passionate, unforgettable career, Tallulah Bankhead did not waste much time on artistic introspection. She was too busy talking, living, performing."

B307 "They Were News." *Theatre Arts*. September 1949, p. 41

This issue paid tribute to the year 1929, and one article featured photos of people who "were news" that year. Tallulah Bankhead, a sizzling stage star in London in 1929, is included.

B308 "*Time*, the Weekly Fiction Magazine." *Fact*. January-February, 1964, pp 3-23.

In this, the premiere issue of *Fact*, nearly three-quarters are taken up by letters from celebrities criticizing *Time* Magazine. "I'm an avid reader of Time," writes Tallulah, "[but] I notice that many of *Time*'s cover stories are full of errors and contradictions... Time is made of of fakery, calumny and viciousness. It is a brutal magazine, with the goddamdest distortion and lies."

B309 "Trial By Stage Whisper." *Time*. December 24, 1951, p. 17.

Another rendition of the Bankhead-Cronin trial, complete with the former secretary's defense and Tallulah's response.

B310 Turnbull, George. "Under Tallulah Bankhead's Spell." *The Spur.* July 1, 1930, pp 40, 97.

A brief profile of Tallulah which reports on her success in London. Turnbull comments on the multitude of young women who have become her fans and tries to explain the phenomenon: "I think it is because she embodies what each soul among them would like to be. They all dream what it is like to be beautiful, graceful, picturesque... and they receive vicarious pleasure in following her, applauding her, doting on her." He relates a few details from a recent meeting with Tallulah, including his asking her if she exercises to keep fit. "I don't anything to keep fit," was her quick answer. "I was born fit."

B311 "Two Tallulahs?" *Newsweek.* March 28, 1949, pp 56, 59.

Reports on Tallulah's lawsuit against Proctor & Gamble, Benton & Bowles, CBS and NBC which resulted from the use of the name "Tallulah" in a radio jingle advertising Prell Shampoo. "I propose to unjingle both Mr. Proctor and Mr. Gamble, their aides, their allies and their echoes," says Tallulah.

B312 "US Helps the Finns." *Life.* February 1940, p. 29.

Reports on former President Herbert Hoover's fundraising efforts to aid the citizens of Finland, recently invaded by Russia. Photographs show him enlisting the support of singer Gladys Swarthout, New York City Mayor Fiorello LaGuardia, baseball hero Babe Ruth and actress Tallulah Bankhead.

B313 Vermilye, Jerry. "Tallulah." *Film Fan Monthly.* March 1969, pp 3-11, 14-19.

An informative article that has been thoroughly researched. Vermilye concentrates on Bankhead's stage career, but her film work is also discussed and her foray into radio and television is included as well. Includes filmography.

B314 "Week's Mail." *Colliers.* March 14, 1953, p. 6

The week's mail brought a letter to the editor from Tallulah Bankhead commenting on the recent editorial listing the advantages of having her manage the New York Giants (see B319.) She writes that if she were allowed to manage the team, three of her new rules would be: spring training on the Riviera; champagne in the water coolers; and uniforms by Hattie Carnegie.

B315 "Where are They Now?" *Newsweek*. March 18, 1968.

Tallulah Bankhead was celebrating her fiftieth year in show business and in this brief interview she gives her opinion of several subjects, among them New York City Mayor John Lindsay ("He should be an actor"); Alabama's George Wallace, a presidential candidate ("He's a disgrace"); and current theatre offerings ("Boring").

B316 "Who is She?" *Picture-Play Magazine*. September 1917, p. 20.

The question was printed above the photo of Tallulah Bankhead that was chosen one of twelve winners in the magazine's "Screen Opportunity Contest," and a portion of the caption reads, "Will the lady of mystery, who is having the door to success in filmdom held open until she arrives, kindly communicate with the editor of *Picture-Play Magazine?*"

B317 Wilson, Elizabeth. "Tallulah's Royal Scandal." *Silver Screen*. February 1945, pp 24-25, 60-61.

An amusing article in typical fan magazine style about Tallulah Bankhead's latest film, *A Royal Scandal*. Wilson writes about how Tallulah happened to be signed (Ernst Lubitsch, the producer, saw her in *Lifeboat*), the problems in having to wait for Charles Coburn to be free, of non-athletic Tallulah's tennis game with Katharine Hepburn and devotes several paragraphs to the skin-tight pants of William Eythe, Tallulah's co-star.

B318 "Woman at Work." *Time*. September 17, 1951, p. 51.

Reports on Tallulah's return to London after sixteen years to kick off the second season of her popular radio program, The Big Show. She celebrated at the Ritz Hotel by drinking champagne from her (size four) shoe, shouted "Winston Churchill is my God!", danced the Charleston and recited Juliet's balcony speech. Said one waiter, "Nothing like this has ever happened here before." [It's a pretty safe guess that nothing like that ever happened there again, either.]

B319 "Would That It Were So." *Colliers*. January 10, 1953, p. 70.

An amusing editorial that makes a pretty convincing case for Tallulah as manager of the New York Giants. "Tallu, we feel deserves to manage the Giants for reasons of sentiment, drama and dollars and cents. She [would be] a bigger thing than night games and television, and she [would] outdraw Musial, Mantle, Satchel Paige and Bill Veeck's midgets, combined." The March 13th issue of the magazine contained her amusing reply (see B314).

B320 Zeitlin, Ada. "The Girl Hollywood Fears: Tallulah Bankhead" *Screenland*. September 1931, pp 32-33, 119, 120.

A fairly routine profile of Bankhead and her uninhibited lifestyle.

B321 Zeitlin, Ada. "Tallulah, Herself!" *Screenland*. October 1931, pp 56-57, 104, 106.

Actually a continuation of Zeitlin's article in the October issue. Again, fairly routine.

B322 Zeitlin, Ada. "Tallulah – So Far." *Screenland*. November 1931, pp 83, 102, 104.

A general report of Tallulah's work in Hollywood, her views and how others view her.

B323 Zolotow, Maurice. "Alabama Tornado, Part One." *Saturday Evening Post*. April 12, 1947, pp 15-17, 87-90.

In the first installment of a three-part series, Zolotow writes an interesting and enlightening profile of the legendary southern actress. "Uninhibited, dynamic, bizarre, Tallulah Bankhead has won fame – and several fortunes – as one of the theatre's most flamboyant stars. Her conversation may curl a producer's hair, but few outdraw her at the box office."

B324 Zolotow, Maurice. "Alabama Tornado, Part Two." *Saturday Evening Post*. April 19, 1947, pp 30-31, 119-20, 122.

In the second installment of Zolotow's entertaining profile of Tallulah Bankhead, he writes that she is "high spirited and obstinate, contentious if crossed," and also that she had a lisp until the age of five.

B325 Zolotow, Maurice. "Alabama Tornado, Part Three." *Saturday Evening Post*. April 26, 1947, pp 28, 134-36.

The final chapter in Zolotow's Bankhead profile, he writes that in Hollywood she was a sensation although her films were not, comments on her ability to survive Broadway flops and says that despite her dedication to the theatre, "she would rather spend her time at the ball park."

Appendix A

Film Roles Considered and Film Tests

Tallulah Bankhead said she was constantly turning down offers to do films, a practice that began while she was in England during the 1920s, so the *complete* list of motion picture offers would be much longer than the one below. The films listed here are those for which Bankhead's consideration was made public either by the studio, another person or Bankhead herself.

1. *Dr. Jekyll and Mr. Hyde* (1920). John Barrymore, set to star in the Paramount picture, allegedly wanted Tallulah for the role of the fiancée, a role that eventually went to Martha Mansfield.

2. *Blood and Sand.* B.P. Shulberg announced in 1932 that Paramount would be remaking the story with Cary Grant and Tallulah Bankhead. (Originally filmed in 1922 with Rudolph Valentino and Nita Naldi, it was remade by 20th Century-Fox in 1940 with Tyrone Power and Rita Hayworth.)

3. *Red Dust* (1932). Louis B. Mayer wanted Bankhead to replace Jean Harlow in the MGM production. Harlow's husband, Paul Bern, had committed suicide and Mayer thought she should take some time off, but Bankhead (whose Paramount contract had expired) turned down Mayer's offer and left Hollywood to return to the New York stage. Harlow completed the film.

4. *Gone With the Wind* (1939). Tallulah Bankhead was the first professional actress actually tested for the role of Scarlett O'Hara. She made the test (photographic only) in Hollywood on December 21, 1936. She was also considered briefly for the role of Belle Watling.

5. *The Rains Came* (1939). Myrna Loy, in her 1988 autobiography,

Being and Becoming, writes that several actresses, including Tallulah Bankhead, were considered for the role of Lady Esketh. (Loy eventually played the part in the 20th Century-Fox film.)

6.   *Mr. Skeffington* (1944). Jack Warner announced in January 1941 that Tallulah Bankhead was being considered for the role of Fanny Skeffington. (Bette Davis played the part instead.)

7.   *Humoresque* (1946). Joan Crawford had, perhaps, her finest hour in this Warner Bros. film, but Tallulah Bankhead was one of the first actresses considered for the role.

8.   *The Sudden Guest* (1946). Tallulah admitted in a newspaper interview that "one studio" was interested in having her appear in a filmed adaptation of Christopher La Farge's play.

9.   *Macbeth* (1948). Orson Welles approached Tallulah about playing Lady Macbeth in the Republic production, but she turned down his offer, allowing Jeanette Nolan to play the famous character instead. (There is some confusion as to whether Welles' offer was for the film, or for the Utah stage production the year before. Miss Nolan played the part in both versions.)

10.   *The Glass Menagerie* (1950). For three days in August 1949, Tallulah made several tests for the role of Amanda Wingfield in the film adaptation of Tennessee Williams's play. Irving Rapper directed, and she was photographed by Karl Freund. According to Rapper, the test was the greatest he had ever seen, but the role went to Gertrude Lawrence.

11.   *Biography* (1950). On November 10, the New York *Herald Tribune* announced that Tallulah might star in the film adaptation of S.N. Behrman's play.

12.   *Whatever Happened to Baby Jane?* (1962) Tallulah was offered the role eventually taken by Joan Crawford.

Appendix B

The Use of Her Name in Books and Films

Tallulah Bankhead has appeared as a character in novels and films surprisingly little, considering the power of her personality. Her's is a name still widely known, and the tales of her sex life, drinking and party antics are so legendary that to have her as merely a character in a story seems impossible. To do justice to the Bankhead personality, she would have to dominate every scene in which she appears. Perhaps that is the reason she appears so seldom, but the following list does include the four books and one film in which she *has* appeared.(She has also been the subject of a stage play, but it was more of a tribute to the actress, and will be found in that section. See A20, 22.)

Books

1)   Kanin, Garson. *Moviola*. New York: Simon and Schuster, 1979.

Kanin has written his own history of the movies, lifting several episodes from Hollywood's past, and dramatizing them. He writes about actual events, but gives them depth by adding dialogue. Tallulah Bankhead makes a dramatic appearance in the chapter on *Gone With the Wind*. She was an early contender for the role of Scarlett, and Kanin has her making quite a spectacle of herself at a Hollywood dinner party, scuffling on the lawn with Miriam Hopkins, and later commiserating with fellow Scarlett rejectees Paulette Goddard and Joan Crawford. (The chapter was made into a television film in 1980.)

2)   Roosevelt, Elliott. *Murder at Hobcaw-Barony*. New York: St. Martin's Press, 1986.

Set during World War Two, a murder is committed at the North Carolina estate of one of President Roosevelt's cabinet members while several celebrities (including Tallulah Bankhead) are visiting. As in most of Roosevelt's murder mysteries, the crime is eventually solved by Eleanor

Roosevelt, the First Lady, and the author's mother.

3)   Baxt, George. *The Tallulah Bankhead Murder Case*. New York: International Polygonics, Ltd., 1987.

Baxt, a former screenwriter and the author of such books as *A Queer Kind of Death*, *Topsy and Evil* and *The Alfred Hitchcock Murder Case*, here allows Tallulah Bankhead to solve a series of grisly murders in New York City. Set in 1952, during the Communist "witch hunts," when almost everyone associated with Hollywood was either being accused of belonging to the Communist Party or accusing others, Tallulah fights to have blacklisted performers appear on her radio program and discovers a connection between the murders and the black list. Baxt admirably captures the Bankhead personality (she utters one wisecrack after another, drinks, swears and flirts outrageously) and he surrounds her with both real and fictitious characters. Dorothy Parker is a major character in the book (which, in some ways, is a sequel to Baxt's earlier *The Dorothy Parker Murder Case*) as are Estelle Winwood and Patsy Kelly. It lacks the suspense of most detective novels, and the reader will realize who the killer is before Tallulah does, but these are minor flaws, and Baxt more than makes up for them by making the book so much *fun* to read. The party, for instance, where Tallulah unmasks the killer, is a treat for any film buff, as Bea Lillie, Basil Rathbone, Grace Kelly, Margaret Sullavan, Melvyn Douglas and even Mae Murray make appearances. Baxt fills the book with Hollywood trivia, and in an afterword explains that all theatrical and film information was culled from his own memories. His memory, unfortunately, is faulty. Tallulah Bankhead did not fly to Hollywood to test for *The Glass Menagerie* (the tests were made in New York), and Sessue Hayakawa did not star opposite Tallulah in 1931's *The Cheat* (he had starred in the 1915 version.)

4)   Steele, Danielle. *Zoya*. New York: Delacorte Press, 1988.

Zoya, the heroine of Steele's romantic novel, is a Russian countess, a cousin to Tsar Nicholas. She escapes the Russian revolution and leads a very exciting life in Paris. She joins the Ballet Russe, almost loses her children in a tenement fire, is briefly impoverished by the crash of '29, buries two husbands and a daughter, opens a successful clothing store and has a perfume named after her. Among the many people she meets during her tumultuous life is Tallulah Bankhead who scolds her more than once for not using enough lip rouge.

Films

5)   *The Scarlett O'Hara War* (NBC) 1980. 105 minutes.

An adaptation of one chapter of Garson Kanin's 1979 novel, *Moviola*, this made-for-TV film traces the heated competition between actresses to land the most coveted role in Hollywood history – Scarlett O'Hara. Tallulah Bankhead was one of them, and although actress Carrie Nye (the ex-Mrs. Dick Cavett) is unlike Tallulah physically, she admirably conveys her flamboyant personality.

Index

This index refers to page numbers as well as to entry codes in enumerated sections. Entries preceded by "A" can be found under Awards, Honors and Tributes, by "B" in the Bibliography, by "D" in the Discography, by "F" under Film Work, by "R" in Radio, by "S" under Stage Work, and by "T" in Television. For page numbers of the coded chapters, refer to the table of contents.

Abbott, George, 15-16
Ace, Goodman, B162, B163, B164
Adams, Abby, B007
Adams, Evangeline, 9
Akins, Zoë, 7, 22
Albert, Katharine, B165
Aldrich, Richard, 38
Alfred Hitchcock Album, The, B063
Alhoff, Fred, B166
Alington, Napier, 8, 11
All About Eve, 35, D9, R91
All Star Revue, 28, 36-37, 167, T1
Allen, Fred, 35
Allyson, June, R78
Alpert, Hollis, B008
Ameche, Don, R108
American Theatre as Seen by Its Critics, The, B107
Amherst, Jeffrey John, 8
Anders, Glenn, 13, 88, S16
Anderson, Mary, F14

Andrews, Ann, 7, 8, F8, S7, S26, S29
Andrews, Bart, B009
Andy Williams Show, The, T37
Angel, Heather, F14
Anger, Kenneth, B010
Anita Loos: a Biography, B030
Annabella, 38
Answer the Call, T2
Antony and Cleopatra, 21, 84-85, S30
Apfel, Oscar, F10
Appel, Anna, F12
Arce, Hector, B011
Arden, Eve, B012, S68
Arlen, Michael, 12
Armstrong, Louis, B154
Arnold, Edward, R96
Arthur, Beatrice, S41
Arthur, Phil, 30
Arthur Murray Party, The, T15, T23

As I Am, B108
Aubrey, John Churchill, B167, B168, B169, B170, B171
Auer, Mischa, F15
Austin, Jere, F4
Aylesworth, Thomas G., B013
Bach, Reginald, 21
Bad Girls of the Silver Screen, B039
Baddeley, Hermione, 40
Bailey, Pearl, T14
Bankhead. Adelaide Eugenia Sledge, 2
Bankhead, Eugenia, 2, 13-14, 42, 45
Bankhead, John Hollis, 2
Bankhead, Tallulah, birth and childhood, 2; film debut, 3; Broadway debut, 4; London, 9-15; suicide attempt, 11; Paramount contract, 14; failure in films, 19; return to stage, 19; illnesses, 19-20; desire to play Scarlett O'Hara, 20-21; marriage to John Emery, 21; divorce, 22; success in *The Little Foxes*, 22-23; summer stock, 26, 30, 39, B219; success in *Lifeboat*, 28; radio success, 33, 35, 152-67; television work, 36; final stage appearance, 40; final film appearance, 42; death, 44; articles by, B148, B149, B150, B151, B152, B153, B154, B155, B156, B157, B158, B159, B160, B161
Bankhead, William, 2, 21, 25, 26, B153
Bannerman, Margaret, 12
Barry, Joan, S17
Barry, Philip, 19, 29
Barrymore, Ethel, 4, 36, B015, B151, F16, R52
Barrymore, John, 7, 21, 36
Barrymore, Lionel, F16, R96

Barrymores, The, B008
Barrymores: The Royal Family in Hollywood, The, B085
Baskette, Kirtley, B175
Bates, Granville, S27
Batman, 42, 168, T42, T43
Baxley, Barbara, S38, S50
Baxt, George, 252
Baxter, Anne, F15
Beaumont, Harry, 16
Behler, Rudy, B016
Behind the Scenes of Otto Preminger, B058
Benchley, Nathaniel, B176
Benchley, Robert, 3
Bendix, William, F14
Bennett, Charles, 74-75, S19
Bennett, Fran, S55
Benny, Jack, R108
Berg, A. Scott, B017
Berg, Gertrude, F16
Berger, Meyer, B177
Berle, Milton, B018
Bernhardt, Sarah, 14
Best, Edna, S13
Bette: The Life of Bette Davis, B070
Bette Davis, B140
Bickford, Charles, 16, F9
Biery, Ruth, B179
Big Broadcast, The, B027
Big Party, The, T29
Big Show, The, 33, 35-36, 153-58, A10, A13, A14, R1
Bing Crosby Show, The, R82
Binney, Constance, 4, 6, S2
Biographical Dictionary of the Cinema, A, B138
Biographies in Sound, R99, R103
Biography, 250
Blackmail, 13, 74-75, S19
Blackmer, Sidney, 6, S2
Bletcher, Billy, F10
Blondell, Joan, 39, S43
Blood and Sand, 249

Blore, Eric, F6, F7
Blum, Daniel, B020, B021, B022, B023
Bob Hope Show, The, R80
Bolger, Ray, F19
Bond, Rudy, S40
Booth, Shirley, F16
Borge, Victor, 42
Borzage, Frank, F13
Bosworth, Patricia, B024
Boyer, Lucienne, 35
Brando: The Unauthorized Biography, B072
Brian, Denis, B002
Bright Lights: A Theatre Life, The, B122
Brook, Clive, 15, F6, R1
Brown, Jared, B025
Brown, John Mason, B026, B183, B184
Brown, Martin, 9
Bruce, Nigel, S9, S12
BS I Love You: 60 Years of Famous and the Infamous, B019
Burke, Randolph Carroll, B185
Burroughs, Don, 8
Busman's Holiday, 21
Buxton, Frank, B027
By Candlelight, 22
Callow, Simon, B028
Camille, R9
Campanella, Joseph, 111-12, S53
Campbell Room, R66, R69, R70
Cantor, Eddie, S68
Capote: A Biography, B032
Capote, Truman, B186
Carey, Gary, B029, B030
Carroll, Joseph, B187
Carvel, Madge, B188
Cary Grant: The Lonely Heart, B073
Castle, Charles, B031
Chalmers, Thomas, S30
Chandler, Jeff, 152, R79
Charles Laughton, B069
Charles Laughton: A Difficult Actor, B028

Chase, Ilka, S25
Chase, Mary, 30, S44
Chatterton, Ruth, S64
Cheasley, Clifford W., B190
Cheat, The, 15, 128-29, F8
Chesterfield Supper Club, The, R61
Chevalier, Maurice, F10
Churchill, Winston, 11, 26
Cinema of Otto Preminger, The, B115
Circle, The, 22, 86-87, S31
Claire, Ina, 13
Clara Bow: Runnin' Wild, B132
Clare, Mary, S10
Clark, Alexander, 30
Clark, Jacqueline, B191
Clark, Kendall, S37
Clarke, Gerald, B032
Clash by Night, 26-27, 90-91, B180, S34
Cobb, Buff, 30
Cobb, Lee J., 26, S34
Coburn, Charles, 29, F15
Cochran, Charles B., 9
Cocteau, Jean, 30, 95, S37
Cohen, Daniel, B033
Cohen, John S., B193
Colbert, Claudette, F10
Cole, Lesley, B034
Cole, Stephan Eugene, S34, S48, S49
Colgate Comdy Hour, The, T7
Collier, Constance, 20
Collier, William, 6
Collinge, Patricia, 25, S33
Compton, Juliette, F11
Conchita, 11, 65-66, S10
Cook, Donald, 29, 30, 33, S38 S50
Coop: The Life and Legend of Gary Cooper, B076
Cooper, Gladys, 69, B035
Cooper, Gary, 16, F10
Cooper's Women, B143
Coote, Robert, S39

Cornell, Katharine, 1, 7, 12, 19, 21, S4
Cotten, Joseph, B036
Coward, Noël, 8, 12, 33, B037
Craig's Wife, 40, 112-13, S54
Crawford, Cheryl, 26
Crazy October, 39, 102-103, S43
Creaking Chair, The, 11, 67-68, S12
Cronyn, Hume, F14
Cross, Robin, B038
Crothers, Rachel, 6, 7, 8, 14
Crouse, Russell, B194
Crowninshield, Frank, 4
Cruikshank, Herbert, B195
Cukor, George, 15, 19, F6
Cukor and Co., The Films of George Cukor and His Collaborations, B029
Da, Lottie, B039
Dalrymple, Jean, 38
Damned in Paradise: The Life of John Barrymore, B084
Dancers, The, 9, 11, 64-65, S9
Danger, 8, 62, S6
Danning, Harry, 25
Dantine, Helmut, 30
Dark Side of Genius, The, B129
Dark Victory, 20, 35, 80-81, S26
Darvas, Lili, 38
Davenport, Harry, F7, S1
David O. Selznick's Hollywood, B067
Davis, Bette, 19, 20, 25, 35, 39, B040, B258
Daydreamer, The, 42, 149-51, F19
Dean, Basil, 9, 11, B041
Dear Charles, 38, 97-98, 110, S39
DeBlois, Frank, B196
Deboinairs, The, B111

de Bosdari, Count Anthony, 14
De Camp, Rosemary, F16
Denton, Frances, B197
Derwent, Clarence, B042, S37
Deschner, Donald, B043
Devil and the Deep, The, 16, 132-34, F11
Dewing, Elizabeth, S27, S28
Dickins, Homer, B044
Die! Die! My Darling! 42, 146-49, F18
Dietrich, Marlene, 15
Dinehart, Allan, S8
Dingle, Charles, 25, S33
Dr. Jekyll and Mr. Hyde, 7, 249
Donnelly, Ruth, F10
Donohue, Steve, 12
Double Exposure, B097
Drew, William M., B045
Drutman, Irving, B046
Duckworth, Dortha, S54
Duke, Patty, 42
Dumas, Alexandre, 14
Du Maurier, Sir Gerald, 9
Dupree, Minnie, 8, S5
Dunning, John, B047
Dunnock, Mildred, 29, S36
Duryea, Dan, 25, S36
Duse, Eleanora, 14
Eagels, Jeanne, 11, 20
Eagle Has Two Heads, The, 56, 94-95, S37
Eames, John Douglas, B048, B049
Ed Sullivan Show, The, T28
Eddy, Helen Jerome, F10
Edgar Bergen - Charlie McCarthy Show, The, 163, 164, R59, R68
Edwards, Anne, B050
Eisner, Joel, B051
Elder, Ruth, F3
Eldridge, Florence, 27, S35
Ellerbe, Harry, 26
Elliott, Robert, 4, 8, F2
Ellis, Zora, 2

Ellrod, J.G., B052
Elsa Lanchester, Herself, B089
Emerson, Faye, S71
Emery, John, 21-22, 25, 26,
    39, R11, S30, S31, S32,
    S36
*Encyclopedia of Movie Stars,
    The*, B033
Englebach, Dee, 36
Engstead, John, B053

Eugenia, 39, 101-102, S42
Europeans, The, 39
Eustis, Morgan, B200
Everyday, 7-8, 61, S5
Exciters, The, 9, 63-64, S8
Exhibitor's Trade Review, 4
Eythe, William, 29, F15
*Fabulous Lunts; A Biography
    of Alfred Lunt and Lynn
    Fontanne, The*, B025
Fairbanks, Douglas, Jr., 7, B054
Faithless, 16, 134-36, F12
Fallen Angels, 12, 68, S13
Fanatic (see *Die! Die! My!
    Darling!*)
Farrell, Charles, T10
*Fasten Your Seatbelts: The
    Passionate Life of Bette
    Davis*, B118
Fate Keeps on Happening, B094
Fein, Irving, B055
Fenton, Leslie. F9
Fields, Gracie, 12
Filmgoers Companion, The,
    B064
Film Encyclopedia,.The, B079
Films of Alfred Hitchcock, The,
    B066
Films of Cary Grant, The, B043
Films of Fredric March, The,
    B117
Films of Montgomery Clift, The,
    B078
Films of the Thirties, The,
    B141
Films of 20th Century-Fox, The,
    B137

Films of World War II, The,
    B103
Finler, Joel W., B056
Fiske, Mrs., 7
Fletcher, Adele Whiteley,
    B204
Fletcher, Bramwell, S31
Flynn, Errol, 33
Fonda, Henry, R9, S44
Fontanne, Lynn, 1
Foolish Notion, 29-30, 93-94,
    S36
Foot-Loose, 7, 59-60, S3
Forbes, Ralph, F9
Ford, Ruth, S45
Forget-Me-Not, 7
Forsaking All Others, 19, 79-
    80, S25
Foster, Phoebe, F6
Fowler, Brenda, F3
Francis, Alec B., F3
Frank Sinatra Show, The, R47
Frazee, H.H., 8
Frazier, George, B205
Fred Allen: His Life and Wit,
    B136
Fred Allen Show, The, R67,
    R76
Frederici, Blanche, S2
Freund, Karl., 33
Friday with Garroway, R98
Friedman, Drew, B057
Frischauer, Willi, B058
Gabor, Eva, F15
Gallagher, Helen, A20, A22,
    S71
Garbo, Greta, 19, 29
Garden of Eden, The, 13, 72-
    74, S18
Garland, Robert, B206
Garnett, Tay, 38, F16
*Gary Cooper: An Intimate
    Biography*, B011
Gelman, Morris, B207
George, Grace, 22; S31
*George; an Early Autobiog-
    raphy*, B144
George Cukor, B114

George Gobel Show, The, T18
George S. Kaufman, B059
Geva, Tamara, 39
Gilford, Jack, F16, F19
Gill, Brendan, 9, 11, 21, B003,
    B208, B209, B210, B223
Glad Tidings, 25, 113-14, S56
Gladys Cooper, B035
Gladys Cooper: A Biography,
    B104
Glass Menagerie, The, 250
Gold Diggers, The, 13, 72,
    S17
Goldstein, Malcolm, B059
Goldwyn, Samuel, 4
Goldwyn: A Biography, B017
Gone With the Wind, 20-21,
    249, B175
Good Company, B046
Good Gracious, Annabelle,
    26, 107, S47
Goodrich, Edna, 118, F1
Goulding, Edmund, R81
Graham, Billy, T14
Graham, Lee, B211, B212
Granger, Stewart, 22
Grant, Cary, 16, F11
Grant, Lawrence, F12
Grauer, Ben, 36
Grayson, Charles, B213
Great Movie Stars, The,
    B123
Great Radio Personalities,
    B127
Great Stage Stars, The, B105
*Great Stars of the American
    Stage*, B021
Green, E. Mawbry, B214
Green Hat, The, 12, 68-69,
    S14
Greene, Bert, B060
Griffin, Merv, 42, B061
Griffith, Richard, B062
Guide for the Film Fanatic,
    B112
Hale, Louise Closser, F12
Haley, Michael, B063
Hall, Gladys, B215

Hall, Porter, R3
Halliwell, Leslie, B064
Hamilton, Margaret, F19
Hampton, Hope, S64
Haney, Carol, S41
Hardie, Russell, S44
Harlow, Jean, 16
Harris, Radie, B065
Harris, Robert A., B066
Harris, Sam, 6, 7
Harrison, Michael, F13
Harrison, Rex, 22
Hart, George Drury, S7
*Hattie: The Life of Hattie
    McDaniel*, B075
Hatvany, Lili, 22
Haven, Scott, B216
Haver, Ronald, B067
Hawthorne, David,. F5
Hayakawa, Sessue, 42, 252,
    F19
Haye, Helen, S22, S24
Hayes, Helen, 1, R96
Hayes, Richard, B217, B218
Heflin, Frances, S35, S40
Heggie, O.P., 7, S3
*Helen Hayes: First Lady of the
    American Theatre*,
    B014
Hellman, Lillian, 22-23, S33
Henderson, Dell, 3, F1
Hepburn, Katharine, 138-39,
    F13, R44
Her Cardboard Lover, 13, 14,
    26, 75-76, 108-09, S21,
    S49
Her Temporary Husband, 8,
    26, 62-63, S7
*Here Lies Leonard Sillman;
    Straightened Out at
    Last*, B125
Here Today, 40, 113, S55
Herlihy, James Leo, 39
He's Mine, 14, 76-77, S22
Hewes, Henry, B220
Higham, Charles, B068, B069,
    B070, B071, B072, B073
Hirschhorn, Joel, B074

His House in Order, 13, 122-24, F5
Hitch: The Life and Times of Alfred Hitchcock, B135
Hitchcock, Alfred, 13, 28, 29, 44, 74, F14, R102, S19
Hitchcock and Selznick, B092
Hitchcock Truffaut, B139
Hobbs, Peter, S55
Hodiak, John, F14
Hoffa, Portland, 35, R1
Hoffman, Theodore, B222
Hohl, Arthur, F8, F11
Hollaway, Sterling, F12
Hollywood: The Selznick Years, T49
Hollywood Album, B082
Hollywood Babylon II, B010
Hollywood greats of the Golden Years, B052
Hollywood Talks Turkey, B096
Holmes, Phillips, F10
Hope, Bob, S70
Hopkins, Miriam, 19, 249
Hottentot, The, 6
House of Barrymore, The, B113
House on the Rocks, 39, 111-12, S53
Howland, Jobyna, S17
Howard, Leslie, S6, S21, S49
Hoyt, Arthur, F10
Hubert, Rene, 29
Hughes, Kathleen, B224
Hull, Henry, 6, 8, 29, 94, F14, S2, S5, S36
Humoresque, 250
Humphreys, Cecil, S23, S31
Hundred Different Lives, A, B101
Hunter, Ian, F5
Hurley, Irma, S42
Huston, Walter, R50
Hutton, Clayton, 14
I Am Different, 22, 87-88, S32
I Blow My Own Horn, B090
Israel, Lee, 13, 20, 36, B004

Ives, Burl, 42, F19
Jack Benny: An Intimate Biography, B055
Jack Paar Show, The, T24, T25, T27, T30, T31, T32
Jackson, Carlton, B075
James, Henry, 39
Janis, Elsie, S64
Jeans, Ursula, S20
Jessel, George, 35, R28
Jezebel, 19
Joe Franklin's Memory Lane, T17
John, Augustus, 15
Johns, Glynnis, 22
Jolson, Al, R71
Joseph Cotten: An Autobiography; Vanity Will Get You Somewhere, B036
Kaminsky, Stuart, B076
Kane, Gail, F2
Kanin, Garson, 251, 252
Karloff, Boris, F19, S68
Karney, Robyn, B077
Kass, Judith, B078
Kate Smith Hour, R12, R55
Kate Smith Show, R9
Kate Smith Variety Hour, R24
Kathy Godfrey Show, The, T11
Katz, Ephraim, B079
Kaye, Danny, S68
Keith-Johnston, Colin, S48
Keating, Fred, 26
Kelly, George, 20, S29, S54
Kennedy, Harold J., B081
Kent, Barbara, S36
Keylin, Arleen, B082
King, Dennis, R106
Kirkland, Alexander, F6
Kirkwood, James, 39
Kobal, John, 19, 36, B083
Kobler, John, B084
Kolk, Scott, F7
Kolker, Henry, F11
Koll, Don, B225
Kotsilibas-Davis, James, B085

Kraft Music Hall, R71, R73, R74
Kruger, Otto, R44
Krutch, Joseph Wood, B226
Lady of the Camellias, The, 14, 77-78, S23
La Guardia, Robert, B086
Lambert, Gavin, B087
Lamparski, Richard, B088
Lanchester, Elsa, B089
Lardner, John, B227, B228
LaRocque, Rod, F4
Larrimore, Francine, S4
Lasky, Jesse, B090
Last Hero, The, B134
Laughton, Charles, 16, F11
Laughton Story, The, B126
Lawlor, Anderson, S25
Lawrence, Gertrude, 1, 33, S68
Lawton, Richard, B091
Leacock, Stephen, 19
Leading Ladies, B099
Leading Lady, B106
Lee, Canada, F14
Lee, Peggy, R82
Lee, Robert E., 21
Leff, Leonard J., B092
Leigh, Vivien, 21
Lennon, John, 42
Leonard, Sheldon, R79
Let Us Be Gay, 14, 78-79, S24
Life, A, B080
Life of Noël Coward, The, B034
Lifeboat, 28-29, 139-41, A7, B177; F14; R79
Lincoln Highway, R20
Lindo, Olga, 11, 12
Linen, James A., B232
Listen, America, R30
Little Foxes, The, 22, 24, 25-26, 27, 35, 36, 88-90, A2, B234, B258, R22, S33
Little Love and Good Company, A, B109
Littlefield, Lucien, F11

Livesey, Sam, S12, S16
Lloyd, Ann. B093
Look at Tennessee Williams, A, B131
Loos, Anita, 3, 4, 44, B094 B237, B238
Louise Brooks, B110
Loy, Myrna, 248
Lubitsch, Ernst, 29, F15
Lucille Ball-Desi Arnaz Hour, The, T21
Lucy: The Real Life of Lucille Ball, B071
Lucy & Ricky & Fred & Ethel The Story of I Love Lucy, B009
Lukas, Paul, 16; F9
Lux Radio Theatre, R4
Lytell, Bert, R4
McArdle, Kip, S44
MacArthur, Charles, 3
Macbeth, 250
McCallister, Lon,. F13
McCarthy, Kevin, R91
McCartney, Paul, 42, T48
McClelland, Doug, B095, B096
McClintic, Guthrie, 19
McDowall, Roddy, B097
McKay, Don, 39
McKegg, William H., B239
MacMahon, Aline, S8
McNamara, Brooks, B098
MacPherson, Don, B099
Main Street to Broadway, 38, 143-46, F16
Make Me a Star, 16, 131-32, F10
Maney, Richard, 36
Mansfield, Martha, 7
Maples, Victor, 6
March, Fredric, 15, 27, F7, F10
Martha Raye Show, The, T9
Marx, Arthur, B100
Marx, Groucho, 36
Mary Margaret McBride Show, The, R53, R87

Mason, Mary, 30
Mason, Sidney, F4
Massey, Raymond, B101
Mather, Aubrey, S36
Maturin, Eric, F5, S12, S14,
    S18, S20
Maugham, W. Somerset, 11,
    20, 22, S27, S31
Mayer, Louis B., 16
Mays, Willie, B158
Meek, Donald, 6
Memo From David O. Selznick,
    B016
Memoirs, B145
Memories, B015
Menken, Helen, R8
*Meredith Willson's Music
    Room*, R88
Merman, Ethel, 35-36, S70
Merril, Scott, S42
Merv, B061
MGM Story, The, B048
Midgie Purvis, 40, 103-105,
    A15, S44
Mielziner, Jo, 21
Mike Douglas Show, The
    T40
Mike Wallace Asks, B142
*Milk Train Doesn't Stop Here
    Anymore, The*, 40, 105-
    106, S45
Mills, Hayley, 42, F19
Mills, John, B102
Milton Berle Show, The, T3,
    T4, T10
Miss Tallulah Bankhead,
    B004
Mr. Skeffington, 250
Mitch Miller Show, The,
    R106
Mitchell, Margaret, 20
Mitchell, Thomas, 19, 80, S25,
    S28, S32
Monitor, R107
Monroe, Marilyn, 91
Montalban, Ricardo, 109,
    S49
Montgomery, Robert, 16, 18,

F12
Montgomery Clift, B024
Monty, B086
Moore, Eva, S18
Moore, Juliet, F2
Moore, Tom, 4; F3
Moorehead, Agnes, F16
Morella, Joe, B103
Morley, Sheridan, B104, B105
Morris, Chester, 26, S46
Morrison, Hobe, B243
Morton, Tom, F16
Moses, Montrose, B107
Mosley, Leonard O., B244
Mossel, Tad, B106
Mother Goddam, B040
Motion Picture Magazine, 16,
    B215
Movie Directors Story, The,
    B056
Movie Stars Story, The, B077
Movie Talk, B124
Moviola, 251
Mud and Treacle, 13, 75, S20
Murder at Hobcaw-Barony,
    251
Murphy, Mary, F16
Murphy, Maurice, 18, F12
My Sin, 15, 126-28, F7
Myerberg, Michael, 27
Myers, Richard, 38
Neal, Patricia, B108
Nesbitt, Cathleen, 35, 71,
    B109, S11
*New Pictorial History of the
    Silent Screen, A*, B022
*New Pictorial History of the
    Talkies, A*, B023
Newmar, Julie, S41
Newton, Robert, S21
Nice People, 7, 60-61, S4
Nixon, Richard, R78
No People Like Show People,
    B146
No Pickle, No Performance,
    B081
Noël, B030
Noël Coward, B037

Nolan, Jeanette, 30
Notable Women in the Amer-
    ican Theatre, B121
Nye, Carrie, 253
Oakie, Jack, F10
Odets, Clifford, 26, S34
Official Batman Batbook, The,
    B051
O'Keefe, Paul, F19
On Cukor, B087
O'Neil, Barbara, S25
O'Shaughnessy, Patrice, B248
Ott, Mel, 25
Owen, Marie Bankhead, 2
Owen, Thomas, 2
Paramount Story, The, B049
Paris, Barry, B110
Parish, James Robert. B111
Parker, Dorothy, 3
Peale, Norman Vincent, R96
Pearce, Alice, 30, S39, S44,
    S50
Peary, Danny, B112
Pedell, Katharine, B249
Pell, Peter, S39
People Will Talk, B083
Perkins, Osgood, F6
Person to Person, T5
Peters, Margot, B113
Phillip Morris Playhouse, R22,
    R25, R27, R31
Phillips, Gene D., B114
Pichel, Irving, 15, F8
Pictorial History of the
    American Theatre 1900-
    1950, A, B020
Picture Play Magazine, 3
Pidgeon, Walter, 20, S28
Pitts, ZaSu, F10
Plowright, Joan, 50, 105
Poe, Aileen, S7
Polito, Sol, 3, F1
Pollard, Snub, F10
Polly Bergen Show, The,
    T20
Porter, Cole, 22
Potel, Victor, F10
Powers, Stefanie, 42, 148-49,

    F18
Pratley, Gerald, B115
Preminger, Otto, 29, B116,
    F15
Preminger; an Autobiography,
    B116
Price, Vincent, 29, F15, S68
Private Lives, 30-31, 33, 96-
    97, 109-10, A8, S38,
    S50
Quadri, Therese, S38, S42,
    S50
Quirk, Lawrence, B117, B118
Radie's World, B065
Radio Playhouse, R8
Ragan, David, B119
Rain, 11-12, 20, 81-82, S27
Rains Came, The, 249
Raleigh Room with Hildegarde,
    30, R49, R51, R58, R60
Ransom, Herbertm S27
Rapper, Irving, 33
Rating the Movie Stars for
    Home Video, TV, Cable,
    B074
Rawls, Eugenia, 25, 26, A18,
    A21, B005, B252, B269,
    F17, S33, S48, S50, T6
Ray, marie Beynon, B253
Red Dust, 16, 249
Red Skelton Show, The, T41
Reed, Florence, 27; S35
Reflected Glory, 21-21, 83-84
    S29
Reid, Carl Benton, 25, F16,
    S33
Reilly, Hugh, S39
Remarkable Woman: A Biog-
    raphy of Katharine Hep-
    burn, A, B050
Rhinock, Joseph L., 4
Richardson, Diana Edkins,
    B120
Rico, Mona, F9
Riordan, Marjorie, F13
Risdon, Elisabeth, 7, S3
Ritchard, Cyril, 42, F19
Robinson, Alice M., B121

Roerick, William, 98, S39, S56
Rogers, Ginger, 35
Rogow, Lee, B237
Romero, Ramon, B258
Roosevelt, Eleanor, 251
Roosevelt, Elliott, 251
Roosevelt, Franklin Delano, 19
Rose, Billy, 26-27, S34
Ross, Herbert, 3
Royal Scandal, A, 29, 141-43,
    B259, B317, F15
Rudy Vallee Show, The, R5,
    R7, R11, R46
Ruggles, Charlie, F10
Ruman, Sig, F15
Ryan, Nancy, S25, S28
Ryan, Robert, 91, S34
Saint Joan, 21
Salad Days, The, 7, B054
Sands, Dorothy, S54
Scarlett O'Hara War, The, 252
Scheff, Fritzi, S32
Schildkraut, Joseph, 26, S34
Schlitz Playhouse of Stars, The,
    T19
Schulberg, Budd, B261
Scotch Mist, The, 12, S15
Screen Directors Playhouse,
    R79, R81, R83
Seawell, Brockman, F17
Seawell, Donald, 25
Second Mrs. Tanqueray, The,
    26, 107-08, S48
Seddon, Margaret, S32
Seldes, Marian, B122, S45
Selznick, David O., 20
Serena Blandish, 20
*Seven Ages: An Autobiography
    (1888-1927)*, B041
Shane, Ted, B262
Shaw, Glen Byam, S23
Shaw, T.E. (Lawrence of Arabia),
    11
Shearer, Norma, 14, 79
Sheridan, Frank, 8
Shipman, David, B123, B124
Shore, Dinah, R16
Shuberts, The, 4, 22, S1, S28,

S29
Shuberts of Broadway, The,
    B098
Shumlin, Herman, 22-23, S33
Sidney, Sylvia, F10
Sillman, Leonard, B125
Singer, Kurt, B126
Skin of Our Teeth, The,
    27-28, 91-93, A4, A5,
    A6, S35
Sleeping Partners, 26, 107,
    S46
Slezak, Walter, F14
Slide, Anthony, B127
Sobel, Bernard, B128
Smallwood, C.L., B265
Smith, C. Aubrey, 68, S12
*Smothers Brothers Comedy
    Hour, The*, T46
Something Gay, 20, 83, S28
Speaking of Silents, B045
Spelvin, George, B265
Spoto, Donald, B129
Springer, John, B130
Spurin, Joe, F7
Squab Farm, The, 4, 57-58,
    S1
Stage Door Canteen (film), 28
    136-39, F13
Stage Door Canteen (radio),
    R32, R38, R40, R44
Stagestruck, B147
Stanwyck, Barbara, 27, 91
Star Shots, B053
*StarSpeak: Hollywood on
    Everything*, B095
Steinbeck, John, 28; F14
Steele, Danielle, 252
Steen, Mike, B131
Stenn, David, B132
Stephens, harvey, F8
Steve Allen Show, The, T14
Stevens, Emily, 7, S3
Stevenson, Adlai, 39
Stewart, Donald Ogden, 15,
    F6
Stokes, Sewell, B133
Stoneman, E. Donnell, B269

Storm, Gale, T10
Streetcar Named Desire, A,
    38, 98-100, S40
Strunk, William, 21, S30
Sudden Guest, The, 250
Sunday with Garroway, R94
Sutherland, Anne, F7
Sutton, Grady, F15
Sutton, Horace, B270
Swerling, Jo, 28, F14
Swindell, Larry, B134
Talkies, The, B062
Tallulah, B001, B003
Tallulah, a Memory, 26,
    B005
Tallulah, Darling, B002
Tallulah, Darling of the Gods,
    B006
Tandy, Jessica, 38
Tarnished Lady, 15, 124-26,
    F6
Taste of Honey,.A, 40
Taylor, John Russell, B135
Taylor, Kent, F11
Taylor, Robert, B136
Tearle, Conway, 21, R8, S30
Tearle, Godfrey, S15
Tell, Alma, 6, S1
Tell, Olive, 6, F4
Terry, William, F13
Tex and Jinx Show, The, T16
Theatre Guild of the Air, R90,
    R91
*Theatre Handbook and Digest
    of Plays, The*, B128
They Had Faces Then, B130
They Knew What They Wanted,
    12-13, 70-72, S16
39 East, 4, 6, 58-59, S2
This Marriage, 11, 66-67, S11
Thomas, Edna, S40
Thomas, Tony, B137
Thompson, David, B138
Thompson, Virgil, 21
Three Phases of Eve, B012
Thunder Below, 16, 129-31,
    F9
Time to Smile, R16, R26, R43

Today, T8
Tonight Show, The, T34,
    T35, T38, T48
Trap, The, 6, 121-22, F4
Tree, Viola, 9, S9
Trevor, Norman, S3
Truffaut, Francois, B139
Truman, Margaret, 35, R1
Tucker, Sophie, S68
Tune in Yesterday, B047
Tunney, Kieran, B006
Turnbull, George, B310
Turpin, Ben, F10
Two on the Aisle, B026
2,000 Movies: The 1940s,
    B038
Tyler, George, 7, S3
Uncommon Scold, An, B007
*Up in the Clouds, Gentlemen,
    Please*, B102
U.S. Steel Hour, The, T6, T33
Van Patten, Dick, 27, 93, S35
Van Sloan, Edward, F9
*Vanity Fair: Photographs of
    an Age*, B120
Variety, 4, 21, 22, 27, 39
Velez, Lupe, 22
Vermilye, Jerry, B140, B141,
    B313
Walker, Cheryl, F13
Wallace, Mike, B142
Wallace, Regina, S30
Ward, Burt, 168, T42, T43
Warner, H.B., S6
Warner, Jack, 33
Warts and All, B057
Warwick, Robert, S64
Watson, Lucile, 8
Watts, Ricjard, Jr., 16
Wayne, Jane Ellen, B143
We, the People, R65, R75
Webb, Clifton, 22, 30
Welcome, Darlings, 39, 110-
    11, S52
Welles, Orson, 30, R8
West, Adam, 42, 168, T42,
    T43
Westman, Nydia, S44

Whatever Became of... ?, B088
*Whatever Happened to Baby
    Jane?*, 42, 252
What's My Line?, T39
When Men Betray, 4, 119-20,
    F2
Whitney, Jock, 20
Whitney, John Hay, 15
Who Loved Him Best?, 3,
    117-19, F1
Who's Who in Hollywood,
    B119
Wilder, Thornton, 27, S35
Williams, Emlyn, B144
Williams, Florence, S33
Williams, Tennessee, 38, 40,
    100, B145, S40
Wills, Brember, S15
Willson, Meredith, 35, 36, R1,
    R88
Wilson, Eleanor, S37
Wilson, Elizabeth, B317
Wilson, Tony, 13
Winchell, Walter, 15, R100
Winwood, Estelle, 4, 8, 22, 28,
    39, 40, B097, B211, R8
Witherspoon, Cora, S25
Without Veils, B133
Wood, Peggy, R106, S68
Woollcott, Alexander, 3, 8
World of Movies, A, B091
*World's Almanac: Who's Who
    of Film, The*, B013
Wynn, Ed, 42, F19, S68, S70
You Never Know, 22
Zadora, Pia, 40, 104-05, S44
Zeitlin, Ada, B320, B321,
    B322
Ziegfeld Follies, 39, 100-01,
    B159, S41
Zolotow, Maurice, 1, B146,
    B147, B323, B324, B325
Zoya, 252

About the Author

JEFFREY L. CARRIER is a creative assistant at Ogilvy & Mather Advertising, New York, and a freelance film historian. His previous book in Greenwood's series on the performing arts, *Jennifer Jones: A Bio-Bibliography* (1990), was called "a superior reference book" by Anthony Slide in *Classic Images* and "one of the best in the series" by John Nangle in *Films in Review*.

Recent Titles in
Bio-Bibliographies in the Performing Arts

Julie Andrews: A Bio-Bibliography
Les Spindle

Richard Widmark: A Bio-Bibliography
Kim Holston

Ann Sothern: A Bio-Bibliography
Margie Schultz

Alice Faye: A Bio-Bibliography
Barry Rivadue

Orson Welles: A Bio-Bibliography
Bret Wood

Jennifer Jones: A Bio-Bibliography
Jeffrey L. Carrier

Cary Grant: A Bio-Bibliography
Beverley Bare Buehrer

Maureen O'Sullivan: A Bio-Bibliography
Connie J. Billips

Ava Gardner: A Bio-Bibliography
Karin J. Fowler

Jean Arthur: A Bio-Bibliography
Arthur Pierce and Douglas Swarthout

Donna Reed: A Bio-Bibliography
Brenda Scott Royce

Gordon MacRae: A Bio-Bibliography
Bruce R. Leiby

Irene Dunne: A Bio-Bibliography
Margie Schultz

Mary Martin: A Bio-Bibliography
Barry Rivadue

Jessica Tandy: A Bio-Bibliography
Milly S. Barranger